For the Love of the Cobbles

Only those who are in top condition can say that the Ronde van Vlaanderen is not hard. For all others, it is the Way of the Cross. —Andrea Tafi

For the Love of the Cobbles

A Journey Inside Cycling's Cobbled Classic Racing Season, and a Ride Across the Hard Surfaces of Belgium and France

By Chris Fontecchio
Founding Editor of the Podium Café

ISBN 978-1-365-01834-3

For all my Podium Café friends;

For Belgium and France and their passionate fans;

And for Stacey, Sage and Sascha,
because it's all about teamwork.

Prologue

On a spring afternoon in 1985, I did what I usually did when nothing was going on. I hopped on my bike and rode to my friend Steve's house. It was spring break and I was home from college with no particular plans, so falling back on my high school routines was like slipping into an old sweatshirt. Those routines consisted of gathering across town -- biking on the nice days -- at either Steve's house or another friend's, and if anything like a quorum could be found, basketball or football or some warped rendition of baseball would happen. But on this day there was no quorum. Steve was home, hanging in his room, watching TV.

"Check this out," he said[1] as he flicked on CBS Sports, showing a bike race from France. I'd caught a glimpse of the Tour de France before, enough to know the name and register some basic comprehension of the need for some people to race their bikes. Back then I poured over the sports pages every morning, and knew from the agate page (the one with the scores, standings, etc. in small type) that Frenchman Bernard Hinault had won the Tour de France a few times, making him the top bicycle racer in the world. Honestly, I haven't the slightest idea how I knew this, but somebody must have said it or written it, and I didn't care to disagree. But this was April, the Tour was three months off, and the race we were watching, called Paris-Roubaix, was unlike anything else I had ever seen, or even expected to see.

---

[1] If you think I, or anyone else writing a book from memory, recalls mundane conversations verbatim from 25 years ago, then... cool! But hey, this is probably pretty close.

Steve got me up to speed: Hinault wasn't around,[2] but a group of international stars was at the head of the race, and an American named Greg LeMond was one of them. No American had ever accomplished anything in European cycling, the hub of the sport, until LeMond came along just a few years earlier, won a surprise world championship, and placed third in his first crack at the Tour de France. This information wouldn't rock my brain for another season, but it was enough to bait the hook. And the roads of northern France proceeded to set it.

The 1985 running of Paris-Roubaix was a classic edition of the Hell of the North, the infamous race over rugged cobblestones through communities known mostly for the devastation they suffered in consecutive world wars. The dark legacy hanging over the region was greatly enhanced that day by intermittent rain showers and thick dark clouds. Mud covered enough of the road so that every spin of a bicycle wheel helped splatter the riders beyond recognition. Videos from that day might confuse a casual viewer as to whether color TV had been invented yet. For the riders, navigating the cobblestones was a brutal, awkward exercise, and the constant threat of crashing kept everyone -- even us first-time viewers -- on the edge of our seats. People like me who hadn't been to war are prone to thinking that the battlefields looked exactly like this.

The American broadcaster CBS did its best to enhance the drama. Anyone who got caught up in the LeMond Era of the

---

[2] Bernard Hinault only appeared sporadically and swore off riding Paris-Roubaix after 1981. Ever the diplomat, Hinault declared the race "bullshit" to the waiting media, seeing no reason to hide his feelings. And he'd just won the race. In 1985, explaining why he was home rather than in Compiègne, Hinault remarked, "I have a wife and two children, so I don't want my skin ripped off."

mid-1980s will doubtlessly remember their approach: selective editing heavy on crashes, uptempo synthesizers, shameless use of dramatic language (you can say "hell" on TV, apparently... over and over...), and the tag-team of John Tesh and some unfamiliar British guy calling the action.[3] I don't know how CBS tried to sell cycling to an American audience back then, but the race was a gift from the Cycling Gods: unfathomable visuals of riders so caked in mud that only their eyes and mouths could be recognized. Action that featured the sport's biggest names, including "our guy." And a fantastic slugfest of a race with all the drama, aggression, tactical nuance and brute athleticism that veteran cycling fans prefer.

The race lead changed hands numerous times, not in the mundane way of cyclists in a break taking turns but in a more serious manner. With the race winnowed down to a dozen or so guys in contention, attacks happened in small groups and failure was constantly an option. At one point mega-stars Eric Vanderaerden of Belgium and Francesco Moser of Italy had broken away from the field, the young Belgian clinging to the wheel of the cagey Italian -- known as "the Sheriff" -- who'd won three previous editions. But suddenly Moser lost his rhythm, veered into a deep puddle by the side of the road, and keeled over. Watching on Youtube thirty years later I still can't believe what I'm seeing: one of Paris-Roubaix's greatest champions unceremoniously kicked to the curb by the infamous cobbles. Vanderaerden, game for a two-man attack, knifed through the headwinds alone, but with 15 miles to go he eventually succumbed to an eight-man group of riders poised to duke it out for the win. The powerful Renault-Elf

---

[3] Phil Liggett, who's no longer even slightly unfamiliar.

squad in their black and yellow stripes were the home team, and they now had two guys up front.

Eventually Renault's young French star Marc Madiot went clear with a well-timed winning attack, step one of his eventual ascent into the pantheon of Cobbles Riders (two Paris-Roubaix wins, marriage to a former Miss France, and knighthood in the French Legion of Honor). Bruno Wojtinek, Madiot's less heralded teammate, escaped for second, and Irish master Sean Kelly outsprinted LeMond for third after the two swerved around a pileup that happened as their six-man group swung onto the wet velodrome track. Intrepid to the last drop, this race. Afterward LeMond was among the 35 riders who survived to finish (officially, at least), out of 172 that started. As he talked to Tesh on the velodrome infield, the layer of mud on his face made the young American look like he'd just stepped in from a minstrel show. Through this mask of shit shone his clear, wet eyes and his satisfied smile, a bizarre juxtaposition of human and inhuman that further drove home the beautiful madness being celebrated on this day. It gets better though: Tesh also interviewed Theo de Rooy, a Dutch rider who occasionally led the race in the final 90 minutes before succumbing:

de Rooy: "It's a bollocks this race! You're working like an animal, you don't have time to piss, you wet your pants. You're riding in mud like this, you're slipping, it's a piece of shit..."

Tesh: "Willl you ever ride it again?"

de Rooy, not hesitating for a second: "Sure, it's the most beautiful race in the world!"

Punctuated by a borderline-insane laugh by de Rooy. I don't remember if this exchange aired in real time, but thankfully it's preserved in legend now. Like the shattered Dutchman, I honestly didn't know quite how to respond to what I'd just seen, but Steve did. He'd talked to some guys who knew about a weekly circuit race in the Boston suburbs maybe ten miles from home, and by summer we were on our beater bikes trying out the sport of cycling. Within a year I had embarked on a fund drive and picked up an entry-level Bianchi racer, gotten completely hooked on the soap opera of LeMond's career, and eventually made myself into a hack racer and permanent cycling fan. The Tour de France was as much the centerpiece of my viewing as it is of the cycling calendar, and with other fans like my big brother Pete and my friend Drew I celebrated the glorious battles on the slopes of the Alps and Pyrenees. We heralded Lance Armstrong's arrival at the front of the Tour, delved deeper and deeper into the sport as the internet grew and dramatically expanded the level of available information. I'm now nearly a decade into hosting the Podium Cafe, a website and community of cycling fans, where we obsess over cycling 365 days a year.

But as great as all that has been, I never forgot that first brush with the sport. I never forgot the sights, the result, and most importantly I never got over the sense that, however great the Tour was, racing on cobblestones was something else entirely.

This book is a journey to the cobblestoned classics, a series of races in Belgium and France that begin with a late February sneak preview and meaningfully unfold over three weeks in March and April. They constitute a season within the season, drawing certain riders (including some who structure their entire year around this period) and certain fans to ride in a particular style of races. They live among the more broadly-defined Spring Classics, which include ancient events like Milano-Sanremo in Italy and the Ardennes races in Wallonian Belgium and the Limburg region of the Netherlands. To people waiting for the grand tours to begin, the Spring Classics are what you watch and celebrate while you wait. But the Cobbled Classics are the heart of spring racing, and they are as unique from Milano-Sanremo or Liège-Bastogne-Liège as the Tour de France.

Apart from the racing style is the fact that they are centered in the Flanders region of Belgium and nearby northern France. The races are inseparable from the area, with its biking culture, its passion for cycling, its endless riding routes, and for a lot of people its massive contribution to the beer brewing universe. The Cobbled Classics aren't merely a thing to watch, but to cozy up to on the streets of Flanders, side by side with many of the sport's most devoted fans. They are a place to visit with your bike as well — the important streets and climbs get reused year after year and have themselves attained legend, even UNESCO heritage status... but they are public streets which you can ride for yourself 364 days a year. Experiencing the intensity of riding the course, of cheering with the home fans, and of absorbing the competition over three weeks — it's a package deal, a cultural and sporting festival that's so memorable, unique, and yet still (for now) so accessible, that it resembles few other sporting events anywhere in the world.

This book is about the whole package. It's a mix of first-person account and something resembling sportswriting. It falls short of being a definitive guide to race history, but deals with enough of the history to (I hope) give readers the full context for the experience of the Cobbled Classics. It was started in 2010 and focuses on those rather memorable editions as a vehicle for telling a more timeless story of the races. And I'd better hurry up and put it to bed before it's time to update it, again, with the 2016 results.

-Seattle, Washington, April 2016

Photo by Elizabeth Freer

Chapters

1: Arrivals

My head reeled from the deadly combination of sunlight and sleeplessness as I got off flight... whatever it was in Brussels to face my first real Cycling adventure. Lo! the banality of adventure. Airports almost never fail to dampen the excitement of a really cool trip, and for one of the world's great transportation hubs the Brussels airport is drab and disappointing. I'd hoped that the runway would be made of cobblestones, or that Sporza announcer Michel Wuyts would deliver the recorded multilingual messages to people in the immigration line, followed by a video of Peter Van Petegem reminding us to fill out a customs declaration. No such luck. A smattering of Dutch and French reminded me that I was in Belgium, but just barely. The airport had been tastefully renamed Brussels International Airport (from Zaventem, I think) just to remind you that you were, in fact, in Europe. And from what I can tell, that's the airport's claim to fame. It's in Europe.

But the reality was that I had just traveled from the non-cycling universe to the cycling one, and things picked up in a hurry. As it was Thursday, I was both early for the big crowds of cycling fans, arriving the day after the initial cobbled classic (Dwars door Vlaanderen), and late for the influx of riders, who trickled into Belgium beginning Monday morning. I'd heard tales of the departure scene at the airport the day after Paris-Roubaix, where the entire sport is being airlifted from Zaventem, but this was something of a dead zone for cycling-related arrivals.

From the rigamarole of entering the country I proceeded downstairs to the rail station, dragging my massive, corrugated white plastic bike box that exceeds the size, weight and inconvenience of just carrying my bike around by several orders of magnitude. But I like train travel, even grimy stations and trains, and the Zaventem station didn't disappoint. Better still, I found an outlet for my undampened excitement -- an American guy dragging a bike box of his own. I'd spied him in the baggage area, we were the only two guys grabbing bikes in that locale, so when he was waiting to catch the same train to Gent, we naturally got to talking.

My immediate assumption was that he was like me, headed over for the classics, joining a new wave of American cobbled classics tourism that I was sure was building and ready to slam into the Vlaamse Ardennes -- the range of small hills in East Flanders -- at any moment. Instead, he was cut from a much more relevant cloth. Steven Gordon was a racer who had left northern Virginia behind for Gent with the hope of chasing a ride in the pro peloton.

In a way Steven's story is both reminiscent of the old days, and something completely different. Like a zillion other would-be pros, ranging from great champions to that universe of guys who remained anonymous, Steven was traveling with little more than his bike in tow and the promise of a place to stay. He had a referral to a team that would give him a jersey and an entree into races, but the rest was up to him. But in 2010 the differences maybe outweigh the similarities. Steven isn't running away from a farm or the mines or some other dead-end life; he's a middle-class kid, I gather, with an MBA. In the world of high-speed networking, he has very real assurances that his team, Kingsnorth International Wheelers, exists and plans to give him a spot. He has sophisticated communications, bank machines that can instantly withdraw cash from his bank back home, video cameras to document his travels and races which he can share worldwide in a matter of minutes. He's American, and that alone would have been astounding 40 years ago before any of the other things I just mentioned existed.

*****

A lot of the old stories have been well-documented: guys arriving in mainland Europe from the UK and eventually the US, but who would grow homesick and struggle to make the cut in the elite peloton. I used to do a podcast with a guy named Graham Jones (not to be confused with the Pugeot rider of the same name from the 1980s), who left London in 1966 after one of his co-workers, attempting to congratulate him on completion of his apprenticeship in electrical engineering, welcomed him to "the rest of his life," a/k/a a factory job. Graham fled this shrunken future in horror, quitting virtually on the spot, grabbing his bike and informing his parents that he needed a ride to the Dover Ferry, which they gave him after they picked their jaws off the floor.

Jones got to the railway station in Gent before the adrenaline gave way and the isolation set in. He had enough money for a short hotel stay, quickly found some races to ride, and before long had moved in with a group of fellow Brits to a building that had been slated for condemnation some time earlier. There was one electrical outlet, a faucet and squat toilet in the courtyard, and that was pretty much it. Graham and his mates raced for prize money to buy food, swarming the kermesse circuit where, nearly every day in Belgium, you could find a purse, hopefully several placings deep. His run lasted two years, cut short by the death of Tom Simpson and pall it cast over the hopes of several young British riders then in Europe, and Graham fell back on his engineering degree to a successful career and life in America. But his and other stories prove that if you were strong enough to leave the nest and fast enough to hang with Belgium's best, you could get your foot in cycling's door.

The better known American stars who made it -- like Greg LeMond, Andy Hampsten, Bob Roll, Lance Armstrong, Tyler Farrar -- all had some form of institutional help to launch their careers in Europe, be it the US National program, the 7-Eleven squad, or what have you. Their talent and the existence of organizations dedicated to willing it out helped shorten the transition and smooth out some of the rough edges. Belonging to a big national program or trade team means you know where your next meal is coming from, at least. And the number of top European teams dedicated to nurturing young American and other foreign talent through high-level development programs continues to grow.

But the story of the marginal or unknown prospect, the long-running tale of local cycling heroes from Europe's quiet corners trekking to Belgium or France with no real lines of support, is an ongoing dream in modern Flanders. In cycling terms it resembles the story of my Italian immigrant ancestors coming to America: the idea that, if you can stomach the process, you can escape the limitations of your inherited situation in favor of a place where you can succeed on your own merits. Not to be confused with some sort of meritocratic utopia, mind you. The locals probably have a leg up regardless, as do the intrepid travelers with a lifeline of support. My entrepreneurial grandfather fled his boring life as a shepherd outside Naples, in part because his brother had already set up a job for him. But he parlayed this start into a dozen small businesses or more, and the rest is history.

In cycling, the past lives on. This land of wieler-dreams lives on in modern Flanders, where you can get race starts, and if you're fast enough, someone will eventually notice. Steven Gordon was off to pursue his own dream. A professional life awaited him back home, but Steven wasn't ready for that, not until he could answer the question: am I a professional cyclist?

****

I didn't see Steven again for the rest of my trip, but I did catch up with him at the end of his season in Flanders. His dreams didn't turn into a movie script, but he had a lot to say about what it's like to pursue them in the Land of Cycling.

First, with a little groundwork and some strong legs, you can start the Belgian chapter of your cycling career pretty easily. "With USA cycling, you get an international license, which if you're racing in America you would only need if you're going to be pro or if you're racing UCI races like Philly or the Tour of California. And then when you're in Belgium all you really need is a $5 card that people just scan at the start at every race and then you're good, then you race. It's really simple. You do need a letter of permission, they're really strict about that. Basically I think what that is, they will only give it to you if you don't have any suspensions for doping or any other suspensions or fines. And then you have permission to ride."

You can ride solo, but finding a team is a viable option too. Steven rode for two of them, Kingsnorth International Wheelers and Team Deschuytter, having been referred to the teams through a friend back at Virginia Tech. This was actually his second trip, having tested the waters for a few weeks the previous year. "There are a bunch of different teams in Belgium, and some of them are targeted toward in international riders, and team Kingsnorth International Wheelers is one of them that has taken American riders, Britsh, Australian, New Zealanders, a Russian here and there, but mostly English-speaking riders. You have to pay for your housing and food and entry fees which are very small, but other than that they have support at the races, they have a guy there to give you water bottles and stuff. You don't have to sign anything, you just tell them how long you're gonna be there, and they tell you where the races are, you just ride there and they'll meet you with the car. There have been some well-known foreigners that have come through the team, such as Freddy Rodriguez and Henk Vogels, to name two.

"We also raced for another team called Team Deschuytter, and that team was a little bit higher level in that that team had invites to some top races. For the other team Team Deschuttyer, the inter-clubs required that a team be invited to the race. And I had two copies of licenses, one copy that said my team was Kingsnorth, and another that said I was Team Deschuytter. So we'd go and do the inter-clubs once in a while. And those are like the longer ones, the races that mimic the classics. We did one race that was like the amateur Het Volk. Another we did was in northern France."

What Steven found, from this daily drumbeat of small races mixed with some bigger, harder events, was a massive opportunity to be racing. Kermesses -- a French term for the town fairs that happen all over Belgium and the rest of Europe in the warmer months -- are a racing staple, offering a constant slate of easy-access races in the 100-140 kilometer range. Criteriums, the staple of American racing, exist too, and even the crits are a robust 90+ minutes long. This simply isn't the case in the U.S., with its smaller scene dispersed across the fifty states, and riders limited by the distances to how many races they can attend. The way people discuss it, it doesn't appear to be the same elsewhere in Europe either. There's a reason why so many development programs from overseas make Belgium their first stop.

The availability and length of races were only a few of the major differences compared to racing back home. "The only place where Belgian racing is at all like the US is circuit races. And they take the corners a lot differently, so it's not the same feel. Like a twilight kermesse, it's just not the same. Everyone wants to attack and everyone does. The mentality in Belgium is, I can win by going to the front and attacking and riding harder. Whereas in America the mentality is, I can win by being smart and staying out of the wind and not do any work unless i have to, and saving myself for the end. So it's a huge difference in mentality and it makes the race totally different.

Is this a cultural difference or just the result of having stronger riders? Both: "The fields there are deeper at any given amateur race, there are always a few guys who are really strong. But it's also just the way they like to race, they way they've seen everyone else win, and it's the way they win. And since everyone else is going to be attacking, I've got to attack. if you want to stay where you are you've got to keep moving up. If you're not moving up, you're moving back. So if you want to actually move up, you've got to attack. because everyone else is doing it you have to too. I don't know how it got started like that, but that's the way it is, and it's not changing. To them that's what racing is. Racing is hard, racing is all out. In the US it's meant to be more of a tactical game where you only go hard later."

The result? Steven returned to the US putting his MBA to work, not cracking the Garmin lineup at Paris-Roubaix. It was always a longshot, but he took his shot and had a good time. He rode the amateur Het Nieuwsblad classic, a race that uses the climbs and cobbles of de Ronde van Vlaanderen, where Steven finished in the main field. In another race he found himself on the Paterberg, where he got caught up in traffic and left behind. Kermesses filled in the spaces in between.

About the only real downside was that he got sick several times and rarely felt like he was truly at his best. Racing three kermesses a week wore him down, and while he was glad for the experience, the cultural exchange and the improvement as a rider, he knew he was heading home to a different life, not to a cycling dream. But cycling is still very much ingrained in his life.

"Back then I thought I would check the box and not want to be racing after. But now I realized, I checked the box saying I don't want to be a pro, that's not really one of my goals anymore, I don't want that for a career, but I do still want to race and train. That's a difference. I could see myself in five years racing pro again, but right now I'm happy to have it on the side."

Photo by Elizabeth Freer

2: Riding the Canals

For us slower, fatter visitors (by cycling's emaciated standards), riding in Flanders[4] is both more mundane and just as mythic an experience as Steven's racing pursuits. American and other non-European cyclists have all figured out that there's great riding to be had in the old cycling nations of western Europe, be it tours of Tuscany or Alpine ascents like you've seen on TV. Further north, the word on the street isn't so much spectacle but proliferation, Go to Belgium, the Netherlands, or Denmark and you'll be blown away simply by the place cycling occupies in daily life, as well as in athletic competition. It hits you the second you exit any train station and see all the bikes lined (or piled) up. And though I was laden by luggage, I was impatient to get going.

Not that it was as simple as it sounds, at first. Getting my bearings after reaching the Gent railway station was the usual tale of traveller's woe: struggling to make sense of transit maps and dragging a massive load of luggage around like a pack horse, trying vainly not to look stupid. The streetcar line fortunately ran from the train depot to the Gravensteen Castle, an unmistakeable landmark in the middle of old Gent, forming the western boundary of the Patershol quarter in which I was

---

[4] So far I've mentioned Belgium more than Flanders, but ultimately this is a Flanders story. As far as I know, Wallonia and all of Belgium for that matter has great riding and a strong cycling culture, but it's distinct and less notorious — if not altogether on another, smaller scale — from that of Flanders. [Actually I've been assured that riding in the Brussels capitol region is an unmitigated disaster, so scratch that off the map.] The tiny roads and canal routes of Flanders are a bit more prevalent around the old textile towns of Flanders than down south, and the cobbles occupy a place in Flemish life that is far beyond that in the rest of the nation. But the love of cycling? Flanders has no national monopoly on that. So at times I'll use "Belgium" and "Flanders" interchangeably, but this chapter isn't one of those times.

staying. So I was quickly within range of my B&B, even if it took another 20 minutes of clueless spectacle to finish the job.

The main culprits were the usual narrow, winding streets typical of old Europe, and my discount bike box which managed to exceed the size of a lot of bikes, without the benefit of anything resembling a handle. My best hope was that people would relate to the sufferings of a would-be cyclist, but I happily settled for my second-best hope on finding that the good people of Gent weren't out and about at 2pm on a quiet, overcast Thursday.[5] I found my place, met my friendly host for the next week, and with no time or energy to summon the bike, I opted to stumble around looking at old buildings and art for a while, hoping I could stay awake til dinner.

It took only minutes before I wandered into the cultural heart of old Gent. I knew nothing about it before landing, but Gent is home to a Flemish primitive painting of the highest order, and I figured out somehow that this should be my first stop. [The soaring belfry and that stands in the old square and dominates the cityscape was a hint.] I'd forgotten most of the content of my art history college survey courses from a couple decades hence, but access to great art was a void in my life now and I wasn't going to miss my chance.

The full work is the *Gent Alterpiece*, a many-paneled 15th century assemblage by Flemish Primitive master Jan Van Eyck depicting various biblical scenes, including *The Adoration of the Mystic Lamb*, featuring a rather nonplussed sheep in the center panel squirting blood into a chalice in front of a

---

[5] Thankfully the tourist-ridiculing season doesn't peak until the weather warms up. The few people on the tramway were too busy getting places to openly laugh at my hapless state. Or maybe too polite, but that's hard to imagine in the age of social media.

complex assembly of admirers. The painting is world-famous, but more importantly is considered a national treasure among Belgians. The tortured history of people's schemes to possess or protect it is pure legend, detailed in a detective-style book called *The Stealing of the Mystic Lamb*. The Altarpiece now sits in an antechamber on the ground floor of Sint Baaf's Cathedral in Gent. It lives in its own special space, where handlers occasionally close or open its majestic panels for viewers to take in its different presentations. Admiring all this kept my mind sufficiently boggled and awake until I could justify dinner, an amazing waterzooi van fis, a/k/a fish stew, and a beer that hit me like a sack of doorknobs, whereupon I called it a day.

Thursday, 2pm in Gent. I want to live in such a place. By Chris Fontecchio

Friday was dedicated to finding my way around East Flanders before the races started on Saturday, with the E3 Prijs

Harelbeke, and taking care of business. Part of my overall plan was to attend at least a few events as a journalist, and I'd made the minimal effort to get credentials via the race websites, ahead of my arrival. The key bit was my need for a press card, an I.D. issued by the International Sportswriters' Association ("AIPS" from the French name), which certifies any applicant whose national association certifies them first. A month earlier I'd called the National Sportswriters and Sportscasters Association, the US entity in charge of unruly sports media types, and they'd signed me right up, with the one caveat that the AIPS cards were issued from Italy, once a month, on a somewhat less-than-reliable schedule. When my AIPS card didn't arrive in time -- it made it to Seattle a full six weeks after my trip *ended* -- I knew I might have some talking to do with the race organizers. So the plan on day 1 was to eat some carbs and sugars, hop on the bike, ride to Harelbeke and Wevelgem in hopes of finding the race organization offices for the weekend's two events, and beg for credentials before a human, face-to-face.

My host had some maps in the room, which were detailed enough for me to pick up on the fact that I hadn't the first clue about how to ride around this country. I don't know that I literally imagined cycling superhighways with neon signs saying "Fietsroute This Way!!"[6] But I am sure I didn't know how complicated things would eventually get. A friend from the Podium Cafe, my cycling website, had urged me to buy some

---

[6] "Fiets" is Dutch for bike. "Route" is route. Not to generalize about Dutch, since I wasn't able to gain full fluency from reading the sports pages over three weeks, but to an Anglo armed with a few key words, it's not especially hard to get the gist of the language, at least when it's written down. For example, take a wild guess what the headline "Wat brengt Big Phil in 2010?" next to a photo of Philippe Gilbert means. I'm sure I'd be over my head pretty quickly if I were on a literature tour or business negotiation, but the cycling lexicon isn't gonna be the heaviest book on anyone's shelf.

fietsroute maps, and it was clear I would never get out of Gent without at least one.

Flanders has a system of bike trails known as the Fietsnetwerk,[7] which has to be on the World Podium of Great Biking Networks. Possibly the top step, though you'll surely get an argument in Holland or maybe Denmark on that score. But to an American cyclist this is like the Ginger versus Maryanne arguments of my pimply youth -- as if anyone I knew had a problem with either. The Fietsnetwerk is a shockingly awesome glut of paths in every direction blanketing the country. The fietsroutes are, at their worst, perfectly acceptable painted lanes on the margin of secondary highways. More commonly they occupy smaller country roads, often barely wide enough for a car, traversing through farmers' fields or up over the famous *hellingen* (hills), or just moseying across the landscape. A few bear the flatness and arrow-straight orientation of a former rail route. Some are simply dedicated bike paths of no obvious origin, apart from something to do with leisure -- being too lovely to have spring from any utilitarian design. Plenty of them are closed to cars.

Among the most notable and easiest to follow are the canal routes, in many cases former towpaths from a time when canals were cash and horsepower had a lot to do with actual horses — in this case, towing barges up or down the canal with ropes. While a lot of fietsroutes connect towns or paths a short distance away, canal routes go on and on, seemingly clear across Belgium, with little to no interruption. Their length, size, straightness and prohibition against cars make them the superhighways of the Fietsnetwerk. Like a good interstate, it's

---

[7] http://www.fietsnet.be/routeplanner/default.aspx

a lot simpler to map out a canal route than using the minor pathways. And after a few hours, it gets pretty dull.

A typical canal route, along the Schelde to Oudenaarde. Photo by Chris Fontecchio

Both of the weekend's races started and finished along the Leie River between Gent and Kortrijk, a smallish city less than thirty miles southwest near the French border. Sunday's Gent-Wevelgem now departs from Deinze, the next discernible town on the way out of Gent, and finishes in Wevelgem, while Saturday's E3 Prijs[8] starts and finishes in Harelbeke -- suburbs that sandwich Kortrijk proper from the west and east. The latter two contained, somewhere in their respective bosoms, a person I could talk to about press credentials, or so I figured. In terms of getting there, all of my stops for the day were connected in a straight line by the Leie River fietsroute. And

---

[8] This is a race of many names, which will be discussed in a moment, but while the original E3 Prijs Vlaanderen seems to have passed out of vogue, E3, E3 Harelbeke and E3 Prijs still seem to work.

having paid more than I can admit without using profanity to fly my bike to Europe for the trip, I sure as hell wasn't planning on taking the train.

So after a few hours spent alternately reassembling my bike, eating, falling back to sleep, eating, and visiting a bike shop, I set about planning the trip down the Leie. Getting to the river from downtown involved choosing between a bunch of squiggly fietsroutes leading out of Gent, signifying God knows what, or the canal route, which initially went northwest toward Bruges for 10km before turning left and making a beeline for Kortrijk. Since "riding the canals" is a time-honored tradition, so the choice was easy.[9]

Mind you, I'm a natural optimist, something I like to think has been good for my soul in the long haul. Sure, I've leaned into more relationship sucker-punches than I would prefer, and growing up a Red Sox fan in the last millennium frequently combined with that sunny outlook to concoct some potent, bitter brews. Ultimately it beats worrying, I think, but if there is one area where optimism is an unmitigated handicap, it's in transportation planning. It's bad enough at home, where after twelve years in Seattle my wife still has to remind me that my bike commute home takes 15 minutes longer than I think. Trying to map out a day's journey in an utterly foreign country? Optimism can be positively crippling.

I started out of Gent a bit past noon for what looked like a 30 mile trek on a straight, fast trail. Ninety minutes seemed

---

[9] Easy if you don't overthink it. For example, the canal route to Kortrijk is spread across three separate maps: Gent, Leiestreek East and Leiestreek West. All routes are numbered, and the Leie canal route changes numbers about a dozen times. I kid you not. But if you just follow the river and don't worry too much about the signs, you can't go too wrong.

sufficient for this kind of trip without a pack, so in my cautious state, allowing for the unforseen, I called it an even two hours. Getting greedy, I figured it couldn't be more than another 45 minutes further west of Kortrijk to Kemmel, home to Belgium's most fearsome climb by many accounts -- the Kemmelberg. So if I moved quickly enough through my agenda I might make it out there for a try up the Kemmelberg, and if 80 miles is too much for the round trip, I could hop on the train back to Gent. I bought the Westhoek Zuid map too, to get me all the way to Ypres. Why not?

Apart from starting after noon and being able to hop on a train, almost none of the preceding paragraph bore any resemblance to reality. Bearing a bulky pack with camera, change of clothes, identification, maps, etc., I turned off the Bruges Canal onto the Schipdonkkanaal -- the upper extension of the Leie route -- and into a headwind that would define the rest of my day. By 4pm I was in Harelbeke, by 5:30 Wevelgem, and when left there an hour later I headed back toward Gent, keeping an eye on the dwindling light and the train map, laughing about the fact that I once thought I could make it to Kemmel. I still haven't opened the Westhoek Zuid map.

The spring winds of Flanders might have messed up my errand schedule and forced me to dig a little deeper than I planned, but I barely minded the inconvenience. These breezes are a timeless, unmistakeable protagonist in the great classics of cycling, an utterly indispensable factor if the race is to be worth watching -- well, that or rain. [Or snow. Preferably all three.] All of Nature's elements matter when you're riding across the open landscape: gravity, precipitation, surface friction. But those things you can detect with your eyes. Wind friction, the

difference between coasting effortlessly forever and reality, is unseen, only felt, and only with some experience can you feel the changes in wind friction enough to be a competent bike racer.
*****

OK, a quick detour to meditate on cycling physics, which are a bit more subtle on the Low Country plains than on, say, Mont Ventoux.

Drafting is to cycling as standing around is to baseball -- namely, its lifeblood, so you'd better be good at it if you want to seize your chance when it finally comes along. Wind resistance calls a lot of the shots, and the stronger it is, the slower you go -- no laughing matter for an activity you plan on doing for seven hours. It messes with your mind too: riding in a bloc headwind for long enough can make the most compassionate person want to run over a litter of kittens, whereas a stiff tailwind is better than the sensation of flying and taking pain medication for the first time, combined.

Even on a still day, moving forward generates wind friction, if you're the first rider in line. The best thing you as a cyclist can do about it is get behind another cyclist. Real close. Behind every person in the pack is a slipstream, a pocket where the rider's body creates a draft of air moving in the same direction, and if you can get in that spot properly you can reduce that all-limiting wind resistance by up to 40 percent. Maximizing this effect calls for riding with your front wheel within a few inches of the closest rear wheel; miss the slipstream by six inches and the aerodynamic advantage is cut in half.[10] Every amateur, and I suspect many a pro, has their comfort zone -- how close to another wheel you're willing to get, knowing that a touch of wheels could put you in the hospital — so getting in that sweet spot can be its own challenge. It gets worse with winds, changing direction or intensity as you move, causing the sweet spot to move with it. The person in front of you knows this, and unless they're being paid specifically to help you win, they will eventually insist on changing places. Add 198 more riders to the pack and let the drafting games begin.

Turning to the Spring Classics, the turbulent winds of March and April are a perfect match for the Flemish race calendar, for a few basic reasons. One, they're inescapable in the lowlands of Belgium and Holland and northern France, ill equipped with much in the way of landforms or tall trees to slow down an onshore breeze. Whatever trees are around probably don't have their leaves yet. And nobody would have it any other way: without the spring winds, a race across the Belgian lowlands would be a long, uneventful day.[11] In spring, the race courses meander drunkenly around Flanders, so a race like Gent-Wevelgem gets plenty of time to experience these winds from the front, the back, and most importantly, the side. Which brings us to the magic of the Crosswind.

---

[10] This applies in a single- or double-file line. In a large peloton, the collective wind break will suck along anything hanging around behind it, within a few feet. This, along with a relative lack of intensity, is why riding at the back is so tempting. It's an armchair ride, until the pack speeds up or a crash causes a split. Then you're in deep trouble.

[11] The ENECO Tour is the big summer race in BeNeLux, and after a few incredibly dull early editions using typical Belgian roads, the organizers figured out that in order to have a summer race there, they'd have to pull out all the stops. Now stages regularly finish atop the Muur van Geraardsbergen, the Côte de la Redoute (from Liège-Bastogne-Liège) and the Cauberg (of Amstel Gold fame). The other notable set of summer races in Belgium consists of post-Tour de France criteriums, which are fun spectacles associated with summer carnivals, and about as legitimate as the game where you knock over the milk bottles, which definitely don't have lead weights attached to them, as far as you know.

Unlike its head and tail counterparts, the crosswind is part of cycling lore worldwide, with a special place in the hearts of Belgians. Crosswinds destroy cycling cohesion like no other natural element, not even hills, which you know about days or weeks in advance. Steady crosswinds can be anticipated, but might also come with little to no warning, and if you're in the wrong position when they arrive, you've got trouble. The thing is, drafting in a crosswind requires you to ride at an angle from the person shielding you, as that sweet spot shifts to the side. A stiff wind from the left means the slipstream of the guy in front of you is behind his right shoulder, and to tuck in efficiently you need to ride not directly behind him as usual but closer to his right hip, wheels overlapping. The next guy in line then gets on your right hip. And so forth until, rather quickly, your angled line runs takes up the full width of the road. This diagonal formation of bikes is known as an echelon, and a properly ridden echelon in motion is an impressive sight.

Strung out single file, each echelon is only as strong as its weakest link. Once echelons form every rider finds himself in a small group of 6-12 riders, battling to remain competitive with the echelons up ahead and behind. So it's crucial to align yourself with an echelon that suits your objectives. If you are hoping to win, get in a group of powerful riders. If a few of your linemates are weak and/or spent, the collective power of your echelon drops, and your hopes are suddenly on the line.

As to the race, crosswinds are an opportunity to change things. If they hit in the first hour, chances of an escape going away are high, since chasing a break is tricky and energy-consuming, not what you want to do with another five hours to go. If they hit in the last hour, the drama that ensues -- or detonates, like a bomb on the peloton -- is what makes crosswinds so famous. On narrow Flemish roads the echelon effect is particularly severe -- maybe five or six guys can fit in line before the last one is hugging the curb, and it's time for the riders behind him to start another line.

The safest choice is to be close to the front before echelons happen, increasing the chances of being in a good position and surrounded by strong riders, and ride out the crosswinds in relative security. But all 200 guys can't fit into the top ten, and in the last hour or so of a race, the urgency of positioning is off the charts. Race radios start buzzing as teams try to figure out which of their main rivals has adeptly positioned himself, or fallen asleep on the job. Managed your way into the first echelon, by luck or skill? If your echelon-mates want to make trouble, the race is in your hands. Made it into echelon #3? That's good news if your rivals are further back, and danger if they're up front. Stuck in echelon #10? May the Cycling Gods have mercy on your soul. Be it ambition or blood lust or anger or fear, when this squall of emotion whips up on the race, everyone has a reason to start hammering.
*****

Back out on my private ordeal, the complete inability to coast meant that every meter from Gent to Wevelgem via Harelbeke was earned, the old-fashioned way. The result was that by the time I made it to the offices of the E3 Prijs, in a small house outside of town, it was close to 4pm on the eve of the race, and for all I knew people were going to start disappearing very soon. Worse, the organization office wasn't in the same place as the press center; that would be at the grammar school by the river that I passed half an hour earlier, where I could find the race-day *salle de presse* and the press officer, a Mr. Van Landeghem.

I am met by a large, older man with a serious demeanor, riding herd over the media as they descend on Flanders. He also seemed very busy, so when I explain my predicament he's not overly impressed. "Internet people with no ID... how do I know you are who you say you are?" as I showed him business cards and explain how far I've come. And of course, he had a point. This is why they have AIPS cards. I don't totally blame him, and perhaps the humbleness of my request came through. "This is all I can do for you!" he eventually said, handing me a press pass.

A press pass — the only thing I needed — was all he could do for me. I guess I was supposed to feel regret about missing out on the hospitality packet, but I hadn't actually flown halfway across the globe for a bag of local chocolates and nicknacks.[12] So yeah, score. On to my next stop: Wevelgem.

The ride was only another 10km or so, but at some point I got off the canal route and into the streets of Kortrijk, only not nice or interesting streets of downtown but perimeter arterial routes. There were signs to Wevelgem though, and if I just kept slogging away at the wind I figured I could get there by 5pm. And maybe, two days before the race, people will still be around. I'd registered for Gent-Wevelgem press creds and received a message saying I could have them, but it still seemed like I should explain my lack of an AIPS card to a

---

[12] Not that I would have said no.

human in advance of the race, if possible. All I needed to do was track down the right one.[13]

In my mind the office of the race would occupy a poster-filled spot at the busiest intersection in Wevelgem, with neon lights announcing their presence and maybe an electronic countdown clock showing how much longer til the race. It's not like Wevelgem is famous for anything else, right? If you go to Green Bay, Wisconsin, is it hard to find the Packers' offices? Why should the headquarters of Wevelgem's lone international calling card be obscured by churches, libraries, pubs and trinket shops? I don't know. But it was.

After an hour of chasing some vague leads I found a bike shop with a bit of a Pro Tour fan-vibe -- i.e., wall-to-wall with Quick Step clothing and trinkets. The shop owner thought the country's fourth-largest race was housed in an office just a block or so away, at the something-or-other bank office. Which it was, a small suite with a few posters and some police tape lying around. And a guy on the phone, being polite enough to me in spite of almost surely wanting to go home. Eventually I stated my business and he put me on the phone with a woman, Griet, who assured me everything would be taken care of. She offered to personally email the press officer and cc' me for good measure. Success, time to point the bike Gent-ward... and start hammering again.

If I've learned one thing from cycling it's the love of turning around after an endless headwind. My all-time favorite ride

---

[13] This was not true. On race day, whoever is checking you in doesn't have time for long explanations. If you're on the list and have ID but not your AIPS card, chances are they'd rather just give you a pass and be done with you. Not that I would try this at a bigger race -- or at all, if avoidable -- but Gent-Wevelgem is a long way from the Tour de France.

was an out-and-back in Vermont on an exposed ridge, probably no more than 15 miles total on farm roads. Out was one of the hardest slogs I'd ever experienced, into the teeth of a firm, steady breeze. I remember crawling along at about 14mph, a pathetic figure even back then in my poorly-trained ways, for what seemed like forever. Then I turned around and sailed home at speeds over 30 mph, flying along, non-stop, absolutely giddy with a sensation just short of flying. This was some thirty years ago, and I'll never forget it.

Now, from Wevelgem to Gent was nothing but wind-aided coasting, probably at some 23mph without much effort. But alas, sailing wasn't in the cards for me in Greater Kortrijk. The sun was sinking fast, and abandoning the road for a train was not a matter of if, but when. The winds were helpful enough and I stretched the return ride to maybe 15 miles, topping 65 for the day (not bad for running errands), and got to the Deerlijk train station just as the daylight levels devolved from "dim" to "grim."

Later that night, the email arrived. From Griet to Marc Van Landeghem, cc'ing me. Different race, same press officer. The world of the Classics may seem puffed up with greatness, but it's still a small, small place. Bottom line is, all systems go.

3: Harelbeke, E3 Prijs and the Cobbled Classic Season

Forty-eight hours in, I began to feel like I was standing in the middle of a movie I'd been watching for 20 years.

The opening event on my three-weekend agenda was the E3 Prijs Vlaanderen race, and as luck would have it, this was the only race I'd planned to see which started and finished in the same place. This doesn't actually happen very often in big-time racing, and the second you start to envy the cyclist's life,[14] up pops another twitter message about how it sucks to wake up in a different town every day. But on this day, the peloton was catching a break, and I was too.

For years I'd seen photo spreads and video coverage, which leave the impression that the two most reliably fun places to catch a race are the start and the finish. Both offer distinct advantages: the morning sign-ins, warmups and milling around that happens at the race start is a good time to say hello to relaxed and often-friendly riders, while the finish offers the chance to see the arms raised in victory and catch a few more impressions of the race first-hand. Start areas are porn for the gear fetishists -- many of the world's most beautiful production bikes, polished and presented for duty. Finishes come with scenes of flying bubbly. In between, everything moves all too

---

[14] Or that of anyone associated with a team, sponsor, or media outlet.

fast. Cycling journalists want to be in both places. That's why they... have cars.

Not that I knew any of this or appreciated how lucky I was. At most I knew I needed to talk myself out of something stupid like "I think I'll take my bike and ride out to the Taaienberg," and having this much action, and the press center, all within walking distance of a stop on the Gent-Kortrijk train line sounded too convenient to pass up. Also, I thought there might be some reporting to be done on Harelbeke cycling pubs. There isn't... but I only learned this through due diligence and a reporter's keen eye.

One thing I did get right was find the race -- follow everyone. I hopped off the train from Gent at Harelbeke Station, a utilitarian facility on the outskirts of the town which, by Flemish standards, is not particularly old or adorable. A block away from the station, traffic flowed through a stone arch beneath the elevated tracks and the granite ridge propping them up. The Kortrijk train line forms something of a Great Wall between the riverside villages to the west and farmland to the east, with just a few gateways. In other words, this archway is the choke point for much of the traffic coming from the E17 highway, which itself connects Harelbeke to the outside world.[15]

Anyway, despite my disorientation I instinctively began to follow a thick flow of pedestrians, traffic, and brightly colored signs pointing "equipes" and "directeurs sportif" down

---

[15] The E17 was originally known as the E3, the motorway whose creation in the 1960s the E3 Prijs Vlaanderen still celebrates with its name. Old habits and iconic logos (a blue triangle with white block lettering "E3") don't die easily in a traditional world like cycling, so the old highway name is still celebrated after its official demise. If you just say "Harelbeke," people will know what race you're referring to.

Stationsstraat (Station Street) into the center of town. As we approached Marktstraat (Market Street -- really, Dutch isn't rocket science) where the race began and ended, a few pubs popped up, simmering with activity. A few older buildings -- churches and municipal structures of some sort -- separated the newer shops and pubs which stretch around the riverfront industrial zone and on into neighboring Kortrijk. People were milling around the barriers marking the race start, as the start time drew near, but the real scene was across the Leie River.

Connected to the start area by a low-arching, four-lane bridge, this part of town was jammed with people. Parked by the side of the road, with no screens or rope lines to keep the fans at a distance, were all of the team buses, which looked like colorful icebergs bobbing in a roiling, gray sea of humanity. Every now and then the sea parted and the even more colorful figure of a rider was disgorged, and I found myself elbow-to-elbow with the Belgian Classics scene.

Harelbeke on Race Day, 2010. Photo by Chris Fontecchio

Within seconds, though, it occurred to me that I had no idea how to recognize anyone, apart from the obvious guys. I had zipped in to the *salle de presse* to grab my packet with the startlist, and using the assigned race numbers I could pick out a few guys. Surely that was Lars Boom, the Rabobank rider with the sleeve piping of a past Dutch champion. With the startlist I could figure out that those Vacansoleil riders passing by were Johnny Hoogerland and Lieuwe Westra. The guys from Team Sky could be identified by their names printed on the ribcage panels of their kits. But mostly the scene was a blur, and identifying riders wasn't as interesting as just soaking in the mob of the fans and stars all jumbled together.

While the team bus area was a free-for-all, back toward the start the streets were fenced off all the way to the finish zone. With a press pass I could walk up the middle of the road, rather than cramming through the narrow sidewalk over the bridge beyond the barriers, but it's a distinction without much difference, save for feeling like I'm walking the red carpet into the Oscars. A stage contained the rider sign-in sheets, and as every rider has to officially sign in, it amounted to a parade past the fans below, dutifully M.C.'d for a good 45 minutes prior to the race. Occasionally a rider of interest got collared for an interview, whereupon some mild-mannered, joking banter and cautious optimism ensued (in Dutch, which on further review I definitely don't speak).

In general there are lots of places to find valuable pre-race information, but asking a rider is about the last place you want to look. This reached comic proportions when the M.C. grabbed Edvald Boasson Hagen, a young Norwegian known for his off-the-charts talent (realized, to a certain degree) and his painfully shy demeanor. Fortunately they switched to English, the common denominator of cycling these days, so I could confirm that he's mumbling about nothing particularly noteworthy. Tom Boonen, of course, was the feature act, and he chatted amiably for the crowd, but the pre-race tension grew anyway.

Alexander Kristoff, Edvald Boasson Hagen and Kurt-Asle Arvesen. Photo by Chris Fontecchio

Eventually the riders mounted their bikes, but it still wasn't time to roll out. So they congregated in the corral, Norwegians and Italians and Belgians from rival teams chatting with each other to pass the time. I chatted with Roger Hammond, a longtime cobbles warrior, and he expressed his hopes (what else?) for a good run. Kids called from the barriers for last-minute autographs, and seconds before we started Russian Serguei Ivanov sauntered over to indulge a persistent kid.

Finally, the whistle blew, the riders rolled out, and the caravan followed. An explosion of activity lasting several minutes til the final bus and car and motorbike were gone… and then the streets went a bit silent. But the littered handbills and Flemish lion flags on the road meant that the Classics Season was underway.

The Classics Season is truly a distinct subset of the cycling calendar.[16] If you ask people when it begins, you won't always get the same answer. The Omloop Het Nieuwsblad -- known as Het Volk for the first 63 years of its existence -- comes on the last Saturday in February or the first in March, and bears the distinction of being one of the most likely races on the world calendar to be snowed out. Twice cancelled (1986, 2004), once postponed, and threatened with disaster almost every other year, the race serves as a preseason event, too early for riders to be on their top form but a nice preview of what's coming in the next few weeks. Fans, on the other hand, don't offer any prestige discounts due to such trifling concerns as "it's February" or "it's snowing," and the Omloop Weekend, book-ended by the flatter Kuurne-Brussels-Kuurne race on Sunday, is celebrated like a major event.

Outside of Flanders, many fans identify Paris-Nice as the start of the cycling season, a nod to its history from the 1930s as the first outdoor event following the winter track season. Paris-Nice is a stage race, covering eight days as it runs from the southern suburbs of Paris to the Mediterranean, and while it is no longer first on the calendar, the image of racing from wintry Paris to the sunny French Riviera very nicely advertises the hope that spring will come soon. To the Classics riders, Paris-Nice serves

---

[16] This was an early working title for the book.

a more practical purpose -- eight hard days in the saddle is critical preparation for the upcoming one-day headliners. Grand Tour mountain goat-types, with no use for the Omloop, will often start their season in Paris-Nice. But riders have their limits, the race is known for horrendous weather and flu outbreaks, and for what it's worth American sprinter Tyler Farrar of Dimension Data[17] insists "everyone hates it," in part because the hotels and food are abysmal. Apparently if a rider is in good enough graces with his team he can get himself sent to Tirreno-Adriatico, an overlapping race similar in profile but warmed by the Italian sun.[18] But you can't show up in Belgium fit for battle if you don't go to one of these week-long affairs.

I suppose you can find others -- Italians, certainly -- who will name Milano-Sanremo as the opening of the cycling season, or at least the classics. *La Primavera* comes before the peloton disembarks for Belgium. Moreover, it's not just a classic, it's the first "monument" of the season, joining the Tour of Flanders, Paris-Roubaix, Liege-Bastogne-Liege and the Giro di Lombardia in cycling's ultimate pantheon of one-day races. Milano-Sanremo is a fascinating race, the longest ride of the year at about 300km, and subtly unpredictable. Thanks to the late climb and descent of the Poggio, just two kilometers from

---

[17] Farrar, who I'll get to in more detail shortly, rode mostly for the Garmin/Slipstream/etc. team before joining MTN-Qhubeka in 2015, before they changed to Dimension Data.

[18] And the team may very well indulge, unless they are angling for a wildcard invite to the Tour de France. The current system (subject to change) has the UCI granting 18 World Tour licenses, which come with an automatic invite to the Tour de France, a race whose economic significance dwarfs everything else, as far as teams and sponsors are concerned. Up to four more "wildcard" invites to the Tour are available, and Paris-Nice is owned by the same private entity, the Amaury Sports Organization, which owns the Tour de France. Lately an understanding has developed that teams hoping to get a Tour wildcard should go to Paris-Nice and prove their mettle, and hope for a Tour invite if you hold up your end. By the same token, Tirreno-Adriatico is owned by the Giro d'Italia's parent company, so if you're angling for that race instead of the Tour, e.g. if you're a second-division Italian team, then your dress rehearsal opportunity lies in the Race of the Two Seas.

the finish, it gives hope to climbers and madman descenders, but if they don't steal the show, the peloton of tireless sprinters take charge.

But Milano-Sanremo, while certainly the first of the true spring classics, is a world unto itself, bearing no resemblance to the Belgian events around the corner. And while Paris-Nice might inaugurate the season, it too has its own story, separate and distinct from the classics. As for the Omloop, let's face it: its purpose is to preview the upcoming season, an indulgence for fans who can't wait for the feature presentation. Same with a new race, the Strade Bianche, a visual feast featuring the white-gravel roads of Tuscany's marble-producing country on the weekend after the Omloop. Like the Omloop, it's great racing and great fun. But it was started in 2007, so let's not confuse it with the real thing.

For my money, the essence of the spring classics is found in the northern events, and the Northern Classics Season starts for real with Dwars Door Vlaanderen, continuing for five weeks through the completion of Liege-Bastogne-Liege. Belgium is the common theme, with every race contained within its borders except for Paris-Roubaix and the Amstel Gold Race, two events which, while culturally non-Belgian, nonetheless finish within biking distance of the border and bear plenty of physical resemblance to the rest. It's a coherent season in which the races hang together, physically and psychologically, connected by the common themes of difficult roads, potentially lousy weather, rugged northern cultures and short, nasty hills.

The season contains 14 days of racing, 10 of which are considered the "cobbled" events, three of which are the "Ardennes" races, and one -- Brabantse Pijl -- that acts as a hybrid. Hardly anyone rides all 14 days, but every top rider can be expected to show up somewhere in that stretch, and for the cobbled classics riders, ten events is enough to define yourself as a cyclist. Here's a brief overview, in order of calendar appearance.

Day 1. Dwars door Vlaanderen

Name: "Straight Across Flanders"
Date: Last Wednesday in March (roughly; sometimes a week earlier)
Course: an impossibly crooked route from Roselare, across the Leie, southeast around the Vlaamse Ardennen, and back to Waregem on the Leie (or, if you prefer, the Gent-Kortrijk axis, a sort-of equator for the classics).
Hellingen (hill) Factor: High. The stars are the Paterberg, Eikenberg, Taaienberg and Oude Kwaremont. Thirteen climbs in all in 2013; 11 in 2014, 12 in 2015… you get the picture.
Cobbles: pretty brutal. The legendary Haaghoek (see below) is among the non-vertical sections of stones that will punish the riders all day. The Holleweg and Varentstraat also feature.
Unique character: Always run on a Wednesday, the only mid-week event previewing the all-important Flemish Ardennes. It's also the official start of Vlaamse Wielerweek.
Recent Winners: Jelle Wallays (2015), Niki Terpstra (2012, 14), Oscar Gatto (2013), Nick Nuyens (2011), Matti Breschel (2010).
Assessment: Opening night is not when anyone wants to reach their peak, but Dwars is a pretty good dress rehearsal for

the bigger events, particularly the Tour of Flanders. If you've spent all spring on smooth tarmac, Dwars will shock you into Flemish reality. Attendance is hindered a bit by Milano-Sanremo, especially with *La Primavera* moving to Sunday in 2013; not everyone wants to hustle up to Roselare right away. But the guys who do tend to put on a great show. In 2014 it was probably the best race of the entire Cobbles season, and there's nothing stopping it from achieving that status again. With the consolidation and reorganization of the warm-up classics in 2013, the race got bumped from a UCI 1.1 event to 1.HC, which meant it could have 70% Pro Tour teams instead of the former 50% limit. This is no longer a warm-up to the warm-ups. It's full on.

Day 2. E3 Harelbeke

Name: Originally honoring the opening of the E3 highway. It's had a few names over the years, including E3 Prijs Vlaanderens and E3 Prijs Harelbeke. Fittingly the E3 has also been renamed to the A14/E17, though the race still bears its old name, because… I don't know why.
Date: Last Friday in March, in all likelihood. [Previously Saturday.]
Course: Vaguely clover-like circuit starting and finishing in Harelbeke, next door to Kortrijk.
Hellingen **Factor:** Very high. This is an unabashed Tour of Flanders preview, albeit in reverse direction and not dramatically different in character from Dwars.
Cobbles: Brutal. All the chef's specials from the Ronde menu, in a diet-sized portion.
Unique character: The only race which isn't under the Flanders Classics umbrella, it's an organizational stand-alone.

So for a couple years it got kicked around a bit, til the UCI gave it World Tour status in 2012.

Recent Winners: Geraint Thomas (2015); Peter Sagan (2014); Tom Boonen (2004-07, 2012); Fabian Cancellara (2010-11, 2013); Filippo Pozzato (2009).

Assessment: Running in reverse direction from de Ronde means you won't get a foreshadowing of the next Sunday's tactics, but your legs won't know the difference. It's the premier Tour of Flanders tuneup. Not everyone is ready to go in time for Dwars, but they're all on the line in Harelbeke, and the podium is generally regarded as an indicator of who the next weekend's favorites will be. But like dress rehearsals, people don't always show their cards, and we've had some bunch finishes.

Day 3. Gent-Wevelgem

Name: Well, it does still finish in Wevelgem, another village on the outskirts of Kortrijk. Gent is a tough place to stage a race though, so it starts nowadays in nearby Deinze.

Date: Last Sunday in March.

Course: A C-shaped loop around West Flanders, often right to the North Sea, before circling back inland with a stop for a few hilly circuits around Ypres. The finish line is a 35km southwest of the start line.

Hellingen **factor:** moderate. The traditional Gent-Wevelgem course de-emphasizes the climbs, employing fewer major uphills further from the finish, in order to give the sprinters a hope of victory. But they still factor in the outcome most years.

Cobbles: Sure. Not the usual suspects, but they get quite nasty at times.

Unique Character: The West Flanders terrain is nothing like the Flemish Ardennes; it's mostly board-flat, wind-swept, and subject to brutal crosswinds which frequently shatter the race. But the hills of het Heuvelland, near Ypres, can shake up the race, and the decisive climb (if there is one) is often the Kemmelberg, a horrid brute. Then it's 35km back to Wevelgem, potentially enough to let the sprinters back in after the hills. For most of its history Gent-Wevelgem was the mid-week event between the two behemoths of de Ronde and Paris-Roubaix, a true Holy Week of cycling... until the race moved to Sunday for 2010, added a bunch of climbs, and tried to become a West Flanders Ronde warmup.

Recent Winners: Luca Paolini (2015); John Degenkolb (2014); Peter Sagan (2013); Tom Boonen (2004, 2011-12); Bernhard Eisel (2010); Edvald Boasson Hagen (2009); Oscar Freire (2008).

Assessment: It's a challenging race, especially in foul weather when tactics take over, but different in many ways from de Ronde: less selective, more open to small-to-medium bunch finishes and other late maneuvering. Fewer cobbles, fewer hills, more wind. So among the cobbles guys, if de Ronde's climbs are just beyond your limits, perhaps this is your race. For many sprinters, this is the #1 priority in Flanders, behind just Milano-Sanremo in prestige.[19]

---

[19] One guy's list of great sprint races, in order (assuming no Olympic or World Championship opportunities):
1. Milano-Sanremo
2. Gent-Wevelgem
3. Final Tour de France stage in Paris
4. Paris-Tours
5. Scheldeprijs

Days 4-7. Driedaagse de Panne

Name: Three Days of De Panne -- but four stages, including two in coastal De Panne.

Date: Tuesday-Thursday before Flanders

Course: An out-and-back route from West Flanders, briefly into the Flemish Ardennes (why not?), before turning back to the coast. Day 1 is a tepid Ronde warmup; day 2 catches or at least mimics much of the Gent-Wevelgem route; and day three is a flat circuit around coastal De Panne in the morning plus a short time trial in the afternoon.

Hellingen **factor:** Only stage 1 features decisive climbing. Stages 2 and 3a are for the bunch sprinters.

Cobbles: Sure, though not overly decisive.

Unique Character: The only stage race on the list, Driedaagse is something to do while waiting for de Ronde. Each day is good training for Sunday, without being overly taxing, if the weather isn't too god-awful (though it usually is). Also, for sprinters who don't want to go home empty-handed, the second and third stages are inviting.

Recent Overall Winners: Alexander Kristoff (2015); Guillaume Van Kiersbulck (2014); Sylvain Chavanel (2012-13); Sebastian Rosseler (2011); David Millar (2010); Frederik Willems (2009).

Assessment: Occasionally predictive of Flanders success (2015, Ballan in 2007). Riders are generally torn between sticking this race out to the end or bailing after one or two stages to ride their own Ronde tuneups. Some of the biggest names (e.g. Cancellara) skip it entirely. Competition level is a cut below the other races listed above.

Day 8. Ronde van Vlaanderen

Name: Tour of Flanders.

Date: Usually the first Sunday in April. The historic 2013 running, the 100th anniversary edition, was March 31, about as early as it gets.

Course: An actual tour of Flanders. Starting in Bruges, the race has settled into a pattern of deciding who wins by forcing the pack to meander around the Flemish Ardennes for the last 100km. But the first 150km changes every year, offering the race a chance to visit the small towns of Flanders and give the country a chance to experience its most treasured sporting event first hand. It's the national race by much more than reputation.

***Hellingen* factor:** if this race isn't their reason for existing, then I don't know my geology.

Cobbles: The race that made them famous. Well, one of the races at least.

Unique Character: Superlatives aside, the Tour of Flanders is the ultimate combination of climbs, cobblestones, a thousand tiny roads, and a million sharp left- and right-hand turns, over the longest distance of the Belgian classics. It's everything you want in a classic, but bigger, harder, longer and lovelier.

Recent winners: Alexander Kristoff (2015); Tom Boonen (2012, 2005-06); Nick Nuyens (2011); Fabian Cancellara (2010, 2013-14); Stijn Devolder (2008-09); Alessandro Ballan (2007).

Assessment: This is really the main event. Paris-Roubaix is the only other cobbled race of equal stature, and the course itself is a bit of an outlier. That's a compliment, mind you. But Flanders defines the cobbled classics.

Day 9. Scheldeprijs

Name: *Grote Scheldeprijs*, Grand Prize of the Schelde.
Date: Wednesday between Flanders and Paris-Roubaix — the Holy Week interlude formerly occupied by Gent-Wevelgem. Prior to 2010 it took place on the Wednesday after Paris-Roubaix.
Course: A toned-down cobbles course just east of Antwerp, with several easy circuits (swinging by the Schelde) at the conclusion of the race. Pretty much guaranteed to end in a sprint.
Hellingen **Factor:** negligible. By the end of the Tour of Flanders, everyone's had enough climbing.
Cobbles: A few servings of them, but they aren't particularly notorious.
Unique Character: All those years following Paris-Roubaix helped define the Scheldeprijs as a sort of light, pleasant dessert course to the Cobbles season. Now, it's more of a mid-course palate cleanser, meant to entice riders out on the road at a very guarded time by promising not to hurt them too much. Not that it's an easy day -- it's still 200km in the spring elements. But the overall intensity of the race is less lethal.
Recent winners: Alexander Kristoff (2015), Marcel Kittel (2012-14), Mark Cavendish (2007-08, 2011), Tyler Farrar (2010), Alessandro Petacchi (2009).
Assessment: Riders for the bigger events will show up here, but don't look for them to play any cards. For the pure sprinters, this is their only sure-fire day to shine, and they do. For the rest, it's marginally considered a classic, and no day for big risks or efforts.
When it followed Roubaix, it gave local boy Tom Boonen a chance to sprint for the home crowd as a sort of victory lap,

but when it changed calendar positions, Boonen switched to setting up teammates.

Day 10. Paris-Roubaix

Name: The Hell of the North (*l'Enfer du Nord*). The Queen of the Classics.

Date: A week after de Ronde, usually the second Sunday in April. Flanders and Roubaix have switched places on occasion but not for a while. Roubaix has also been known as the Easter race, though that's only sometimes accurate.

Course: By cycling standards, it's a pretty straight line heading north-north-east, before bending a bit west after Valenciennes, for the business end of things.

Hellingen **Factor:** Nonexistent. Little-known fact: Paris-Roubaix did have some hills back in the day. Pretty good ones. But no more. And I doubt anyone misses them.

Cobbles: If de Ronde made them famous, Paris-Roubaix made them infamous. Riders don't often curse their sport, but you can start a pretty good argument in the peloton about what constitutes a road that's "fit for a bike race" here.

Unique Character: "Unique" only begins to tell the story. No race favors larger-bodied riders like Paris-Roubaix. The punishing cobbles, strong winds, and total lack of hills add up to the Revenge of the Draft Horses. Unlike Flanders, there aren't a zillion twists and turns. Just get up front and grind.

Recent winners: John Degenkolb (21015), Niki Terpstra (2014), Fabian Cancellara (2006, 2010, 2013), Tom Boonen (2005, 2008-09, 2012), Johan Van Summeren (2011)

Assessment: Plenty of riders have done the sainted Flanders-Roubaix Double, and more have come close, but the races favor different characteristics. Top riders in the classics talk all the time of favoring one of the Monuments over the other, and Roubaix specialists are pretty easy to find. If you're over six feet tall, strong as an ox, and don't care for all the climbs at de Ronde, today is likely your Super Bowl.

Day 11. Brabantse Pijl / La Flèche Brabançonne

Name: The Brabant Arrow -- a race across the Brabant Region of Belgium. Time to say goodbye to Flanders.

Date: Wednesday after Paris-Roubaix. Formerly much earlier in the rotation, but this is a better spot.

Course: another horribly twisted "arrow" route, meandering around Brabant.

Hellingen: yes! And they're longer than the Flemish climbs.

Cobbles: It's Belgium. There are cobbles. But they don't define the race, by any means.

Unique Character: This has long been a lower-key event among the breathless stretch of esteemed races, and placing it after Paris-Roubaix hasn't changed that. However, it's also a chance to draw out some riders who are perhaps just trickling into the area in anticipation of the Ardennes Classics coming up. Brabantse Pijl celebrates the landscape of Brabant, which itself is a nice microcosm of the event. The historical Province of Brabant is wedged between Flanders and Wallonia, straddling the linguistic border, and since this is Belgium it had to be split into two separate provinces, in 1995. Fittingly, the race (which is split maybe 2:1 between the Flemish- and French-speaking areas) is a hybrid of Flanders and Ardennes classics, open and windswept, lightly cobbled, if at all, and featuring about 25-30 short climbs.

Recent Winners: Ben Hermans (2015), Philippe Gilbert (2011, 2014), Peter Sagan (2013), Thomas Voeckler (2012), Sebastian Rosseler (2010), Anthony Geslin (2009), Sylvain Chavanel (2008), Oscar Freire (2005-07).

Assessment: Of the cobbles riders, the Paris-Roubaix draft-horses have little hope here, while for the medium/small-ish riders who climb very well but have the power to handle the cobbles, this is their day. The mountain goats who dominate the next week in the Ardennes don't tend to invade Brabantse Pijl, or if they're here they often guard their form.

Day 12. Amstel Gold Race

Name: Sponsor Amstel, the Dutch beer giant, founded the race in 1966 to give the Netherlands an enduring, major classic race. Sorta like bringing the World Cup to Brazil -- how did this not happen sooner? Anyway, AGR is a recognizable acronym.

Date: Third Saturday in April, a week before the Koningsdag (King's Day) holiday — which was formerly Queen's Day, and which the race was originally scheduled for, only to have logistics and protesters from the Provo Movement force a change to a week earlier. Somehow this seems like a day when Dutch fans are entirely ready to party, holiday or not. Anyway, unlike most races which forge traditions out of whatever mundane circumstances they confront, the AGR was carefully targeted to be good fun.

Course: A spaghetti-like scramble over every cute little road outside Maastricht. There are multiple circuits, but each lap is different. The finish atop the Cauberg favored purely climbing... and waiting. But after hosting the 2012 World Championships, with the finish a couple km further up the road after the climb levels off, Amstel followed suit starting in 2013, and the new finish has made for a more interesting finale. It's not just a climb-sprint to the line anymore.

Hellingen: Indeed, although the terrain of Limburg Province[20] is more like the Ardennes in Wallonia -- longer climbs, smoother surfaces, good for the pure climbers... but short enough for at least some of the power riders to stay in contact. AGR sets the record for rated climbs in a classic, typically including about 33.

Cobbles: Nope. And frankly, after the last month, the image of smooth roads is a little jarring.

Unique Character: The roads themselves. AGR is made up of endless tiny roads snaking in, around and over the verdant hills of lovely, pastoral Limburg. To win you have to be a pretty dominant climber, enough to race from the very front of the field, because the idea of moving up from the back seems ludicrous.

Recent Winners: Michal Kwiatkowski (2015), Philippe Gilbert (2010-11, 2014), Roman Kreuziger (2013), Enrico Gasparotto (2012), Serguei Ivanov (2009), Damiano Cunego (2008). Gilbert also won the 2012 World Championships on a semblance of the AGR course.

Assessment: The little climbers who are almost universally absent from the cobbled classics suddenly appear in Maastricht a few days ahead of this race, like a sudden high pressure system moving in overnight after three stormy weeks.

---

[20] That would be the Dutch Limburg Province, not to be confused with the Belgian Limburg Province right next door, which is flatter and not known for any major pro events. At least one part of Belgium, besides downtown Brussels, has to not be known for pro cycling events. Right? Anyway, the two Limburgs used to be one Limburg until 1839 when the Treaty of London split the province between Belgium and Holland. Oh, and the name comes from a fortified town in... Liege. If you really want a headache, you might look up Dutch Brabant, which they call Noord-Brabant (North) in the Netherlands, the implication that the Belgian province is Zuid Brabant (South), and it was, until 1830 when newly-independent Belgium severed the nominal tie. To recap, Brabant was comprised of two Dutch provinces until the Netherlands and Belgium split. Then each country had one Brabant. Then the Belgians split theirs in half. Got it?

But that is no assurance of great racing, and my beef with this crowd, starting at Amstel Gold and continuing through the grand tours, is that they can be very cagey in their approach. With La Fleche Wallonne and Liege-Bastogne-Liege in the coming eight days, the latter being a monument, the mega-stars sometimes seem to hold their fire a bit at Amstel. At its best Amstel Gold is a great, unpredictable race, barely distinguishable in both character and prestige from Liege, as long as people show up to battle.

And here we wander off into one of cycling's never-ending arguments. "He should attack!" "Why aren't they attacking?!?" is a common refrain in races, both the cobbled classics and the hilly ones, where in recent editions the top riders have mostly waited until the final minutes of the race to launch anything like a definitive attack. "Because I was tired," usually comes the rider's answer (skipping over the unseen complexities of a long race which sapped his strength in the first place). Cycling is no exception to the rule that fans want and expect action, but how realistic those expectations are at any given moment is nearly impossible to pin down. Sure, some guys thrive on launching dramatic accelerations, and if they're not doing so, you can be pretty sure their chamber is empty. Another group of riders, particularly sprinters who have little incentive to break up the race, can be counted on to do anything but attack, since their best chance is from a bunch sprint.

But for a larger percentage, even among the top guys, the wisdom of attacking is subject to constant reassessment, based on the race situation, the relative exhaustion of whoever is on hand, and of course their own reserves. Riders in this category will always explain the lack of attacks in any race they lose by saying "well, sure, of course I would have if I could have." How convinced fans are on hearing that... it's not often pretty. No doubt some riders need to be called out to take chances, and naifs like me might give some guys more credit than they deserve. Then again, presumably close to 100% of those riders have team directors doing exactly that -- yelling in the rider's earpiece, no less. So when the inevitable fan criticism comes rolling in, questioning the desire of a guy who just burned 15,000 calories he didn't have to spare in an all-out war on the bike, it can be a little hard to watch.

Day 13. La Flèche Wallonne

Name: The Wallonian Arrow. Another non-arrow arrow. But whatever, we're finally in Wallonia.
Date: Third or last Wednesday in April. At present, with Gent-Wevelgem migrating to the weekend, La Flèche is the biggest mid-week classic of the year.
Course: About 198km of ups and downs through the beautiful, brooding forests of Namur Province, before the endgame, a 2km slow-motion sprint up the Mur de Hûy.
Hellingen: Er, check your Dutch at the linguistic border. It's all côtes and the occasional Mur from here on out. Côte is French for "coast," a word meant to evoke images of horse-drawn sleighs careening down a snowy hill. Mur is a special distinction, like the Flemish "Muur" (meaning "wall") in Geraardsbergen, reserved for truly leg-breaking ascents. And the signature event of La Fleche is the Mur de Hûy, a 2km beast straight into the gradient, averaging 10% and topping out at 17%. Possibly the hardest climb in Belgium, at least when it's ridden in an all-out, race-ending sprint.
Cobbles: Nope.

Unique Character: Of the classics, only this and Amstel finish on a climb, and between the two the finishing climb at La Fleche is far more decisive. In fact, it's pretty much the whole race. Earlier climbs, including an initial trip up the Mur de Hûy, help separate the wheat from the chaff, but the race is on for good with about 10 or 15 km to go, as teams prepare for the final 2km climb -- which takes forever -- by either launching maneuvers or saving their strength. Of all the classics, apart from the underwhelming Scheldeprijs, this is by far the most predictable. Except for once that's a good thing: the slugfest on the Mur is truly spectacular, every time.

Recent Winners: Alejandro Valverde (2006, 2014-15), Dani Moreno (2013), Joaquim Rodriguez (2012), Philippe Gilbert (2011), Cadel Evans (2010), Davide Rebellin (2009), Kim Kirchen (2008). The race gained its first Spanish winner in 2003, and its second, third, fourth, fifth and sixth in pretty quick succession.

Assessment: La Flèche is a bit of a specialty race even among the climbers' classics, since it's basically a 2km uphill sprint which decides the event. For the pint-sized guys who aren't necessarily as strong as the riders who win in Limburg or Liege but who can kill it for ten minutes or so,[21] this is their day. Patience is a major ingredient -- the trick is to get an armchair ride to Hûy, then not to attack at the start of the Mur but to stay within range when the inevitable attacks are launched in the first half of the climb and be the last man standing at the top. In the few events I can picture by memory, nobody has been able to sustain an attack from the lower slopes of the Mur all the way to the finish. But guys always try,

---

[21] It isn't quite fair to describe the race as 200km of wandering aimlessly and 2km of utter madness. The race action is subject to ebbs and flows, like any, and on the final run-in to Hûy the temperature rises steadily anywhere inside the last, oh, 15km. The real action is on the Mur, sure, but there is definitely a bike race happening throughout the final stages.

and the result is a slugfest the length of the Mur, over about five absolute edge-of-your-seat minutes.

Day 14. Liège-Bastogne-Liège

Name: Liège and Bastogne are two cities in Wallonia, which more or less still represent the terminal and turnaround points of this ancient classic. Also known as "La Doyenne," the old lady, as it's the oldest of the classic professional cycle races still in existence.[22]

Date: Last Sunday (usually) in April.

Helling... um, Côtes? Whoa yeah. The longest climbs of the classics season are found in this great race. Not as numerous as Amstel and nothing as clearly determinative as the Mur de Hûy, but La Côte de la Redoute is one of the hallowed places in all of cycling.

Unique Character: L-B-L has spawned numerous imitators around the world with its format of starting in point A, heading out to point B on a nice, lovely ride, and returning back to point A via all of those nasty hills you avoided on the way out.[23]

Recent Winners: Alejandro Valverde (2006, 2008, 2015), Simon Gerrans (2014), Dan Martin (2013), Maxim Iglinsky (2012), Philippe Gilbert (2011), Alexandre Vinokourov (2010), Andy Schleck (2009).

---

[22] The key word is professional. What is the world's oldest bike race? Paris-Rouen is generally recognized as the first race, in 1869, but that event went amateur and then disappeared. Paris-Brest-Paris, begun in 1891 and continues today as a randonnée, part race and part marathon, and strictly amateur. But the longest-running race is something called the Catford CC Hill Climb, an amateur hill dash in Kent (south of London) that dates back to 1887.

[23] For years there was an utterly brilliant version outside Tacoma called Tahuya-Seabeck-Tahuya — mostly rolling on the way out across the interior of Kitsap Peninsula, then just littered with climbs on the more coastal return leg.

Assessment: With the biggest climbs a good 20km or more from the finish, L-B-L is a true classic in that riders can employ a variety of attributes to win -- climbing, descending, attacking on the flats, and even the occasional sprint from a small group. Moreover, being in the Monumental 250km range means that a true strength is required to win, more so than La Flèche. The finale often contains one or two strong classics riders not known for climbing. If you want to see everything cycling has to offer in a single day, this is the best race in the world.

A point of order -- this book is about the Flemish Ardennes (Vlaamse Ardennen) -- not to be confused with the better-known Wallonian Ardennes of Liege province -- as much as anything else, and the series that revolves around them. The four days spent probing the Vlaamse Ardennen are Dwars door Vlaanderen, E3 Prijs, the first stage of Driedaagse de Panne and de Ronde -- three hors d'oeuvres and the Tour of Flanders, constituting a season within the season [within the season]. Check out this chart of the 2013 climbs:

Where Are the Climbs?

Name	Length (m)	Gradient Avg/ max	Cobbled? Y / N	Ronde Climb #	E3 Climb #	Dwars Climb #	Omloop Climb #
Tiegemberg	750	5.6/9%	N	1	14	--	--
Taaienberg	530	6.6/18%	Y	2	8	--	8
Eikenberg	1300	6.2/10%	Y	3	6	6	9
Molenberg	463	7/14.2%	Y	4	--	--	12
Berendries	940	7/12.3%	N	6	--	4	2
Valkenberg	540	8/12.8%	N	7	--	5	6
Oude Kwaremt	2200	4/11.6%	Y	8, 13, 16	12	9	--
Paterberg	360	13/23%	Y	9, 14, 17	11	10	--
Koppenberg	600	11.6/22	Y!	10	--	--	--
Steenbekdries	700	5.3.6.7%	Y	11	--	7	--
Kruisberg	2500	5/9%	N	12	--	--	7
Leberg	850	4/15%	N	--	1	3	1, 11
Oude Steenweg	900	9/19.8%	N	--	2	--	5
Knokteberg	1530	5.3/13%	N	--	13	8	--

Using 2013 as a representative sample, no "preview" race imitates the sequence of climbs in the Ronde too closely, but all three of E3, Dwars and the Omloop Het Nieuwsblad include five of de Ronde's 14 different ascents. Climbing the Paterberg in race conditions is critical training regardless, and E3 Prijs incorporates it with the Oude Kwaremont (in reverse order) late in the game. As dress rehearsals go, this is the one you can't afford to miss. Dwars too. The message of this feature is clear: if you want to win Flanders, it starts in these other races.

Back in Harelbeke, my first day as a cyclo-journalist went smoothly. The press liaison Mr. Van Landeghem forgot about me, occupied by the more obviously working press (the guys sitting around drinking coffee). He's sort of like the Macy's Santa at the start of the Twelve Days of Christmas -- a can't-miss character, the familiar symbol of a special day and season, right up there with the actual players in the drama. I popped by to thank him again, and that seemed to take the edge off our "relationship."[24] I grabbed a ham and cheese sandwich, ordered an espresso, and settled into a cold press-room chair. Beefy wifi translated quickly into some live posts to my Cafe

---

[24] [24] Van Landeghem was something of an institution in the small world of Belgian cycling journalism, starting as a writer with Het Volk — organizers of the Omloop Het Volk — before starting his own press agency and eventually taking over management of press matters for Flanders Classics. He also helped run the Gent Six-Day Race, one of the biggest winter events, and was said by his colleagues to be especially passionate about Cyclocross. I last saw Van Landeghem in an elevator in Louisville, where he'd accompanied the Belgian team to the 'Cross world championships in 2013, and with a captive audience I reminded him of our past meeting and how fondly I remembered his taking care of my flimsy credential request. We had a good laugh together, which is nice, because the following year Van Landeghem passed away unexpectedly, en route home from the 2014 Road World Championships in Spain. I mention him in part because of my personal experience, and in part because, as we'll get to shortly, a surprising number of cycling's great traditions can be traced back to passionate, influential sportswriters. Van Landeghem's career connects directly to the legacy of the sport's most notable pioneers.

friends, but the race wasn't on the big screen for a while, and surely there was something better to do out on the street.

Out on the race course, with the peloton several hours from returning, the scene had been taken over by kids. They were kitted out in the fully-matching, colorful garb of their local racing club, boys and a few girls, ages ranging from maybe 7-15 years. They straddled their road bikes with big bulky numbers strapped to the bars, with "Vlaamse Wielerschool" -- Flanders bike school -- in prominent letters. Flandrien class was in session, though as iconic as this seems to me the kids themselves struck a variety of poses ranging from nonplussed to boredom. There were some tables set up in the street with water bottles (bidons) on them, and the kids gathered in lines at both ends of the course. Eventually the drill commenced, and the contestants rode slowly and carefully enough to grab a bottle from one table and put it down on the next -- a bike-handling contest. Flemish racing is all about mastering the finer points, boys and girls, though I doubt this was the first time they'd heard that lecture.

Another large group of older kids was gathering further up the road, all the hallmarks that a race is imminent, though I didn't wait long enough for the action to begin. Instead, I walked around to take in the street scene on Harelbeke's big day. Sensibly enough, the residents seemed to be pacing themselves, with the race finish a ways off. Some of the bars right on the course were armed for battle, with tables on the sidewalk and non-threatening dance music pumping out at a casual volume. Since my status as a journalist was pretty tenuous, I decided to exclude myself from professional codes of conduct long enough for a beer in a townie pub. For years --

decades? -- I'd been conditioned to imagine Belgian pubs serving a thousand fabulous national brews, like those I'd already tracked down in Gent, but this was a Jupiler bar, starting with the sign, and they serve Jupiler. There is nothing special about Jupiler, but I shouldn't have been surprised to discover that even in Belgium, people need a gulping beer to wash down a long day of watching sports. Few mortals, with three hours to kill before the peloton returns, could afford to spend the time quaffing 12%-alcohol trippel ales, or not if they want to remember anything at least. Also, after waiting in endless lines for carefully-poured craft beers in the US, I strongly suspect Jupiler exists so Belgium's fans can whet their legendary appetite for beer that can be served in under ten seconds. Jupiler... a slamming-quality Belgian ale.

Sitting alone in a quiet pub with a forgettable beer didn't hold my interest for long, so I turned to food. Out on the street there was dried fish of some sort, sausage grilling from another cart, and frietes. That's about it. This was a pretty big contrast to sports-food in the US, which started out in my childhood as hot dogs and pretzels but has lately exploded into a multicultural arms race to see who can offer the widest variety of options. Undoubtedly this varies by region, and surely there are places in America where the beer-and-a-brat option still rules the roost. But I can't remember the last sporting event or street fair I went to in the US that didn't have a spread of options including Chinese, Thai, Jamaican, Ethiopian, Mexican, something that looks like Mexican (but is actually Salvadoran, Honduran or Guatemalan), Indian, Himalayan, and a few regional American themes (Cajun, chowder, hippie burritos, etc). In Seattle you can add Piroshkys to the list and count on practically every one of these options somewhere in the lineup. But in Flanders, sausage, dried fish and frietes still get it done.

Everyone on the street politely ignored me, but I did manage to attract the attention of one couple, an elderly pair standing in front of a hand-marked board full of racers' names and numbers. It wasn't immediately comprehensible, but looked like some sort of book-making system. I'm pretty ignorant of Belgian law pertaining to gaming, but they must have some laws, because these people made it clear to me in gruff Flemish that they had no interest in being photographed. Is there a mob in Flanders? Probably. And I decided I might try to make it through the weekend without crossing them.

Back to hanging around the press room, which was more essential than voluntary. At a stadium sport, the press have a lounge to hide in when the game isn't drawing their attention, and the press box or table row where you catch the live action. Cycling has a few options for media types. First are the cramped, cylindrical commentary boxes perched on the street, inspired by medieval Europe's affinity for confinement and torture, and broadcasting elites can get a front-row seat to some 30 seconds of the race. For written press, there are team and support cars following on the heels of the race, which you can maybe get a ride in and see — live and in person! — everyone who gets dropped or crashes out of the peloton. Finally, for the rest of the media horde there's the press room, where you go not to hide from the race but to actually see it and cover it. From the moment the TV cameras deem it engaged enough to broadcast -- usually the last two hours or so -- the race is projected onto a large screen in front of rows of tables.

On this day not everyone was captivated by every move, but the chatter suggests the folks in the room were paying very close attention to the developing story. On the road, Liquigas were on the front, broadcasting their ambitions. Roger Hammond attacked, looking strong, but his Cervelo Test Team had spit the bit, with Thor Hushovd pulling out and Andreas Klier hitting the deck. The tenor in the room rose and fell as key moves were made. In theory the assembled media weren't doing anything (just then) I couldn't do at home, and with English commentary to hold my hand, but there is something to be said for catching the reactions of the sport's seasoned critics, in case you weren't sure anything important was going on. I'm not great at reading a race in real time, but this is a skill I might acquire if I spent enough time in press rooms.

The race split up on the Taaienberg, the sixth of the day's eleven climbs, affectionately called Boonen's Berg for the regularity with which the Quick Step thoroughbred has attacked on the climb. The Taaienberg is steep and cobbled, but there's a concrete rain gutter along the side if you want to get off the stones -- which, if you're climbing this thing for a living, for results first and last, you do. Boonen attacked up the gutter, and a Quick Step lieutenant sat behind him, maintaining a slightly slower pace in order to force Boonen's rivals to let the gap out or come past the teammate, on the cobbles, and close it. Boonen got a gap, but was joined by Fabian Cancellara and Juan Antonio Flecha, forming a threesome that dueled all the way back to Harelbeke.

Given their stature this was a splendid, exciting development, and as the trio of ace riders approached the finish, something had to give. Boonen was then, for years, a world-class sprinter, not too far removed from being hailed as the world's fastest man. His wild, head-bobbing sprint had won him about 80 pro races by 2010, including a world championship dash in Madrid and a points competition at the Tour de France. Those days were receding, but he still owned a massive edge over Flecha and Cancellara if it came to the last 100 meters. Flecha would be no match for either of them in any real respect. Not to disparage his career, in which he's earned the title "the Spanish Flandrien," but Flecha's highest accomplishment is second at Paris-Roubaix, and on this day he was sandwiched between a three-time winner (Boonen) of the Hell of the North and a guy with a win and a second (Cancellara) on his resume.

Boonen's strategy was obvious to all -- hold things together for the easy sprint win -- but the cagey Cancellara was unlikely to play along. He's a master bike handler and a guy who can launch and sustain absurdly powerful attacks, if you blink an eye and grant him a meter of space. On this day he already had three time trial world championships to his credit (and another waiting), as well as some other devastating performances -- a shock move at Milano-Sanremo to steal victory from the sprinters with a 2km solo attack; a similar steal-one-from-the-sprinters move to win a stage of the 2007 Tour de France, while wearing the yellow jersey; and my all-time favorite, his prologue around London at the start of the 2007 Tour, when the motorcycle up ahead, charged with filming him, couldn't get through the corners quickly enough to keep out of his way.

Fabian Cancellara wins E3 with nobody else in the photo. By Chris Fontecchio

Rolling into Harelbeke, seconds before the 1km to go banner, Cancellara unleashed a pretty typical attack up the left side of the wide, straight Bavikhofseestraat, a four-lane road coming to a traffic circle. Boonen and Flecha sprung straight into action, seemingly ready for this move, but a gap of a couple meters had opened nonetheless. Boonen's power alone might have been sufficient to close the gap, but the race turned left through 90 degrees of the circle, with concrete curbs sandwiching the traffic lanes and squeezing the chasers through a tight, devilish bend. Cancellara, the legendary bike handler, swept through like a tornado, but Boonen cut a bit too hard left, touched his brakes to correct his course around the curb, and essentially the race was over. This wobble cost the chasing duo a few more precious meters and a blink of momentum -- a fatal error against the world's best time triallist. Back in the press room, Belgian announcer Michel Wuyts breathlessly hailed "de tank, de tank, de *pletwals* (steamroller)," as the Swiss Bear flattened the Belgian champion and the Spanish Flandrien. One minute later the result became official, Cancellara comfortably alone for the victory, while Boonen outsprinted Flecha handily for second.

The crowd didn't stick around long in Harelbeke. A foreigner (albeit a respected one) had rained on their parade, and the riders don't linger after a race, giving the fans little to do. The podium finishers made their obligatory appearances, onstage and in the press room, but everyone else beat a hasty retreat to nearby hotels in Kortrijk or Gent, or their homes, for dinner and rest. The team buses lined up in the driveway behind the press center, positioned for a quick getaway. A few fans sought out the cyclists, but it was Saturday evening, and people had some place else to get to. There were a few hellos, I had time to ask fifth-place finisher Lars Boom (then a much-heralded hopeful) a couple questions, before the scene packed up and absconded like the mobile carnival it is. After a half-hour or so I headed back to the train, by which time nearly everyone else had cleared out and the overnight work crews were disassembling the barriers, staging areas and grandstands. Even the bars seemed half empty. For Harelbeke's biggest day of the year, nobody seems all that intent on savoring the moment.

4: Deinze, Gent-Wevelgem, Crosswinds and Calendars

The next morning came around all too quickly. Not in some metaphorical way, but literally, in the sense that I was still making a major time zone adjustment when Europe decided to skip its clocks ahead and begin daylight savings. Further complicating matters was the fact that the train line to today's race had some sort of outage between Gent and De Pinte, so my tram to the train ended with me on a bus... then a train, and finally to Deinze, starting place for the 72nd running of Gent-Wevelgem.

Not unlike E3 Prijs being named after a highway that doesn't technically still exist, Gent-Wevelgem never sets foot in Gent, not anymore. There's a trend in cycling that the oldest races with place names in them almost never actually start or finish in those places. Sure, Paris-Roubaix finishes in Roubaix, Paris-Tours finishes its autumn course in Tours, but neither starts anywhere near Paris. Liege-Bastogne-Liege finishes in Ans.

Gent held on gamely as the starting point for today's event for some 70 years, until 2003, when it was moved to Deinze, about 15km down the road in the direction of Wevelgem. I can't find any definitive explanation about the move, but the usual culprits are the cost of staging a race in large urban areas, and the willingness of other, smaller towns to pay for the privilege of playing hosting to a start or finish. Take your pick.

Regardless, upon arriving in Deinze, it was immediately apparent that they run a different kind of show here than at E3 Prijs. Not surprisingly -- E3 is the only race among the big Belgian spring races that operates outside the Flanders Classics cooperative, a marketing entity whereby organizers of the member races coordinate and fight for the best calendar spots. That's a whole other subject, but for now it's fair to say that the Flanders Classics including Gent-Wevelgem and de Ronde make E3 feel a bit mom-and-pop, with a bandbox stage, big screen hanging from a rented crane, and no cordoned off area for the teams, who spend the morning being swarmed by the public. E3 *is* a bit mom-and-pop. Here in Deinze, things were different. Slicker, more managed, more of a show. Welcome to the big-time.

An MC entertained the crowd from a stage looked that like a crosscut of an airplane hangar, beefy and elevated well above the crowd with a soaring aluminum arch overhead announcing Het Nieuwsblad, the large Belgian daily newspaper, as the primary sponsor. Between the stage and the press area, where I signed in for the day's action, was a corral of steel fencing, virtually unbroken for a quarter mile except for a few crossing areas.

The press center connected to an indoor VIP area, which I was shooed out of until I explained that I was trying to find the teams. They were on the far side of the VIP hospitality section, in a large dirt lot fenced off from the fans. If E3 represented the epitome of cycling's lack of barriers between the stars and the fans, Gent-Wevelgem by comparison feels a bit like a Habitrail.[25]

No doubt this made for a slightly more peaceful start to the day for the participants, who could warm up on a trainer untroubled by anyone save the VIPs and press folks wandering around. But Belgian fans can only stand so much separation from their heroes, and there was some subtle, if serious, payback in the fencing arrangement.

Some young Topsport Vlaanderen guy milling around. Photo by Chris Fontecchio

---

[25] This awesome metaphor (OK, simile) will likely be lost on any reader under 40. A Habitrail is a modular housing system for hamsters and gerbils that was wildly popular back in the 1970s, where your little rodent could go from one room to another via tubular hallways, etc. Apparently they still exist, though I haven't heard anyone talk about them in a few decades.

Once a rider warmed up and was ready to sign in, they had to follow the trail of fencing to the sign-in area, which was the width of the road, but as you approached the stage, the pathway devolved into a human slot-canyon about five feet wide and a good hundred feet long, swarming with autograph-seeking fans on both sides. This made for one hell of a gauntlet, and reminded me of a famous samurai castle I once visited, which used a similar setup to lure attacking armies into a congestion trap where they could be doused in boiling oil.

Riders managed to survive, and the race start scene was politely joyful. A band played to keep the crowd's spirits high. Outside the fan gauntlet a young rider from Topsport Vlaanderen idled by the barriers, chatting with family members, a moment charmingly reminiscent of practically every local criterium scene in the world.

I made my way around the stage to the ramp where riders exited for the race start and watched the famous names roll by. I managed a quick hello with George Hincapie, America's most-decorated classics rider[26] then with the BMC team, once he was done exchanging friendly greetings with Spanish sprinter Oscar Freire, of Rabobank. Moments later, as Tyler Farrar was cheerfully pressing the flesh, shouts came up that the race was starting. Farrar excused himself and was off in a flash, as were Tom Boonen and Saxo Bank's Matti Breschel, Fabian Cancellara's lieutenant, having a chat on the ramp when they heard the word. Cancellara himself, star from 24 hours ago, was still up on stage talking to the MC. Before I

---

[26] Submitted without comment: Hincapie's greatest achievements were all nullified in 2012 as a consequence for his testimony in the Lance Armstrong USADA investigation, wherein Hincapie admitted that he used performance enhancing substances during his peak years.

could move off the ramp exiting the stage, Cancellara hurriedly signed in for the race, then used those bike-handling skills to plummet deftly down the ramp, pinning me and the other VIPs and journos milling around in place against the rail, and took off chasing the race. Not an ideal way to start, for him, but I think my adrenaline rushed more than Cancellara's. Standing there an inch from the speeding champion was a bit like an F-15 stadium flyover, experienced from the top row.[27]

Tom Boonen and Matti Breschel depart just after the race has left. Photo by Chris Fontecchio

Of course, as hectic as that sounds, all the late-starters rejoined with no difficulty. The race is 220km long, a solid five hours in the saddle, so nobody charges out of the gate very quickly, even with a prospect as tempting as leaving a couple heavyweights like Boonen and Cancellara behind. Within

---

[27] In hindsight, I am glad to have dodged his bike and a place in history as the guy who took out the favorite for the Monuments in a stupid pre-race mixup.

minutes the caravan was gone, and with the finish 40 km down the road in Wevelgem, there was no setting up in the press center. Deinze was done hosting the race, and the action shifted to Belgian Rail.

I'm pretty sure I have never experienced a public transportation interlude in the middle of a major sporting event that I was trying to attend, but this turned into another one of cycling's charming wrinkles. I was one of the first people to arrive at the platform, like a clueless, anxious tourist, so I settled in to munch my feedbag from the press center, the highlight of which was a box of soy milk whose "heart-healthy" label was covered by a sticker with Russian writing on it, placed there apparently to protect Russian consumers from knowingly doing something healthy. By the time I finished my standard-issue ham and cheese sandwich, the platform was starting to fill up for the short hop to Kortrijk. From there we changed trains onto something of a race-special, a double decker car set aside for people who bore Gent-Wevelgem VIP tags around their necks. I doubt the press was part of that plan, but I had my official lanyard and wasn't going to walk back to coach until someone made me. Wevelgem was only a few stops up the line, and the ride passed without incident, unless you count several women breaking spontaneously into song at the sight of Bissegem Station.
*****

Gent-Wevelgem may be a keystone event in the Flanders Classics lineup but the parcours (race course) is something of an outlier for Vlaamse Wielerweek. Races like E3 and Dwars door Vlaanderen and even Driedaagse de Panne all employ portions of the Ronde van Vlaanderen course in a sort of week-long patchwork dress rehearsal.

Gent-Wevelgem, by contrast, trades the Flemish Ardennes for West Flanders, avoids the Ronde course entirely, and in the process carves out a stature second only to the Cobbled Monuments. In fact, for years, starting in 1960, Gent-Wevelgem was routinely spoken of in the same breath as the Tour of Flanders and Paris-Roubaix. Raced on the Wednesday between the two Monuments, Gent-Wevelgem occupied a sort of near-monument status in a week-long Holy Trinity of racing.

The only downside was that being the mid-week event meant it could never be on par with the Sunday headliners. The most ambitious classics champions tended to make half-hearted efforts in Gent-Wevelgem, for fear of physically overdoing it prior to Paris-Roubaix. By the new millennium contenders for the two bigger weekend events were expected to start Gent-Wevelgem, for training purposes, but duck out at the first sign of misery. Not since 1985 had the Tour of Flanders and Gent-Wevelgem shared a victor. Nobody ever won all three in a single week.[28] Few riders with a realistic chance ever tried.

But the Wednesday position between the main events had its benefits too, branding the race as the unchallenged #3 classic, best of the non-Monuments, and starting in 2010 the organizers decided to cash in on that stature by moving the race to the Sunday before Flanders -- a direct challenge to the previous day's E3 Prijs, which had carved out a niche over the

---

[28] All of these records fell in 2012 when Tom Boonen won everything in sight, but over three weekends, not in a single eight day period, per the old calendar.

years as the preeminent Flanders warm-up race. Indeed, if successful, Gent-Wevelgem could bill itself as the second of six major races spanning consecutive weekends and encompassing four of the five Monuments of cycling -- from Milano-Sanremo to Liège-Bastogne-Liège. Keeping this kind of company would be good business for Gent-Wevelgem.

But in 2010 the riders were unimpressed with the calendar change, and subsequent editions of Gent-Wevelgem have failed to elevate the race to *the* pre-Ronde event. A certain class of riders won't easily give up on the E3 dress rehearsal, and Gent-Wevelgem is unlikely to scrap its formula, the thing that gives it its character, to be more of a Ronde preview. But if being unlike the other Flanders previews, Gent-Wevelgem is like no other race in the world... isn't that good enough? Because if there is one common element to the top classics that makes them so cherished, it's that each one is basically unique.[29] E3 and Dwars door Vlaanderen will probably always be really good, fun races, but events like Gent-Wevelgem are what keep cycling from becoming a formula.

Gent-Wevelgem began in 1934 as a tribute to Flanders/Roubaix double-winner Gaston Rebry, citizen of Wevelgem,

---

[29] My favorite race on the uniqueness score is Milano-Sanremo, the Italian spring monument. It's the longest race of the year, just a hair under 300 km. It's pretty flat and doesn't disintegrate like the cobbled races do -- and some people complain about this. Often it ends in a sprint -- another thing people complain about. But it's not an ordinary sprint, it's a longish, wide-boulevard sprint by guys who have been riding a good two hours longer than they would before any other sprint. The sprint is preceded by the Poggio, a climb of 4km followed by a twisting, squirrelly descent. So among the ways you can win MSR are by attacking on the climb, attacking on the descent, attacking from a few km away, and sprinting. No major classic is open to more different potential endings by a wider group of riders than MSR. Even when it does end in a sprint, there is plenty of drama in the battle to make that happen.

and being on the west side of the Leie (Lys) River[30] became the race's identity. Unlike the slew of races passing through Oudenaarde en route to some portion of the Vlaamse Ardennen, Gent-Wevelgem has mostly stayed out in West Flanders. Not always, and it's had its Ronde-knockoff editions back in the early days, but by 1945 the race was featuring climbs in the region around Ypres, due west of Kortrijk, and by 1957 climbs in French Flanders, just over the border from Ypres, had mostly replaced the Flemish Ardennes. Recent editions have circled all the way to the North Sea, with the fearsome Kemmelberg in the Heuvelland area near France as the major upward obstacle.

As horrible as the Kemmelberg is -- a long, cobbled, winding pathway that hits 23% gradient -- the race has acquired a reputation for favoring sprinters. A 2008 entry on the UCI website describes the course as "almost completely flat," which has been true, but the windswept environs of West Flanders offer their own unique set of challenges to the peloton. Well, one challenge, really. A one-word obstacle that strikes fear in every weaker rider's heart. The crosswind.
****

Crosswinds, in cycling, are simply winds coming at the riders from the side, but their effect is nowhere near so straightforward. Drafting is what makes the sport a game, for the simple reason that riding in the slipstream of another rider reduces your wind friction, and riding behind a pack can make you feel like you're being sucked along by a vacuum. Knowing when and how to draft, at least until it's time to make your

---

[30] Or, if you prefer, the Gent-Kortrijk axis, a key line of demarcation in understanding the classics.

move, is the key to victory, or at least survival. But crosswinds upend the normal order where riders can hide for hours in the shelter of a large pack in a long, flat race. When the wind hits from the left, for example, the slipstream of the guy in front of you moves around to his right. Not directly, since you're still rolling forward, so locating the slipstream can take a moment. But let's say the sidewind is strong enough that the slipstream is now at a 45-degree angle from the guy you're drafting. Anyone not 45 degrees to the right and rear of him, or you, or somebody, is stuck out in the wind, burning precious energy reserves just to keep up.

So echelons form -- diagonal lines of riders across the road, one behind another at just the correct angle. From the air they look like rolling back-slashes of flesh and machinery. But echelons line out across the road, and to make matters worse the roads in Flanders are exquisitely narrow, so a single echelon might only offer shelter to half a dozen guys, gutter to gutter. When one echelon runs out of space, as it quickly does, it's time for the other riders to drop back and form another.

To a racing pro, you not only need to be ready to form echelons, you also have to pick the *right* echelon. Your sextet or octet or whatever of guys has to sink or swim on its own, and if the echelon in front of you is setting a stronger pace, they are going to disappear up the road and leave your race-winning hopes for dead. If you fall in with a weak or ambivalent group, you might as well be in the wind all by yourself, because if you don't your day is over. Worse, everyone knows this, and often they know when crosswinds are coming, so the competition to make it into the best group is strong, and the guys who succeed are gonna hit the gas and weed out anyone weaker or less attentive. Positioning counts for an awful lot in cycling. But in the Tour of Flanders, you know where the decisive climbs are about six months before the race starts, and when to get in proper position. In Gent-Wevelgem, you may or may not get much more than a two-minute warning from your team car that there are crosswinds ahead.

In mellow-weather years, the race really isn't very hard, and the honor roll includes plenty of pack sprinters not known for winning classics. The great Mario Cipollini only won a handful of one-day races among his dozens of grand tour stage sprint wins, but he won three times in Wevelgem. On occasion the win is contested among large groups of 30 or more riders. Most years, though, the weather converts the race into a challenge nearly on par with the Monuments, and the finale features one or two or a handful of riders sprinting for the win. Some years, it's a war on the level of the world's hardest races. In 2009's grim, storm-lashed affair, the race broke up very early, in the first 45 minutes, and 99 of the 186 starters abandoned prior to Edvald Boasson Hagen's two-up sprint win over his Kemmelberg breakaway partner, Alexander Kuschynski.

The wild-card nature of the race, counting on the elements to define it, sets Gent-Wevelgem apart from the other non-Monuments. Races are usually measured in geographic terms -- how hard are the climbs? -- but closer up riders will frequently mention how weather played a role, and Gent-Wevelgem showcases this fundamental element of Cycling as well as any race on the planet. Still, the endless tinkering goes on, and beginning in 2010, along with the move to Sunday, G-W's organizers added six additional climbs to the Monteberg-

Kemmelberg circuit, which is run twice, bumping the number of climbs from four to a Ronde-like sixteen. Some additions, such as the Rodeberg, merely returned to the race from editions in the 1950s and 60s, so the effort to beef up the course is not without some historical connection. But in 2011 the climbs totaled 18, again more than Flanders. It would be a shame if the race morphed into yet another Flanders dress rehearsal. Gent-Wevelgem is an oddity. That's a good thing.[31]

My first stop in Wevelgem was checking in at the press area, a grammar school complex not far from the train station with a few rooms set aside for our use. To the right was one room for the English media, with a 19" TV and enough people to fill a phone booth... maybe. To the left was the Flemish room, with a giant screen broadcast, food, coffee, and pretty much all the journalists, including the English speakers, despite the fact that the thermostat timer was set on "Monday." The broadcast came on, and on cue VacansOleil's Johnny Hoogerland went on the attack, confirming every cliche about cyclists playing to the TV cameras. Amusing, but I needed to see the sights, grab a sausage, eat some frietes, and down a beer (ah, unpaid work...), so I headed out to join the crowds.

On Menenstraat, where the finish line stood, a juniors race was going on, but I couldn't tell what was happening in any respect. Riders passed through the finish area solo or in small groups, frequently enough and spaced widely enough that I had no idea who was chasing whom. There was no peloton to speak of. I didn't get it at the time but talking later with Stephen Gordon, the guy I met on the train, he described the

---

[31] Spoiler alert: it hasn't. By 2012 the race was back to only 11 rated climbs, and in 2015 the number further shrank to nine. Meanwhile the race added to its name, now officially listed as *Gent-Wevelgem: In Flanders' Fields*. Maybe it's hit on an identity after all.

dominant racing style, from junior levels on up, as all-out attack. "It's just the way they like to race, they way they've seen everyone else win, and it's the way they win. And since everyone else is going to be attacking, you've got to attack. If you want to stay where you are you've got to keep moving up. If you're not moving up, you're moving back. So if you want to actually move up, you've got to attack. because everyone else is doing it you have to too. I don't know how it got started like that, but that's the way it is, and it's not changing. To them that's what racing is. Racing is hard, racing is all out. In the US it's meant to be more of a tactical game where you only go hard later."

Ah, the social contract. The kids racing around Wevelgem on this breezy spring day were born into a system that bred them to bolt away from any peloton that showed a danger of forming. So round and round they went, hammering into the wind, racing all out. Racing in an attacking style is doomed if you're the only one thinking that way, but in Belgium that doesn't appear to be an issue. Aggressive riding is infectious. The cliche'd description of a Belgian rider's ambition is to win with nobody else in the picture, and that seemed like a probable result for these kids.
*****

Today's edition of Gent-Wevelgem unfolded under nondescript weather conditions, and consequently the pack survived intact through the entire western swing of the race and the first of lap of the climbing circuit, the set of eight ascents that would decide the race, or at least set up the finale. Without major crosswinds the sprinters were licking their lips and thinking if they could bomb it down off the

Kemmelberg and close up whatever gap the stronger guys have opened up, it could yet be their day.

But the classics studs had other ideas. With Astana's Max Iglinsky and Liquigas' Daniel Oss up the road, Matti Breschel, the striking victor four days earlier in the Dwars door Vlaanderen, blasted away from the pack on the Rodeberg to join in the lead. Sensing the moment, US champion Hincapie and treble world-champ Oscar Freire, two former winners here, followed suit and joined the front. This move meant too much firepower was up the road for the remaining contenders to sit back, and next to arrive were Sep Vanmarcke, a 21-year-old rider from Topsport Vlaanderen, and HTC's Bernhard Eisel, a veteran Austrian sprinter who likes these races. Then came the move everyone was waiting for -- Silence-Lotto's Philippe Gilbert, one of the sport's most dangerous riders on any day and a perfect rider for the newly reconfigured Gent-Wevelgem, came thundering up to the lead with the help of his teammate Jurgen Roelandts. When Gilbert goes, this late in the race, it's business time.

Or so you would think. Cycling's one-day, all-or-nothing races are about playing your cards and hoping for the best. It's easy to look back on any classic and point to the split-second moment where the winning move occurred; the dozens of stories in the press across Europe, Australia and North America will all come up with the same answer later that day. But recognizing that moment as it's happening is another matter. If you attack late enough in the race to draw some companionship, your move's success often hinges on who else comes with you.

There's the team makeup -- a group off the front of the race will be left alone, all the way to victory, if it contains at least one top rider from all the teams who are strong enough to have any say in matters. Or, to put it another way, breakaways fail when the strongest team misses out and is forced to chase the leaders down. Today, the lead group contained more or less the best hopes for BMC, Liquigas, Omega Pharma, HTC, Saxo Bank, Rabobank, Astana and Topsport. Powerful Quick Step missed out, but their man Boonen kept his leg warmers on all day, a subtle sign that he was just getting in some training after a hard ride yesterday.

Also missing was Garmin-Transitions, the American squad aiming to boost its credentials in the classics. Tyler Farrar would be their top choice, but the native of Wenatchee, Washington hesitated when the top guys headed up the road, in ones and twos, and in the end his patience wasn't a virtue. Farrar did chase madly all the way to the finish line, but the firepower up the road was simply greater than anything he could muster in support.

When trying to gauge a break, the individuals involved is the other primary factor. Big names don't make pointless attacks. When the leaders go, it's time. Here, Breschel and Hincapie were the designated leaders of powerful Saxo Bank and BMC squads. Freire, with a blazing sprint and a knack for one-day races, was Rabobank's best hope. And Gilbert is the main attraction at today's race, Belgium's athlete of the year in 2009 after running off a string of victories that boggles the mind, including the rare "Autumn Double" -- victories in the esteemed Paris-Tours sprint and the ultra climby Giro di Lombardia monument -- a victory sandwich nobody had tasted for nearly 50 years. The leaders even contained a couple extra teammates, Roelandts for Gilbert's Lotto squad and Kuschynski for Oss' Liquigas, which meant two guys in the front to do the dirty work. This group wasn't coming back.

Nothing changed much over the Kemmelberg, though the scintillating riding of Breschel undoubtedly raised some alarms in the other camps. But his rivals caught a big break when Breschel suffered a flat with 16km to go and dropped back to the Farrar chase group. Then the leaders got a bit testy with Freire: having a sprinters' pedigree means that nobody besides other sprinters is interested in arriving at the finish with you. So Liquigas dispatched their spare rider, Kuschynski, to cut the chord. With Freire riding at the back of the group, Kuschynski found the Spaniard on his wheel and took his foot off the gas, allowing a gap to open up. This is a game of chicken: one rider seems willing to let the race disappear, daring the other rider to do something about it. The other rider, aside from getting angry, has to calculate whether he wants to sprint back on to the field and tow the guy who created the problem in the first place along with him. Kuschynski didn't care, his sprinter mate Oss was up ahead so he was quite pleased to put himself out of business if he could take Freire with him. Team tactics aren't for the shy. A few conversations ensued, but Freire knew he had been played, and he drifted backward to the Farrar chase group.

Approaching Wevelgem the leaders were Gilbert and his helper Roelandts, Hincapie, Oss, Vanmarcke and Eisel. Vanmarcke showed his doubts in the sprint -- or his Belgianness by trying to win with nobody else in the picture, as they say -- launching a breakaway with 3km remaining. But he seemed to cramp up before long, and the sprint was back on. Hincapie tried an early run, futilely, and in the final meters Eisel took the win by a full bike length, with Vanmarcke recovered for second place over Gilbert.

Bernie Eisel, Sep Vanmarcke, Philippe Gilbert. Photo by Chris Fontecchio

Eisel was a solid winner, climbing and sprinting well and showing that HTC could count on him in the classics after losing Hincapie and 2009 Gent-Wevelgem winner Edvald Boasson Hagen from their squad. But the story of the day was Vanmarcke. A young Flemish kid stepping up to take second on the big stage, pretty much in his first major race, was exciting enough. But for him to beat Gilbert was like a quiet rookie dunking over LeBron James.

Charmingly enough, it turned out Vanmarcke was the kid I'd seen leaning against the fence in Deinze, talking to his family or close friends or whomever, about four hours earlier. Lots of riders sit around beforehand looking relaxed and smiling, but rarely do you catch a guy enjoying his last few moments of anonymity. Vanmarcke has evolved quickly into one of the regular challengers for cobbles glory, with a second at Paris-Roubaix in 2013 and an Omloop Het Nieuwsblad win in 2012.

Anyway, photos were my challenge of the day. After a single stab at playing reporter, I decided it wasn't possible for me to add much value to the cycling discussion with a who-what-where and some post-race quotes. I like all of those things, but the straight news sites can do them perfectly well, and my friends back at the Podium Cafe had already seen the race and listened to the interviews. What would go over better would be some bits from the sidelines, beyond talking about frietes.

Not being exactly a professional photographer (ahem), I didn't have permission to get to the photo well -- the mosh pit of official photographers just past the finish line, to one side -- and it didn't take much Dutch to understand the guy near the well who was telling me to get bent. Writers get to wait at the far end of the finishing straight. Ever notice how the end of a sprint consists of riders crossing the line at full speed and then immediately slamming on their brakes to avoid running into a human wall? Those are the writers. They're sort of a fleshy safety net in case of brake failure.

I decided my goal was to get a shot from the sideline, as close to the finish as possible. By then, I guessed, either guys will be bearing down on the line or in the early celebration phase, so the chance of a striking image was good. For the first (but not last) time I noticed that races often have a truck parked in the vicinity of the finish, across from the VIP grandstands. Once the easily accessible vantage points are spoken for, you can expect people to start wedging themselves into some uncomfortable spaces for a good view, but much of the space between the truck parked maybe 40 meters from the finish and the steel race barriers was unoccupied. The main issue involved some cement posts built into the sidewalk, which had to be climbed to get to the open space next to the truck. The police didn't seem interested in whether or not anyone got in there, and with some hand signals I made it clear to the kids blocking the opening that I planned to slip by them. With little more than bruised ribs, I had myself some grade-A real estate as fine or better than any opening in the surly photogs' well.

The finish of the race was kind of a blur, though I got a prize picture of Bernhard Eisel bearing down on the finish line, with Vanmarcke and Gilbert in a line over his left shoulder. It took another minute to extract myself from my ad-hoc photo well, then a few more minutes to salmon my way through the crowd to where I could get past the barriers and talk to a few riders. By then the leaders were off to their interviews and doping controls, before stopping by the media center. After two days, I got the routine, and as an experience it didn't do much for me. I stuck around the press room for Eisel's appearance but packed up pretty quickly thereafter and headed into the darkening streets.

The party in the main street pubs seemed centered around a bar with a bunch of Quick Step posters in the windows and maybe a mural or two on the brick wall overlooking the parking lot. It was a cycling bar, though without much Dutch I could tell when I peeked in that my interaction was going to consist of being in a bar, drinking another Jupiler, and heading out. So, duly noted, but that's it. In a few different directions there were other buildings without signs -- rec centers? private clubs? -- whatever. But the sounds of VIP socializing were unmistakeable. I wouldn't use the word festive, I was a long way from Bourbon Street, but Wevelgem and the cycling fans of Greater Kortrijk were enjoying their Sunday of racing, no doubt. For me, though, I was relishing a day off from the race routine tomorrow, so the train back to Gent beckoned. At the station, surrounded on a few sides by more well-attended pubs, I got to the open-air platform, an island of peace until a gang of tipsy Norwegian kids ambled up to wait. So far I hadn't detected much of an international flavor to anything. With Flanders-Roubaix week still several days from starting, that was likely to change, and the outsiders were slowly beginning to straggle in.

By 2012 Gent-Wevelgem and E3 Prijs had learned to coexist as neighbors on the cycling calendar. My visit in 2010 coincided with the first Sunday edition of Gent-Wevelgem in a while, just one day after E3. That was too close for comfort, and riders complained about having to choose one or the other. Things got worse a year later, when G-W's top-level UCI status and

E3's lack thereof meant that pretty much everyone was forced to go with the former, even though the latter was considered the better prep for de Ronde. Most strikingly, Tom Boonen was pulled from the E3 roster, after setting the record, and told to go after UCI points in Wevelgem (which he did, by winning). The organizers of E3, disgusted, threatened to shut the race down.

Only in 2012 did a solution appear -- a brilliant one, moving E3 to Friday, enabling riders to recover and go hard in Gent-Wevelgem too. Fans had an excuse to start their weekend a few hours early, a modest demand on the race's part. The organizers of E3 had compromised, moved off their Saturday spot, but in exchange for UCI World Tour status -- equal footing. Boonen obliged by returning to Harelbeke, then winning it. Two days later he became the first rider to win E3 and Gent-Wevelgem in the same year. And everyone agreed, it was a win-win solution.

Do people actually enjoy this? Photo by Chris Fontecchio

5: *De Vlaamse Ardennen*

Nothing in Belgium is without needless cultural complication, at least to my American sensibilities. So in this regard it makes perfect sense that the centerpiece of Flanders and its world-famous biking regions is *de Vlaamse Ardennen*, the Flemish Ardennes. Yes, the word "Ardennes" is generally associated with the region of Wallonia known for its forests and hills. And for hosting the Battle of the Bulge. And for the coal which transformed Belgium into the second great industrial power of the world. It's a French name derived from the former *département* of France in which the Wallonian Ardennes is situated. So what could possibly be confusing about the Flemish region adopting that French name for *its* geological crown jewel too?

Maybe there is a logic to it, beyond mere one-upmanship. Maybe the word has come to mean "hill in Belgium" or "hill that's awesome for riding up on a bike."[32] Anyway, officially the blame for this confusion is laid at the feet of Omer Wattez, a local writer from a century ago, who allegedly penned the nickname merely to point out that Flanders has hills too. He died in 1935, so there no longer seems much point in arguing.

The Flemish Ardennes are geologically part of the central plateau of Belgium, between the sand dunes and polders to the northwest and the more rugged Ardennes to the southeast. They are comprised mostly of long, narrow ridges, with parallel horizontal clusters of hills from Oudenaarde to

---

[32] I have taken to labeling some of my local climb-sets that way: the famous Norway-Big Finn-Juanita-Kirkland climbs at the north end of Lake Washington, along the Sammamish River, are now known (to me) as the Sammamish Ardennes.

Brakel and to the south from Geraardsbergen to past Ronse. Beyond and between these clusters are several more hills, alone or in waves, amidst flatter open areas, and to a cyclist passing through there are few alternatives to climbing. The hills themselves don't tend to soar much higher than 100 meters, and at times don't soar at all so much as roll gently. The scenery is pastoral and pretty, with small villages and neatly-kept farms tucked into quiet corners throughout the region. If rural Flanders were your idea of a vacation getaway, this is probably where you go.

The Tour of Flanders website lists 59 *hellingen* (hills) which have appeared at least once in the race. Some of these climbs may lie outside the region, but apart from those, the number 59 represents a low estimate of the number of actual hills or roads going through them found in the Vlaamse Ardennen. Just the ones that have made the race. The actual number is... er, I'm not sure how you could count. More than enough.

But if the peaks and valleys of the Vlaamse Ardennen don't instantly conjure cycling legend, the slopes sure do. At the edges and tucked into the folds of the hills, the Vlaamse Ardennen often drop suddenly, and the roads in these drops are some of the sport's most hallowed ground. Sunken into the landscape, these ancient farming paths often go straight into the grade of the hill, often using cobblestones to slow the ravages of time, water, and encroaching forest or farmland. Exploring them under grey spring skies feels a bit like stepping into a grainy cycling history film.

By cycling standards the climbs are short, but that does not mean easy, not even close. The Koppenberg has gained worldwide fame for causing the best road cyclists in the world to do something you never see: get off and walk their bikes. Other climbs have that potential, and lesser cyclists will find all sorts of roads worth walking up.

In between the climbs are other features which make cycling in the Vlaamse Ardennen unique, and which shape bike racing in Belgium. Roads in all directions are often very narrow and constantly twisting and turning. For a cyclotourist, this is a big part of the charm, but to a swarm of 200 racers these turns constantly choke the speed of the pack, which accelerates again as soon as the path straightens out. Speed up; slow down; speed up; slow down... all day long. Wind tends not to matter on the climbs, which enjoy some shelter, but it does tend to matter, sometimes a lot, once you've climbed to the exposed hilltop, just when you really don't need it.

And then there are the stones. Iconic hillsides aren't the only stretches of road made of cobblestones. There are endless stretches, from a few meters to several kilometers, of cobbled roads: flat areas, winding areas, uphills, downhills -- they're simply part of the road infrastructure. Rarely do they contain something dramatic, like the soul-crushing Arenberg forest "stones" in Paris-Roubaix. But no matter how tidy they are, the cobbled roads kill a bike's momentum and force you to pedal harder than you would on tarmac. They jar your hands and shoulders. Like the changes in speed, to even the strongest rider they add up over time.

Monday was the first chance to sleep in, start the day slowly, collect my head... and ride. No errands, no races, nothing between me and the Koppenberg.

OK, not nothing. First there were the streets of Gent to navigate, which aren't challenging once you figure out where you're going. I intended to head south to Oudenaarde, gateway to the Vlaamse Ardennen and a stone's throw from the Koppenberg, as well as a few other famous ascents. Gent and Oudenaarde are connected by the Schelde River, so the path of least resistance would be the canal route all the way. But the Schelde is most of the way across Gent, to the south, requiring a tour of the city's historic center, as well as its less historic off-center, and finally its not all that historic industrial fringe, before finally connecting up with the river. Like most old cities, the roads don't make complete sense to the uninformed visitor, so I praised my years of racing combat for blessing me with the ability to ride steadily one-handed, with my map in the other hand.

I've known about the Schelde, or Scheldt, since a college geography course, where the professor shocked me with a speech about how some river in Belgium was the key to economic power in Europe. To this day I don't fully understand why -- isn't the Meuse or the Rhein much longer, and therefore important? Not sure, but he seemed like he meant it, enough so that it remains among the dozen or so facts I remember from college. When I finally reached it, I couldn't help notice the placid atmosphere, completely devoid of warring German, British or French armies. Had I been lied to? Perhaps, but in late March daylight doesn't last forever, so the lack of controversy and barbed wire was probably for the best.

Oudenaarde is about 30km from Gent by car, slightly shorter by canal fietsroute, and for the second time in two bike trips I found myself heading generally south and a bit west... straight into the teeth of the wind. Counting the large pack on my back[33] and the occasional stops for sightseeing (is that a muddy cyclocross track heading into the woods?), it was close to two hours by the time I pulled into Oudenaarde center for a quick bite to eat. Oudenaarde is a medium-sized town, a speck next to Gent but something of a destination for people visiting the Vlaamse Ardennen, or living there and seeking a night out. Or at the very least, the Centrum Ronde van Vlaanderen is located in town, so it must be important enough. The town square is classic Flanders, reasonably large and ringed with well-kept old buildings, including the dominant presence of the Old Town Hall, a structure dating back to the 14th century with a six-story belfry that towers over the entire city.

Fed and watered isn't exactly ideal prep for the Koppenberg, but I approached the entire outing expecting trouble to come at me in plenty of other forms, so eating a sandwich figured to make little difference. I crossed over to the south bank of the Schelde and pedaled upstream, past the sand pit on the edge of town, back into the wind, in the direction of Melden, home to a pathway connecting the canal to the civilized world... and the Koppenberg. Eventually I could see a hill rising up, and within a few moments I could see the familiar little lane through the trees that is on the cover of nearly every Tour of Flanders video. There simply isn't much else on the horizon besides the Koppenberg, and the business end of this wonder of geology faces the river, for passing cars, bikes and barges to pay their respects. At this point the canal fietsroute was on a dike, dropping off in both directions, and it took a little time to

---

[33] No way was I going to the Koppenberg without the rather large camera that had been lent to me by the 1980s.

determine where to jump off. I half-expected breathless signage saying "KOPPENBERG This Way OMIGOD TURNHERENOW!!!" but the Flemish style is subtle, and the most I could find was a sign with the number 18 on it, marking the fietsroute spur to Melden.

This connector was a dirt path between farmers' fields, ending with a cobbled driveway around Sint Martinuskirk (St. Martin's Church), a dark, lovely, brooding old stone edifice whose sharply pointed steeple was made more majestic by the building's location on a hill above the fields. It was the perfect entry point to the Vlaamse Ardennen: a silent, stately old presence matching the customary gray spring skies. Even better, the driveway had about a 12% pitch or so, with some bumpy old cobbles. *Welcome to town, and don't try anything foolish until you've at least warmed up a bit.*

By now my heart was racing a bit, but there was little time for the anticipation to build. The road from the church met the town center in the space of about two blocks, and another block further is your destination. At this point there are signs directing visitors to the Koppenberg, should they be reluctant to simply look up at it. A slight right, then bear left, and suddenly you're standing at the foot of the great, stony beast.

From the bottom the scene is disarming, with a pub on the right sporting a "Koppenberg" banner in case you had any doubts. The rest of Melden might feel deserted -- in four visits I can't remember seeing anyone in the actual town, or even the pub -- but the Koppenberg enjoyed a steady trickle of visitors, pilgrims really, mostly on bikes. I snapped a couple pictures, then tried to stop thinking about what I was doing and proceeded up the hill. It's just under 700 meters from the pub to the top, and at first the pitch feels gentle, the stones nothing unusual. A hundred meters or so along, though, and it's business time. The next 120 meters take you from an 11% grade to over 16%, over rough stones packed in dirt, and between steep embankments that wall you into the climb. This is seriously hard work, yet all it does is soften you up for the main trench.

Bottom of the Koppenberg. Photo by Chris Fontecchio

Roughly 325 meters or so into the climb, the cobbles change utterly: the pitch juts violently up to 20% and the stones get even uglier. The dirt setting has given way to cement, or something impermeable, so at least you don't have mud to contend with, or not a fresh supply of it anyway. Daylight appears at the top of this stretch of the climb, ground zero for Flanders cycling, but before then you've got to muscle up over the part of the road where you often see the world's best riders start to walk. The problem for some is that the road is too steep to climb, at least under the circumstances, such as slippery conditions. But in the race the far bigger problem is simply traffic: If the people on the front of a large group slow down, the rest of the group loses all its momentum, and with no momentum and no room to maneuver, on an often slippery 20% cobbled hill, you have no place to go but toppling over on your side.

Center of the Koppenberg. Photo by Chris Fontecchio

The fact that the center stretch is cemented now is a slight historical oddity. The Koppenberg was included in the Tour of Flanders starting in 1976 through 1987, but excluded for the next fifteen years, thanks to an episode that is both a cycling legend and a YouTube classic. In the '87 Ronde, Dutch rider Jesper Skibby was the first to reach the Koppenberg, and began climbing up the hill in the concrete gutter that formerly existed on both sides of the road. Riding gutters is an old trick in Flanders, kind of cheating to a purist, but irresistible to a pro who's been riding at his/her limit for six hours and is looking for any little break. Anyway, Skibby got to the mid-point of the climb, but then wobbled helplessly out of the gutter and into the arching crown of the road, switching over to what were some truly horrible stones, and keeled over. The race director's car came along beside him, but for some reason the driver failed to stop -- probably fearing that loss of the car's momentum will see them all slip backward down the hill in a multi-car pileup. The car squeezed left, knocking a policeman into the embankment, and then crunched straight over both of the wheels of Skibby's prone bike, barely missing running over the rider in the process. Skibby lay in shock, the fans turned quickly from shouts of encouragement to Skibby, to incredulous yells, to a loud chorus of booing when they saw the destruction wrought by the car. Someone came up to help, pounding at the wheel to dislodge it from the bike, but Skibby ultimately shouldered his chariot and started walking.

After this incident, the Koppenberg was pulled from the race. As iconic as it may be, fans and officials have long debated whether it is simply too beastly a route to warrant inclusion -- is this cycling or a sideshow? -- and after WheelcrunchGate the anti-Kopp forces temporarily won out. The Koppenberg returned to the race in 2002 and has been used every year except 2007. But Koppenberg 2.0 contains a few differences. The gutters are gone, and cobblestones fill the road from one bank to the other. However, the road no longer sports a pronounced crown in the center with the sloped margins that made a bad situation even worse; horizontally, it is now close to flat. Most importantly, the stones are now fixed in place, discouraging thieving tourists and sinkholes alike. The ravaging Flemish winters make no guarantee that the road will remain intact, and in fact the stones have already started loosening and tilting again, but for now the annual decay is mostly under control, enough to suggest the possibility of safe racing.

Anyway, Skibby's Trench is the halfway point. Once you've emerged from it, the embankments level off a bit and the road feels like it opens up. But you still have some 200 meters of gradient that "slackens" to 13%, then 11%, before cruelly kicking up to 14% just to twist the knife. Finally, the embankments level off, the trees peter out, and you emerge from the trench to the top... and you still aren't done. The stones keep going and the road rises just enough, maybe 3% gradient, to keep you working, and now you're exposed to the crosswinds.

Most years the Koppenberg has come with more than 100km to go in de Ronde, so it has not been regarded as overly strategic among the top contenders, though having a large peloton arrive made it disruptive enough anyway — the more people involved in a potential traffic jam, the more walkers you get.[34] Even among the leading riders, this arrangement of blow

---

[34] In 2015 it was 70km closer to the finish, enough so you'd think it would decide the race — and it might, if it were the ultimate or penultimate climb. But coming just after the first Oude Kwaremont—Paterberg combination, and with five more climbs remaining, it

after blow, gradient, stones and finally wind, means that only the strongest riders can emerge from the climb, into the open (often windy) hilltop, and still stay in contact. It's a beast no matter what the circumstances.

My first attempt really was pre-doomed. I'm not the most aggressive cyclist to begin with, despite having started racing about a year or two before Lance Armstrong. In my mind, crammed with images of Skibby and other fallen pros, I was probably already beaten by the time I got to Melden. But riding hills is about putting your head down and turning the pedals. I might have survived. If not for the mud.

The Koppenberg is a "*holle weg*," a hollow way, a nice description of the trench I described above — where the road is sunken down between two high, steep embankments. When leaves fall or rain sets mud in motion, a good deal of it heads for the road. Dead leaves aren't abundant in spring,[35] but rain had been coming and going since I'd arrived, so although this Monday afternoon was dry, the still-muddy dirt packed around the cobbles on the lower slopes did me in. I got through the first two sections, though it was exhausting enough so that things weren't looking great as I hit the middle section, the deep, hollow trench. Mud from the lower slope had coated my rear tire, smearing my skinny Gatorskin every time it slid between the stones, which was about three times per second, so that when I reached the section where the stones were set

---

wasn't where the winning move was made, though it saw its share of losing ones. Assuming it continues to occupy a late position, you can count on the Koppenberg to end the chances of a few big names every year.

[35] Which reminds me of another enduring image of the Koppenberg, laden with dead leaves and mud during the KoppenbergCross, raced every November 1 at the site. The route typically includes some 200 meters of the cobbled road, before turning right into the farmer's fields and doing cyclocross-y things.

in concrete, the tire had acquired a nice reddish-brown coating. Once the pitch was steep enough to shift virtually all my weight to the rear wheel, that tire started slipping on the stones as I stomped on the drive train for power, and I stuck out a foot before I could keel over. My first attempt at the Kopp was done and dusted.

From there it became face-saving time. If you ride the Kopp in late March, you won't be alone for long -- someone will come past you looking annoyingly comfortable. At that moment, the only thing worse than stopping at all is walking the rest of the way, and having come so far to be here, I started trying to saddle up again just above the trench. Remounting on a hillside means you need to push yourself forward to start moving and stay upright, then shift as needed, quickly, on a rear tire that's lost its grip, no less. At my dismount point, this wasn't happening, but I walked up a bit until the gradient leveled off to the low double digits, and after a few tries I was back up and, moving, grinding slowly up the remaining part climb -- still no picnic. A couple riders spun past, including one in an HTC kit, just as I managed to reboot my dignity. I got to the top and stopped to surveyed the scene. Looking down the hill, you can see several miles in most directions. You can see bits of Oudenaarde, to the north, and the nuclear power plant near Ruien to the west. You can see more green fields and the blue Schelde. But you can't see the road you just came up. From the top looking back, the Koppenberg seems to drop straight down into an abyss.[36]

---

[36] And that, or a hospital, is probably where the average cyclist would end up if he were foolish enough to *descend* the Koppenberg on a cool, wet day.

Looking back down. Photo by a now very tired Chris Fontecchio

Next on the list was the Kortekeer, a climb I knew nothing about, but it lies on the western shoulder of the same lump of rock that hosts the Koppenberg, it was scheduled to be raced in Driedaagse De Panne the next day, and I wanted to hit as many race-ready climbs as I could. So after cresting the Kopp, I swung right, made a lovely, curving descent through the trees, came to the center of the rise, climbed back up a bit more to Nukerke, and finally dropped down level with Melden again, at the foot of the Kortekeer. Familiar signs for KBC, the Belgian bank which sponsors Flanders Classics and Driedaagse, lined this stretch of the road as the organizers of tomorrow's stage prepared the Kortekeer for racing. So, not hard to find.

The Kortekeer has spent the last generation serving as plan B for the Tour of Flanders when the Koppenberg is out of service. In 2010, there were rumors on race day that the Kopp could be scrapped on short notice, in the event of snow or sleet, and undoubtedly the race would have done what it did in 2007, or from 1995-2001, 1988-90, all years when the Koppenberg was unavailable -- from Melden center, where you'd turn left to get to the base of the Kopp, turn right instead, keep right at the next intersection, and from there make a beeline for the Kortekeer. The summits of both climbs, running parallel a kilometer apart, are joined by the N60 route, as well as some smaller lanes that you could use to pick up the Ronde route where the Kopp climb would have left off.

But while they're logisitically interchangeable, that's about where the connection ends. The Kortekeer isn't too different from the skinny rural roads you could find in plenty of other countries, save for things like the fietsroute signs and other trappings of cycling. It's paved, extends for about a kilometer, averaging six percent (my internal tipping point, by the way, when climbing goes from being fun to some sort of survival experience), and hitting 17% in the road's gentle bends.[37] The approach is wide open and subject to heavy crosswinds, but the upper half, with a mix of tree cover and small openings, is really just a lovely spot, particularly if your most recent experience was the hell of the Koppenberg. At least a third of the Tour of Flanders pack would be grateful to see this climb on the agenda instead of the Kopp. And as I got up the Kortekeer in one piece, I could sympathize.

---

[37]"Kortekeer" means either "short time" or more likely "short turns" -- the local meaning isn't too apparent, but the zig-zag bends which characterize the climb give a good hint.

The graceful bends of the Korte Keer. Photo by Chris Fontecchio

By this time it was around 4pm, and my tour of the Vlaamse Ardennen was getting scaled back quickly. I'd hoped to hit some of the iconic climbs, but the Paterberg was too far southwest, the Muur too far southeast, and I wasn't too sure where the Molenberg was. Since I was scheduled to ride every last one of them in five days' time, I decided to err on the side of making it home before total darkness. That left the Taaienberg as my last major destination for the day. It's a short, nearly "straight" line (by local, meandering standards) from the Kopp to the Taaienberg, via a long stretch of sloped cobbles known as the Steenbekdries in one direction and the Stationsberg in the other.

Heading toward the Taaienberg, I'm officially proceeding via the Steenbekdries, which takes in parts of three roads, mostly over the rugged cobbles of Mariaborrestraat, before tipping upward, making a juncture, and sloping down the path to the silent little train depot on the outskirts of Etikhove. Climbing the Steenbekdries, which tops out at 6%, is pleasant, another quaint, pretty spot tucked into the folds of the Vlaamse Ardennen. But things turn a bit ugly after the summit, when I face my first cobbled descent. It's only about half a kilometer or so before the Stationsberg jogs right, crosses the train track, and mercifully levels off in the train depot plaza. But any downhill pitch, even the modest 3-4% Stationsberg, forces you to choose between letting gravity thrash you helplessly down the stones or fighting these forces the whole way. Should you choose the latter, which I vowed to do until I got better acquainted with the whole cobbles experience, this means maintaining a very tight grip on the bars while the rest of your body chatters violently.[38] By the bottom, unclenching my hands from the death grip they'd assumed took half a minute or so.

Moments after remounting, signs began to tell me I was approaching the Taaienberg. Boonen's Berg, as it's known nowadays, thanks to the tendency of the Belgian star to attack here in the E3 Prijs [he did so again two days earlier, which eventually led to the winning break he formed with Cancellara and Flecha]. The approach is a slight descent into a small forest, so the road itself is hard to see until you reach the start of the climb, where it turns cobbled, forks, and lurches upward toward the narrow opening and distant daylight. The climb is 800 meters averaging six percent, but after a slight warmup, it's a full 200 meter grind over the cobbles as the gradient

---

[38] A small cottage industry has arisen in recent years consisting of slow-motion YouTube videos of riders' bodies while they traverse cobblestones. Even the fittest pro cyclist will look like he's got Grandma's upper arms as flesh he couldn't possibly have been aware of sways hither and yon.

goes from eleven to a thigh-snapping eighteen percent. When that's over, the road keeps rising for another 400 meters at a gentler grade, but it and the relentless cobbles are enough to stop you from recovering after the main wall.

Photo by Chris Fontecchio

The road has concrete gutters on both sides, and for kicks I rode up them for a bit before feeling like I was cheating and jumping back onto the stones. Warmed up now, I made it to the summit without interruption, drafting the last 100 meters or so behind a pickup truck full of kids and their bikes, leftovers from a rag-tag youth ride that was scattered around the paths up ahead. But those few moments in the gutter were enough to help me understand their strategic importance. It's simply a lot faster for anyone with enough power to climb up that gradient in a straight, narrow line to use the smooth concrete gutters instead of the cobbles. If you want to attack on the Taaienberg, that's where you do it.

During the Omloop Het Nieuwsblad, which employed the Taaienberg in February, 2010, there was much chatter about Boonen taking the lead up the gutter while the second-placed rider, a Boonen teammate, allowed Tommeke's acceleration to open up a gap between them. The speculation was that it was planned: Boonen would go, his teammate would fail to accelerate and effectively block the rest. Old-school hardball tactics, know among Flemish roadies as *"het gat laten vallen,"* let the hole open. But having ridden briefly in the gutter, it's so simple and effective you can't imagine them not pulling this maneuver. Quick Step are simply saying to other riders, if you want to match Boonen's acceleration, not only do you have to go around me, but you have to jump on the cobbles to do it, where you'll have to work significantly harder than Boonen is right now, just to keep him in sight. Ultimately the attack was too far from the finish, and Boonen was done in by a flat tire before he could get in position for the OHN win. But for the home team, it's always a good day for a little gamesmanship.

Anyway, with my day's mission done, it was time to race the fading sunlight on my way back to Gent. The fastest way, as far as I could tell, from the top of the Taaienberg to downtown Oudenaarde was to circle around to the Stationsberg, climb up and over that, and veer north off the Steenbekdries to the N60, heading back to town. By the time I got to Oudenaarde and back on the canal route, I figured I had an hour of daylight or so. And no lights. Still, for the first time since I arrived, I actually had a tailwind to take me the whole way there. The kilometers ticked off pretty quickly, and at the end of what amounted to a one-hour time trial I was back in Gent under the streetlamps just as the last hint of daylight disappeared. Adopted Gentenaar Tyler Farrar has often spoken approvingly of staging rides around the Vlaamse Ardennen from Gent. Plenty of riders set up shop in Kortrijk or in the middle of the Vlaamse Ardennen, steps from the climbs, but Farrar's perspective was that the 30km before and after your climbing route is great fitness. After hustling back to my room in Patershol, I couldn't agree more.

Gent at night. Photo by Chris Fontecchio

6: Oudenaarde, Driedaagse De Panne and Hans the Warrior

Packing carefully was the key to Tuesday's adventure. On the menu was the opening stage of Driedaagse De Panne -- Three Days of De Panne, named not after bread but rather a village on the North Sea coast, De Panne, which owes *its* name to dune hollows. Or pans. It's a little confusing. Anyway, the North Sea has a thing or two to say about Flemish cycling, from the weather to the occasional seaside events.[39] Driedaagse is its biggest festival, with stage one departing from De Panne for points inland, a second stage that turns and goes back to De Panne or neighboring Koksijde, and a final day of double-stages, a morning circuit around De Panne and a short time trial in the afternoon. Gent-Wevelgem and occasionally the Tour of Flanders will graze the coastal area, albeit at a safe distance from the dunes. And maybe the biggest recurring event out at the seashore is the legendary Koksijde cyclocross world cup event, known as the *Duinencross*, the Dunes Race, where in typical cyclocross fashion they don't so much avoid the natural hazard of sand as wallow in it. For Koksijde, De Panne and Ostende, these are the main events.

---

[39] The Tour de France has staged a few finishes along the North Sea in recent years, whenever it has started in the Netherlands. In 2015, for example, with the Grand Départ in Utrecht, stage two ended on the Oosterscheldekering, a storm surge barrier and part of the Delta Works which are listed on the Seven Wonders of the Modern World. Basically, a modern dike used to hold back the sea. The finish line was halfway across the nine-kilometer barrier, and the combination of rain, sea spray and crosswinds caused the stage to end in chaos, with André Greipel leading home the handful of remaining sprinters among the GC contenders (Froome and Contador) who took advantage of the broken peloton.

Anyway, today's inland stage of Driedaagse isn't about the coast, it's about trying to entice the Cobbles guys to take an interest in the overall classification by sending them around the Vlaamse Ardennen, where they can maybe create a little separation in the standings prior to the next two board-flat sprint-fests. This opening stage was to finish in Oudenaarde, which bills itself as the "Pearl of the Flemish Ardennes." Not for nothing either: the Koppenberg is visible from town, the city itself (soon to become my home base for a week) is small but lively, and the city plaza sits beneath an immaculate, towering, 500-year-old late Gothic *Stadhuis* (Town Hall) structure that represents the grandeur of Flemish architecture as well as anything else this side of Gent or Bruges.

Stepping off the train in Oudenaarde I got my bearings and started to look for a place to lock up the bike, eventually settling on the police station, though mostly because the town square was overtaken with trucks, steel fencing, and bodies. Even if there was a place to park it by the Stadhuis, heading out would only mean slaloming through the crowd back toward the police station anyway before I could manage to ride.

The "Presse" signs directed me to the second floor of the Stadhuis where I encountered the most beautiful location in the history of cycling press rooms. It was like having a friend give you random tickets to a game, and as you arrive not knowing where you are sitting, the usher keeps walking down the steps to the front row. Indeed, we were to be lodged in a room the size of a small auditorium, with 20-foot sculpted-wood ceilings, stone walls and stained glass windows, the latter two adorned with depictions of... medieval looking people of some sort. Knights? Royalty? Religious figures? All of the above? Can't say for sure. I know that sounds ridiculous, but on the big stone wall are two painted figures. One wears a white robe and a crown, but holds a sword. Another is wearing armor and a crown, but holds something with a cross on it. Nobody actually knows who these people are or what they're doing, I think.

Oudenaarde Town Hall and the Driedaagse De Panne finish line. Photo by Chris Fontecchio

But everyone knows *Hanske de Krijger*, a/k/a Hans the Warrior, the 17th century figurine sitting way up high on the belfry's peak. Hans is kitted out like Don Quixote, for some reason, but otherwise bears the standard of the town, with an "A" in his lowered left hand for "Audenarde," an archaic spelling of the town's name (which means "old Earth"). The statue depicts the town guardian of old legend, who was best known for having fallen asleep -- thanks to one too many beers -- on the day Emperor Charles V arrived in town. Why he's dressed in Spanish armor is glossed over. In these lovely, ancient, historic Flemish villages, everything has a story. Just don't count on it making sense.

Anyway, this was the People's Hall, where the citizenry have gathered since the mid-16th Century to celebrate, entertain VIP outsiders, and debate cloth prices. Compared to the arctic middle school classrooms of the past weekend, the grandeur of the setting was hard to get over.

The Driedaagse organizers were comparatively laid back, not seeming too worried about my lack of a press card and even offering me a photographer's vest without much convincing. This is the holy grail of press access, or so the photographers would have you believe, so I was looking forward to a fun day.

Back down in the square, under the watchful gaze of Hanske, the city hummed with activity. Vlaamse Wielerweek had pointed the spotlight at Oudenaarde a couple times already, and the city's place in the sport of cycling was growing by the day. The race-week curtain-raiser, Dwars door Vlaanderen, passed through town twice, and the E3 Prijs Vlaanderen came by as well. Hosting a stage finish of Driedaagse De Panne boosted the town's profile, but the biggest prizes were scheduled for Sunday, when the women's Tour.of Flanders would start in town, as usual, and the men's Tour of Flanders would pass through as it does occasionally. And the other 50 weeks of the year, Oudenaarde is known as home to the Centrum Ronde van Vlaanderen, the museum dedicated to preserving the race's history.

A year later, things took a dramatic turn for the town's relationship to cycling, when Flanders Classics flipped the script and redirected the Ronde van Vlaanderen finish to Oudenaarde. All of this is alluded to above, but apart from the race character and the shelving of the incomparable Muur, there's the backstory. The organizers had long been at odds with the people who own the pub atop the Muur, *'t Hemelrijk*, and perhaps the owners of other locations along the route over VIP access, and word is that by switching to the Oude Kwaremont/Paterberg finishing climbs, with fully three circuits passing by, profits are being maximized by the race. That's an endless argument; all one can say for certain is that the crowning moment of *Vlaanderen's mooiste* fell into the laps of Oudenaarde.

Anyway, back to the comparatively nondescript *Driedaagse* stage, I had decided to mix things up with the day's plan and catch the race out on the road. The Kortekeer was just past the Koppenberg, close enough for Hans the Warrior to spot on any sort of a clear day. So I planned to bike out for the first run up the Kortekeer, which the race would ascend twice. The second trip up would occur only 12km from the finish -- and I did want to catch the finish -- so that was out. But there would be 70km left after the first ascent, more than enough time.

After getting my bearings, I found a place to change into bike clothes -- not standard journalist behavior -- and slunk out as discreetly as possible. I grabbed my bike and headed toward Melden and the Koppenberg, though as I got there I could see helicopters across the river, obviously marking the front of the race. Whether that meant they had gone by the Kortekeer or not, I had no idea, so I rode on to the bottom of the Koppenberg, took a right turn before the climb, and headed toward where I thought the Kortekeer was. About ten minutes later I was no closer to the climb, even after asking virtually every person I saw (both of them) while winding around the tiny farm roads. The helicopters seemed to be getting further away, and by the time I came across a road marked with the ubiquitous KBC signs indicating that I'd found the course, there were only a few people and cars around, and no sign of helicopters anywhere in the sky.

Admitting defeat wasn't easy. I'd lugged around a lot of gear, ridden 20km on a day when I had other things to do, and accomplished nothing whatsoever. In hindsight, it might have been more fun to stay put and see the race out on the course instead of the finish line, but since I had a photo vest I was determined to wedge myself into the finish line photographers' pit because... well, because. So back to town it was.

Now, I'm pretty averse to making an ass of myself, and as poor a grasp as I had on playing journalist, I knew far less about the etiquette of playing photographer. I could guess that my total lack of credentials would be plain as day to any working photographer who looked my way, starting with my non-massive camera and going downhill from there. It wouldn't have taken much for me to feel intimidated about thrusting myself into a crowd of dusty blokes just off the back of a four-hour moto ride, sporting massive amounts of gear and an air of entitlement. But my friend Mark had sent me a few simple pieces of advice. Don't get greedy about where you position yourself. Don't block the shot of anyone who takes pictures for a living. Make it clear you're not planning to fight for anyone's spot and they won't have a problem. I stood back far enough, lined up my viewfinder between the cannon-sized lenses, and waited.

The photographers' pit is about as anticlimactic a place to watch from as one can imagine, with the possible exception of the fans lined up behind the photogs' pit. Of which there aren't too many, because 20 meters after the finish line is way worse than 20 meters (or 50 or 100) before. There is no video screen, no system to keep you in touch with anything beyond what you can see with your own eyes. And when the riders arrive, it is literally all over but the shouting.

It serves the photographers well enough, however, yielding pictures of riders in joyful celebration mode, every crease of their smiling visage captured by massive zoom lenses that, taken together, look like the broadside of a 19th century battleship. Most pro riders I'm sure treat the photog pit as nothing more than a potential crash hazard after the line, but I'm sure a neo-pro or two has done a double-take the first time he saw all those lenses trained on him.

Finally, with all of "us" working photographers tensed like jungle cats for a while, the conclusion of the race was upon us. First came a few motorbikes, with photographers coming in from the course to get their finish line pics, but that was well ahead of the peloton. Next a few more cars and motorcycle cops came through, sweeping any interference off the course. A couple minutes and several more waves of motos later, the PA announcer took his voice up from a steady chatter to something more urgent, then a fever pitch. And *down the stretch they come!*

The sprint was from a seven-man breakaway, having separated itself on the last ascent of the Kortekeer (dagnammit). Bouygues Telecom rider Steve Chainel, a favorite here for his cyclocross exploits, timed his jump to perfection and left two Italian classics stalwarts Luca Paolini and Enrico Gasparotto in a lurch. Chainel gained enough of a gap to sit up and fire three right-fist pumps, a two-arm salute, and one more right arm forward thrust before he crossed the line. Not the kind of combination that would get him through a round with Manny Pacquiao, but as far as Paolini and Gasparotto were concerned, it was just as devastating.

Steve Chainel. Photo by Chris Fontecchio

Chainel bubbled with enthusiasm for the rest of the day's proceedings. This was his first significant victory on the road, after a dozen cyclocross wins over the previous decade, and Chainel, training his focus on Belgian road races, seemed at home over the border from his native France. He smiled almost sheepishly as the organizers presented him wiht one jersey after another. At present Chainel is a B-list cobbles specialist, with top-twenty placings in both Flanders and Roubaix, and while his Cross pedigree has faded a bit nowadays, he's still pretty well-known -- as the husband of 2013 French national cyclocross champion Lucie Chainel-Lefevre.

Chainel would go on to surrender his lead in the overall classification of Driedaagse de Panne two days later. His fatal mistake was dragging Garmin's David Millar with him on his day-one escape, as Miller would then time-trial his way to victory. Me, I took a detour to Amsterdam, for 24 hours of culture and to prepare for the next round of events, including moving my base to Oudenaarde, picking up my brother, and gathering with Ronde van Vlaanderen fans from around the world as the big day drew ever nearer.

Chainel sprints to the win in Oudenaarde. Poor, grainy photo by Chris Fontecchio

7: Ronde van Vlaanderen Week, and the climbs of *Vlaanderens Mooiste*

Great races all have romantic beginnings. The Tour de France was invented to unite France and show the world its diverse beauty. Right? OK, it was to sell newspapers. The Giro d'Italia was modeled after the Tour de France: a beacon of newspaper-selling success. Liege-Bastogne-Liege is today the oldest race still in existence to capitalize on the glorious newspaper-sellingness of cycling. You get the idea.

By the way, there is a bit of chicken-and-egg to the influence of the newspaper business. The Tour de France capitalized on several existing races linking the major cities of France and just put them all into a single event. Henri Desgranges, the best-known of the Tour's founders, did in fact editorialize about the virtue of discovering the many regions of France, in the process of riding the mother of all long-distance races. And not every great race from antiquity has the same genesis; Paris-Roubaix, preceding the Tour de France by seven years, had the temerity to ignore the newspaper racket entirely, inspired instead by the desire of the Roubaix town fathers for their provincial town to enhance its standing (and that of its velodrome) with Parisians.

But the origins of Belgium's two biggest races fall in line with this familiar creation story... as well as another common theme of Low Country Life: language politics. Liège-Bastogne-Liège was sponsored by the French-speaking *L'Expresse*, stamping this race across Wallonia with a clearly (and appropriately) French identity. This left Flemish Cycling a bit out in the cold until the *Sportwereld* sports newspaper was founded in 1912, heralding the event with a race around Flanders. On May 25, 1913, the Ronde van Vlaanderen was officially born.

The language and cultural divisions of Belgium have long been a major driving force behind the race's importance, so let's back up a bit. Belgium's language politics are legend, so excuse this is the short (and mild) version, but throughout the 19th Century and into the early 20th the country was dominated economically and politically by French-speaking Wallonia, then home to some of Europe's most important steel production as well as other heavy industry. This was in essence a reaction to the previous phase of Belgian history, when King Willem of the Netherlands, then in control of Belgium, declared Dutch to be the official language of the country, with little regard for the French speakers. When Belgium gained its independence, largely at the hands of Wallonian troops, the newly minted independent nation went into linguistic backlash mode, declaring French the sole tongue. This worked out about as well as King Willem's idea, with resentments boiling on both sides of the debate.

Economic divisions exacerbated the matter. The new country's Flemish region was mostly agricultural lands, culturally and economically distinct from the factory-fueled engine running the economy of Wallonia. All these divisions drove the Flemish in search of ways to preserve and promote their identity.

Cycling was an ideal vehicle for the Flemish to use in their quest for justice. At the turn of the 20th century, passion for cycling was sky-high in France, and the French newspapers couldn't invent races to sell their broadsheets fast enough. Paris-Rouen begat Paris-Bordeaux, Paris-Brest-Paris, Paris-Roubaix, and finally the Tour de France in 1903. *L'Expresse*,[40] a rival French publication to the Tour de France organizers *L'Auto-Velo*, transferred that passion across the border to Wallonia, founding the beautiful Liege-Bastogne-Liege race in 1892. But despite the exclusively French nature of the sport, it was Flemish cyclists who broke through the barriers and set the standard for Belgian cycling.

Odiel Defraeye, from Rumbeke in West Flanders, became the first Belgian winner of the Tour de France in 1912, the last Tour ever decided on a points basis as opposed to accumulated time, by winning three stages, placing second on another three, and third on three more. He was succeeded by Phillip Thys of Anderlecht, near Brussels, who won the next two Tours and would nab a third before he was done.

This iron grip on the world's biggest cycling spectacle gave Flemish fans plenty of reason to love the sport -- but they already did, enough to supposedly inspire the founding of *Sportwereld*,[41] a weekly sports magazine and the first of its kind in Flemish, in 1912, the same year as Defraeye's historic win. Its founder, August De Maeght, brought in a young Carolus Ludovicus Steyaert, writing about cycling under the pen name Karel Van Wijnendaele (Charles from Wijnendaele)

---

[40] Information about this publication is a bit hard to come by, so consider this assertion not very well confirmed.

[41] Sportwereld, meaning "sport world," continues to this day as a section of the newspaper Het Nieuwsblad.

after his West Flanders village. Van Wijnendaele proceeded to organize the first Tour of Flanders in 1913, in part to break the French-speaking leadership's stranglehold on the national cycling federation in Brussels.

In hindsight this was a stroke of pure genius. The race quickly became the focal point of the season (besides the Tour de France) for Flemish cyclists and fans. From the beginning it functioned like its name says -- a tour of Flanders[42] -- showcasing towns in the modern-day provinces of East and West Flanders along a route in excess of 330 km.

But "brilliant" and "easy" are infrequent bedfellows. The first two editions of the Ronde van Vlaanderen were marked by the absences of great riders like Defraeye, who rode for teams sponsored by French bike companies which ordered them to stay out of the new Flemish race -- either actively perpetuating the anti-Flemish prejudice or at least yielding to it.

Still, the reduced field managed to produce charismatic winners. Paul Deman, the victor in the inaugural Ronde, rattled off subsequent victories in Bordeaux-Paris, Paris-Roubaix and Paris-Tours, sandwiched around a wartime stint in the Belgian espionage service smuggling documents by bike to Holland. Next up was Marcel Buysse -- a rising star at the 1913 Tour de France -- who defied his powerful (French) Alcyon team's

---

[42] By the way, the term "Flanders" means either these two modern provinces, or the entire Dutch-speaking half of Belgium, or the ancient "County of Flanders" stretching from the southernmost polders of Holland to northern France. Even the simplest political concepts in Belgium are confusing. De Ronde goes the easy route, staying more or less inside the two modern provinces.

admonition against riding the race to take the last pre-war Flanders win.[43]

When the war ended, the race resumed and grew in stature, and as a symbol of Flemishness. Flemings dominated the winners' circle, with only Swiss star Heiri Suter breaking their grip, temporarily. Flemings weren't quick to forget the isolation heaped on them -- for example, on several occasions the organizers defiantly held de Ronde on the same day as Milano-San Remo. But isolationism only gets you so far.

As with so many other European features, World War II wrought significant changes to de Ronde. The race actually continued during the war after the fall of Belgium to the German Army, and claims of collaboration with the Germans briefly tarnished the image of the race, even leading to the creation of the Omloop Het Volk as a protest against the Tour of Flanders' cozy coexistence with the enemy. After the war several journalists from *Sportwereld* were punished for collaboration, and Van Wijnendaele was actually given a lifetime ban from his profession, which was retracted when he produced proof from the British Air Force that he'd hidden downed English pilots in his house.

The stench of war politics eventually died away, even if Het Volk didn't, and the Tour of Flanders evolved slowly into more of an international monument. Italian Fiorenzo Magni became the second foreigner to win with his 1949 victory, which he then doubled up in 1950 and tripled the next year -- a record

---

[43] Needless to say, the race was not held at any time during the First World War. German forces occupied much of the country beginning in summer, 1914, and were not defeated until 1918. That the race *could* continue during World War II is an indicator of the difference in the nature of the two conflicts.

that's never been equalled. Since the Second World War ended Belgians have won 40 times and foreigners 27.

What this race means to Belgians is a little hard to summarize. *Vlaanderens mooiste*, Flanders' greatest, as the Belgians call it, is a beloved *sporting event*. It may have been born out of linguistic rivalry, but its significance has soared well beyond addressing a grievance. It is, quite simply, the Super Bowl of Belgian sports, with a bigger place in its fans' hearts than that of the great Cycling Powers of Europe. True, cycling in Belgium doesn't have to fight as hard for attention as compared to its soccer-mad neighbors -- including even France. But the real beauty of the Tour of Flanders, surely a primary source of the special love that exists for the race in the country's collective bosom, is the nature of the race itself, the way it took a beloved sport and carved out a truly unique niche within it, one that connected with the people and their land.

And this hasn't gone unnoticed outside the borders of Flanders either. The success of foreign riders has accompanied the rising foreign interest in de Ronde. In 2010, as one race after another fell into foreign hands, the Belgian media spoke frequently about the internationalization of their sport -- the full three weeks from Dwars door Vlaanderen to the Scheldeprijs. Fans now come from all over, as do riders. The 2010 edition consisted of four Belgian teams, equal to the number of American teams.[44] To the hordes of invaders, the political struggles which marked the original Ronde mean nothing. They come anyway, with no regard for the need to connect with the Flemish countryside or its lovely little towns. They

---

[44] The numbers were the same in 2015. The top ten finishers represented seven different countries, including three Belgians as well as the first Norwegian winner.

come because the race itself is so hard, so beautiful, so utterly unique. So Flemish.

The race is truly a creature of the geography, history, weather and culture of Flanders. The geography of the Flemish Ardennes tend to dictate the tactics in the end, but all of that is set up by the skinny roads of this farming country, roads which twist and turn a thousand times and force riders to slow down and speed up at nearly every corner, an effort which drains precious energy reserves and calls for aggressive strategy to remain close to the front, away from the deadly accordion effect of those speed changes at the rear of the pack. These are the roads of Old Flanders, and the race pays homage to the ancient agrarian scenes of the country as it winds through many of the region's old towns.

And old roads mean cobblestones. The legendary *kasseien* come in roughly thirty servings in de Ronde, varying in length from 15 to 2400 meters. For the 2010 edition, by the end of the day the peloton crossed over 26km of the infernal stones, 26km where wind friction is the least of your problems as each stone absorbs a bit of your momentum. 26km of bouncing across the stones, at speeds which decrease the pounding effect but increase the danger. 26km to snap the strength in your legs well beyond the experience of riding on smooth pavement.[45]

The cobbles of Flanders aren't the big stars of the race, the way they are in Paris-Roubaix, in part because at their worst they are still rideable. In Flanders, cobbles can be roughly categorized in three varieties. Actually the Centrum Ronde van

---

[45] Another variable figure; in 2015 there were approximately 24km of cobbles.

Vlaanderen, the race's historical society, rates the cobbles on a 1-5 scale, a concept borrowed from Paris-Roubaix, but the range of difficulty isn't comparable. The stones in town centers or more modern villages, set in concrete, are bumpy but of no real concern. These are your category 1-2 cobbles. More common are the rural stretches of large stones set in dirt. These cobbles, sometimes called *kinderkopje* ("baby heads") when time and weather rounds and smooths their tops, will throw you around pretty good, and as they make up all of the longer stretches (2+km), they make a pretty big difference in the race. Lastly, on just a few occasions (such as the Koppenberg) you will get hit with a mix of big, bumpy, uneven stones set in dirt on a steep slope. Really, they're only different in gradient, not grade. In Belgium you simply don't encounter cobbles in the state of utter disrepair that you find in France.

Weather comes in next, adding a layer of challenge on top of the hills, corners, narrow roads and stones. Wind scatters the field into echelons, which get chopped down to size on the skinny pathways. Rain means that your next corner may be your last. That's life in cycling. But on the cobbles, it's mud that really ups the ante. Nice weather on race day is great, but if there's enough moisture in the ground from earlier storms, the dirt packing the stones in place will get picked up by every tire (cars and motos along with bikes) which crosses over them, making them slick and treacherous. Worst are the climbs, like the Koppenberg, where your tire can pick up a coat of mud just as you're about to hit the steepest section. Slipping sideways is bad enough, but any rider whose weight goes too far forward will feel their rear tire spin out on the smooth granite, and in the blink of an eye their momentum -- and their chance of staying in contact with the leaders -- is gone.

All of this adds up to a story of Flemish culture. The popular stereotype of the Flemish people is that they are stoic, hardbitten and industrious, not particularly given to comfort or excess. Regardless of how accurately that describes them -- it is a stereotype, after all -- there is little doubt that they celebrate stoicism with gusto, and the Ronde van Vlaanderen is the primary vehicle for doing so. A "real Ronde" is one lashed with wind and rain, at least for a portion of the day, and which faces an unending array of obstacles. You can argue whether this or Paris-Roubaix is the hardest day of the season, but the last 100km of Flanders is an experience in a class all by itself.

While the riders will cite all of these challenges as what gives de Ronde is brutal splendor, to the fans the *hellingen*, or the *bergs*, are the stars.[46] On the ultra-steep cobbled slopes of the *Vlaamse Ardennen* is where fans see the most dramatic scenes: riders slipping and walking, rocking side to side, bouncing off fans who crowd in on top of them and, if necessary, push them up the hill. At the business end of the race, the climbs are where the decisive maneuvers happen. In race reports across the world, writers will credit the Muur or the Bosberg or the Valkenberg as having dictated who won. By the road, crowds will descend in massive numbers on the slopes, standing shoulder to shoulder to sheer on the heroes. If the story is of 250km of suffering, it's those few stretches of 300 or 600 or

---

[46] I'm pretty sure it's only us English speakers that talk of the "bergs." First, Dutch pluralization rules don't work that way; it would be *bergen*. Second, "berg" means mountain, while "helling" is hill — a bit more accurate. The "bergs" is a reference to how all the hellingen are named in a way that ends in -*berg*, but to the natives they are hills, not mountains.

800 meters which compress all the day's drama into a dose of pure Flanders.

When Andrea Tafi says that the Ronde is "the way of the cross," he is saying the *hellingen* are the stations. It's a great analogy, walking the holy trail of suffering, and pausing, or at least slowing, to savor the agony.

The stars of the show are as follows:

1.   Muur van Geraardsbergen

Stats: According to the race historians, "the Muur" is 1075 meters long, 9% average grade, 19% max. There is some debate as to what is "the Muur," because it's not a discreet road/ascent, but rather the worst path or paths up the steep ridge which cradles the small city of Geraardsbergen in its arms. It's best to think of the Muur climb in three separate segments: the approach, the true Muur, and the Kapelmuur. The modern approach comes up the Vesten, a wide, cobbled plaza through town, to the foot of Oudebergstraat. Here begins the true Muur, narrowing and lurching upward, eventually becoming a cobbled trail through a dense forest. Finally, as you emerge from the trees, a right hand turn sends you up one last short rise, the Kapelmuur, past the old chapel. All told, the Muur is fairly long by Flanders standards, particularly when you consider that the median and maximum slopes are among the day's steepest stretches.

Cobbles? Yup. Big ones. Actually, the cobbles on the modern approach, the Vesten, are no big deal; they're packed in concrete and made for modern traffic. [Before being resurfaced in 2009, they were a lot bumpier.] But near the top, when Oudebergstraat turns into the woods in the last 300 meters, the stones get big and nasty -- *kinderkopje* -- smoother on the top, and set further apart for maximum effect. In all, there might be a few moments of pavement, but not for long. These aren't the worst stones in Belgium, but they're close, and they hurt.

Photo by Chris Fontecchio

So How Bad Is It? One of the advantages of putting this rating system into the hands of a marginal athlete like me is that being near or just past one's breaking point is a good way to make the otherwise fine distinctions between the *hellingen*. Sure, Tom Boonen knows these climbs infinitely better, but readers deserve more of an answer here than "Oh, it's pretty hard I guess."

The Muur is hard. Top five for sure. The length is a big issue, and the 19% section comes pretty far into the ascent. There is a saving grace, however, in a few flat spots where you can take off the pressure before blood starts trickling from your ears. Also, the stones aren't quite as muddy as, say, the Koppenberg, so on a treachery scale they're more like an 8.

History: While the road itself probably dates back hundreds of years (Geraardsbergen is over 1000 years old), "the Muur" came into Ronde existence in 1950 and has been the main attraction for much of the time since then. As mentioned above, despite being the bearer of the most simplified, no-elaboration-necessary moniker, in fact the Muur is shorthand for the three stages of the Geraardsbergen ascent, with plenty of variation in the route. For fourteen editions (1950-'52, '70-'80) the approach was off to the east a bit on Abdijstraat (formerly Kloosterstraat), straight into the gradient of Geraardsbergen on what could fairly be called city streets. In some years that was enough, or Oudebergstraat was unavailable, and the true Muur was off the program. In others, the brutality of Kloosterstraat followed by Oudebergstraat served up several minutes of pain. Eventually Kloosterstraat was paved over, renamed, and taken off the menu, replaced by the tamer Vesten approach, which itself used to be a bit harder than it is now. But the true Muur, the upper portion, is as rough as ever, and to compensate for some of the taming of the lower slopes, the Kapelmuur (chapel wall) was tacked on. It's not terribly hard, but ten more seconds on the stones is an eternity at that point.

Strategic Importance: Formerly massive. This was the last truly painful ascent in the race for many years. The Bosberg, a lesser climb, typically held the honor of coming last, but it's the Muur that so often served as the final, fatal blow to the hopes of all but the winner and maybe a companion or two.

Or that was the case prior to 2012, when the race organizers decided to move the finish to Oudenaarde. A rift between the property owners along the Muur and the race organization led the latter to pull the Muur from de Ronde. Seems impossible to imagine, even after four editions without it, and the impetus to return it to de Ronde will never die. For now, though, there are no plans to bring it back.

Most resembles: Oude Kwaremont? Not in a physical way, more in spirit. It's alive with spectators, and it's a rite of passage in the race. Physically, the Molenberg is maybe closer, with equally nasty stones and a hard, steady gradient. But the Oude Kwaremont, repositioned as the penultimate climb of the race (for now), has recaptured the madness of the Muur.

Take-Home Message: The Muur has really done great things for the sport. The scene at the top is like no other: a sea of humanity and banners on an open, grassy hill which is half-circled by the race course. There is a pub at the bottom of the Kapelmuur and a tiny chapel at the top (great place to kill a

Sunday?). Up to the pub, the scene isn't radically different from the other great climbs -- narrow, lined with fans between the trees, lovely enough. But the pub -- named, awesomely enough, 't Hemelrijk, the Kingdom of Heaven -- suddenly appears out of the forest, packed with bodies hanging from every window and only a steel fence preventing them from literally pouring out of the patio and onto the road. The serene chapel rising above this madness is the perfect touch, anointing the climb with a spiritual grace, and the open space on the hill is a mass of sheer human joy.

So why did this change? The wisdom of tinkering with this will take a little time to understand, if it's to be understood at all (besides something on a balance sheet somewhere). Races do change, virtually all of them, dramatically and repeatedly, so in that sense this shouldn't come as a shock. And further on the plus side, the finale after the Muur has tended to allow the race to regroup, and the possibility of a bunch sprint isn't one the organizers would likely welcome. Not in a country where winning with nobody else in the picture is a national virtue. So the changes to the course have favored strong climbers and reduced the finale each year. But there is an uglier side, for sure: the race owners have long resented their lack of control at the Muur, and they didn't like missing out on the revenue that can be generated by this kind of precious real estate, which people will gladly pay to occupy for a few hours. The race has found that opportunity for control at the Paterberg and the Oude Kwaremont, and rerouted the course to suit the tastes of the VIPs. In this way, the Muur actually became its own worst enemy.

As lovely as the Muur has been, if that energy and excitement just re-creates itself along the Paterberg, then great. If instead the best part of the best race gets commodified and sold off to the highest bidders, then cycling's greatest asset -- its accessibility to everyone -- will have taken a foolish hit. Personally I don't see the Paterberg taking the place of the Muur, and the race can't quit Geraardsbergen for too long, but we shall see.

2.　Koppenberg

Stats: 682 meters long, 9% average grade, 19% max (or 22%, if you believe everyone other than the official Flanders website). Possibly the only climb in Flanders with its own website [http://www.koppenberg-oudenaarde.be/]. The steepest part is in the middle, but the bit before the maximum grade is only slightly less, as is the part after, with "easier" sectors at the beginning and end. Sort of like an Oreo cookie, only replace the smooth, creamy filling with 60 seconds of terror, and the cookie parts with searing pain.

Oh, and "Koppenberg" is a bit of a misnomer. The climb itself is up the Rotelenberg, a sort of conjoined twin hill to the actual Koppenberg. The race goes straight up the face of the former, summiting both, then descends rapidly down the latter. The name switch probably has to do with the road, which starts off as Steengat before the name changes to Koppenberg. So yeah, the most famous scene in the present Ronde van Vlaanderen actually takes place on the Rotelenberg. And if you meet anyone who cares about this bit of information, tell them I said hello.

While we're on the name, another suggestion is that the climb is named after the grisly "kinderkopje." Sounds great to cycling fans, but race didn't exist until the last century, and the hill has presumably been there, and been called the Koppenberg, far longer. So this explanation sounds implausible. My version is that sometime in the 14th century, a farmer accidentally ingested a mushroom from his pasture in present-day Melden, and while waiting for his senses to return he uttered the Dutch phrase for "Whoa, that hill looks like two giant heads coming out of the Earth!" If you have a better explanation, I'd love to hear it.

Cobbles? Yup. Worst ones of the race, at least among the ascents. Scroll back to Chapter 5 for more.

So How Bad Is It? Bad. I wouldn't rank it the hardest climb on a nice day, but it's as treacherous as a Kung Fu villain. Survival is the only objective, and to achieve it you either need an extensive stretch of dry weather (which still might not be good enough) or ideally you need to be at the front of the race when this climb starts. Because a zest for treachery is the Koppenberg's signature.

Once someone discovers this first hand -- a rear wheel slip, a blocked pathway as riders careen back and forth -- momentum is gone and all that's left to do is climb off and walk. And once one rider walks, anyone unable to squeeze past him has little choice but to do the same. I don't know if it's the mud between the lower stones or the polished stone surfaces or both, but the Kopp seems to be the slickest of the climbs, and the only thing worse than a 22% gradient is having to do it sitting firmly in the saddle to keep enough weight on the back wheel.

History: No course-planning topic has been more hotly debated than the inclusion of the Koppenberg (at least til 2012), and while the race has become more comfortable with it since the renovations of 2002, when its famous middle section was refurbished, it still evokes mixed feelings. Older Ronde purists have long scoffed at it as a gratuitous spectacle, while the rest of the cycling world celebrates it as... well, a gratuitous spectacle. Koppenberg 2.0 is no less steep than ever, but the crown of the road is not nearly as pronounced; there are no longer concrete gutters to escape the stones; and the middle 100 meters or thereabouts is set in concrete, to stave off degradation and thieving tourists.

The Koppenberg was originally added to the festivities in 1976, but it was removed before the 1988 edition, after the famous incident the previous spring where a commissaire's car almost ran over a fallen Jesper Skibby.[47] It's been back since 2002, with the exception of 2007, when more renovations were needed. Being steep, wet and run over by tractors all year means it's often in need of some fixing, concrete casting or no. And even then it's not always enough. In 2010 there were rumors of a switch to the Korte Keer (or maybe the Rotelenberg, skirting the southern edge of the Kopp), if the weather got awful enough. Even when they plan to run it, the organizers stand by, ready to pull the plug.

Strategic Importance: Variable. In the pre-2012 race it happened around 60km to go, and ended a lot of riders' day,

---

[47] This incident is YouTube GOLD.

but tended not to weed out many contenders. Then for two years it was set back to 100km to go, further lessening its impact. In 2014, however, the Koppenberg got bumped up into the big time, with about 45 km to go in an 8km stretch connecting it with the Steenbekdries and Taaienberg. That was a dry day, and nothing too memorable occurred, nor did much happen in 2015 or 2016, but it won't take too many editions styled this way before we see fireworks there. And at a minimum it's putting a dent in a lot of people's hopes before the final moves are made. Suddenly those scenes of riders walking translate into hopeful winners being eliminated.

Most resembles: For treachery, I'd say the Kemmelberg, which has never featured in de Ronde (though it's the symbol of Gent-Wevelgem). Physically, it's a bit like the Taaienberg, in that it keeps going up for so long after you think you're through the difficult part.

Take-Home Message: One of the unique features of the cobbled climbs is that typically team cars aren't allowed on them, certainly not on the steep ones. For a car, or a motorcycle, there is quite a bit that can go wrong on a wet cobbled climb barely wider than my Subaru. The exclusion of support vehicles throws yet another mischievous splash of gasoline on the bonfire of Koppenberg treachery. For example, in 2009 a half-fit Fabian Cancellara broke his chain on the steep midsection of the ascent, and started walking up like everyone else at that point. But then he realized he couldn't get a team car for quite a ways beyond the visible top, and wound up walking down the hill to find... either a chain or a lift home. When you're walking your bike in the opposite direction of the race, that's a sign your day may be over.

3.   Oude Kwaremont

Stats: 2500 meters long, 3% average grade, 11% max. Of the hills that matter, this is by far the longest.

Cobbles? Mostly, yes. The first 600 meters or so are on pavement, but the rest is classic old Flemish stones. They're bumpy and it gets difficult on the two steep patches, in the middle and the last 50 meters, but the rest of the stones have no real trick to them. Apart from continuing on and on.

So How Bad Is It? Sneaky bad. There are no special tricks to make your brain freeze or your mouth fill with profanity. After a middle section where the gradient briefly hits double digits, it's a pretty easy ascent. But this is the genius of the stones at work. 2500 meters is a good 4-5 minutes of climbing for the top guys and probably double that for the average cyclotourist. Multiply that by the number of times per second that every bit of loose flesh on your body is violently shaken and, well, it takes its toll. Stone by stone.

History: Added to de Ronde in 1974, the Oude Kwaremont path replaced a parallel path -- simply, the Kwaremont -- that had been a fixture in the Ronde since 1919. That stretch of cobbles was paved over in 1965 in a fit of progress, but de Ronde has never had much use for progress, so the race was relocated to restore the bumps on the ride out of Kluisbergen.

Strategic Importance: In previous years, it acted as a gatekeeper for the real Ronde, the juncture of the race where the pack comes in like a lamb and goes out like a lion. The narrow roads of the low countries define the spring classics, acting as choke points for all but the strongest and smartest riders who know to stay close to the front when the pace picks up. Well, on the old course, with some 160km in the books before the Oude Kwaremont, the pace was bound to pick up, and the climb itself is long enough to that the pack would stretch out a long, long way on the ascent. Chances were, if you weren't in the first 50 places, you'd emerge from the Kwaremont chasing like mad... or packing it in. These junctures are known by all, well in advance, so the battle for position before the Kwaremont starts was said to be ferocious.

As of 2012 the Oude Kwaremont now appears not once, not twice, but three times, including serving as the penultimate climb in the entire Tour of Flanders -- in effect playing the role formerly granted to the Muur. In this format, it has already given us one winning break and is sure to serve up more. In 2012 the last trip up the Oude K is where Alessandro Ballan and Filippo Pozzato made their decisive attack, drawing only Tom Boonen (oops) for company. Expect a steady diet of favorites battling here for the win, either physically or psychologically. The strongest and craftiest teams will take the lead on the lower slopes, where it's paved, controlling the pace and blocking anyone from moving up... but when the cobbles start, so will the attacks. Maybe the Paterberg, the last climb, will anoint the winner, but the Oude K will narrow down the list of contenders.[48]

Most resembles: The Nieuwe Kwaremont, only cobbled. Not helpful? OK, the Kruisberg. The Oude Kwaremont is a bit

---

[48] Together, the Oude Kwaremont and Paterberg are now considered the "Executioners," while the previous climbs of the Taaienberg, Kruisberg and maybe Koppenberg are potential places for race-altering mischief.

rougher and longer, but its neighbor just to the south sports the same profile, more or less: long, cobbled, but not very steep.

Take-Home Message: The Oude Kwaremont is a bit like some great actor doing Shakespeare in the park for eons, only to be discovered after a few decades and given a leading mega-budget film role. After 38 inclusions in the Ronde, always overshadowed by the Muur, its time has come to take center stage. You can hate the new Ronde but you can't hate this grand old climb.

4.   Paterberg

Stats: 361 meters long, 12% average grade, 20% max. The only rated ascent in Tour of Flanders history, out of 59 entries, with an average gradient in double digits.

Cobbles? 100%. They are nothing too awful, being all new since 1982 or later.

So How Bad Is It? From my amateur perspective it's the hardest climb, at least until weather factors in. It didn't seem as slippery as the Koppenberg or sections of the Muur, so in bad weather you're more likely to get done in by one of those two than the Paterberg. But for sheer oxygen deprivation, my legs and lungs were screaming afterward for at least twice the amount of time it took to climb the bugger. As for the pros, it doesn't seem to trouble them too much. Guys get gapped, but at this level 361 meters is covered in the blink of an undernourished eye. It has a gutter, where you can avoid the cobbles, and when the Paterberg shows up in some races like

E3 the gutter is often available. Not so in de Ronde, where short-cuts are frowned upon. Fencing now covers the gutter during the race.

Photo by Chris Fontecchio

History: Anticipating the future, when his actions could be breathlessly recounted at the Podium Cafe, a local farmer is alleged to have plowed a strip up the steep incline of his pasture, covered it with cobblestones, and declared his property open for cycling business. In 1982. By 1986 the race responded and 26 inclusions later the Paterberg, like the Oude Kwaremont, is having its day in the sun. You sort of wonder what message that sends, and why the farms of East Flanders are not by now criss-crossed with hundreds of cobbled goat paths. I guess those Swedish cobblestones aren't cheap.

Strategic Importance: Historically, minimal. Like the Koppenberg, another semi-outcast to the purists, it was consigned to the middle of the race until the grand reorganization of 2012. But after three decades of existence its dues are paid and now the Paterberg is nothing less than the final climb of the entire race, with all the strategic importance that implies. Prior to 2012 it generally has not been worth attacking here, given the short length and the looming Koppenberg just 7km or so later. There is also a winding descent back down to the valley floor most years, so the gaps close up quickly.

But at the end of a seven-hour race, it can definitely matter. Brevity notwithstanding, under the right circumstances (e.g., a small breakaway involving at least one superior climber), even 361 meters of that hell may make all the difference. It certainly did in 2013, when Fabian Cancellara ditched Peter Sagan and Jurgen Roelandts on the climb, and it played a role in 2012 (when the chase group got tangled up coming onto the climb) and 2014 (when Cancellara reeled in Greg Van Avermaet and Stijn Vandenbergh on the climb, setting up the final sprint). And in 2016, it was where Sagan got free of Sep Vanmarcke and soloed home to win.

Most resembles: The middle section of the Koppenberg, minus the prologue, epilogue and penchant for treachery. If the Koppenberg is a Kung Fu villain, the Paterberg is a sumo wrestler: short on guile and subtlety, long on pure pain.

Take-Home Message: The Paterberg is at the center of the cultural crisis enveloping the race at present. Before this decade, its lack of historical significance (or even existence) didn't trouble anyone; it was just a nice, nasty little hill in the early wave of truly painful ascents, raced hard but not final-hour hard. But one of the most enduring traditions in cycling is the trashing of the sport's most enduring traditions. Alpe d'Huez was a short-lived publicity gimmick for a single hotel, before it became the symbol of the Tour de France, starting in the 1970s, while the Ballon d'Alsace (the first-ever mountain stage of the race) has been largely forgotten. Paris-Roubaix was nearly paved over in the 1950s, in the name of progress, and has been furiously reworked to retain its character, over a completely different route. The Vuelta a Espana used to be in spring. Same with the Giro di Lombardia. Everything changes, and we find new ways to keep loving cycling regardless.

5.   Molenberg

Stats: 462 meters long, 7% average grade, 14% max... depending on where you stop counting. Those are the RondeToerism numbers, presumably calculated by someone who knows something, but a narrower view of the climb would call it 325 meters averaging 9.8%.

Cobbles? Yes, and truly nasty ones, but not quite all the way up, which is the root cause of the numbers dispute. Anyway, they're old, with a nice, classic crowning in the center, and pretty bumpy, but uniformly and tightly packed. They were tidied up a bit in 2014, but still quite nasty.[49]

So How Bad Is It? To a tourist who's headed around the course, the Molenberg will leave a mark, but not a permanent one. The gradients simply aren't the worst of the worst, and the length is nothing unusual. That said, on a slippery day, the jarring stones and the slight crowning will make any rider have to concentrate a bit. If you're in a group, you may not have room to let the crown slide you toward the curb. And if it seems narrow, it is, a fact reinforced by 10-foot hedges lining some parts of the road, as well as a complete lack of gutters. Once you start, there aren't many options besides finishing.

History: The Molenberg is actually a protected monument, presumably owing to its ripe old character, but it has only featured in the Tour of Flanders since 1983, albeit with regularity. It is also a key climb in the Omloop Het Nieuwsblad, the late-winter classic which starts the madness in Belgium each year. In 2011, the Molenberg was the final climb of the day, albeit separated from the finish line in Gent by about 40 flat km.

Strategic Importance: Middlin. The Molenberg falls into the next category of hard-hitting climbs: those that can be handled with ease or used to put a hurt on the field, depending on how the riders choose to approach it. The hardest gradients happen after a short introduction to the

---

[49] Why God? Why? What's the point of tidying up a road whose chaotic state is the source of its charm? Because the stones move — due to weather, vehicle traffic, thieving cobble tourists, and whatever else. Cobbles rise and fall, or start sliding gradually down the slope, opening up big gaps. So fear not — just because the Molenberg has been tidied up now, it won't last.

cobbles, and by the time the Ronde reaches the tarmac section you'll typically see guys getting a bit wobbly. Like the Paterberg, it's very narrow with a choke-point of an approach, a sharp 90-degree turn with no way to cut the corners, so guys at the back of a big bunch are in a spot of bother. If it's wet, expect to see people walking.

Like any of the climbs, the key is placement, and for years the Molenberg has enjoyed a spot in one of the more concentrated clusters of *hellingen*, thanks to its proximity to so many other climbs, particularly the Leberg, Wolvenberg, Tenbosse, Berendries, Kapelleberg, Valkenberg and so on. Cancellara made his winning selection here in 2010, attacking hard enough to shatter the field and draw only Boonen for company. Nobody else ever saw them again. As for the future, it's also very close to Oudenaarde, and yet -- for now -- the course organizers have decided to put it early in the race, at about the halfway point, where it serves as a mere *amuse bouche*.

Most resembles: Taaienberg, in shape and in character, thanks to the upper reaches being paved. In strategic significance and difficulty too, I suppose. Heck, it even has a nice gentle curve to it.

Take-Home Message: If you're watching at home, don't sleep on the Molenberg, at least when it's in the last 50km of the race. If you're riding it, make sure your water bottle is fit snugly in the cage before you start up.

6.   Bosberg

Stats: Officially 986 meters long, 5% average grade, 10% max. Honestly, there are two halves to the Bosberg, a fairly easy 3% false flat for nearly a km, followed by a 400 meter wall, mostly 10-11%

Cobbles? On the hard 400 meter part only. As Kappellestraat, the road ascending up the Bos, is more of a serious car track than several of the tractor paths on this list, the stones are reasonably uniform and non-threatening, having been mashed down by traffic for however long.

So How Bad Is It? 400 meters on cobbles at 10% or so is nothing to sneeze at. Also don't be fooled by the wide, smooth approach, which is a false flat and has a headwind most of the time in spring. It's harder than it looks, so *grinta* up and climb.

History: The Bosberg made its cycling debut in the 1950 edition of Het Volk (now Het Nieuwsblad), and joined the Ronde party in 1975, where it has held its place every year but one, and usually as the final climb.

Strategic Importance: On the old route, high. Usually "last climb" is synonymous with "game-decider," but that was always a bit of an overstatement in the case of the Bosberg. When Michael Phelps swims the third leg of the relay, the anchor guy is no longer the key to victory. But on occasion the riders didn't make the race on the Muur, and even when they did, us fans watching at home didn't always know it right away. So there was almost always tension and excitement on the race's final rated climb. And it's not exactly naive: Edwig Van Hooydonck won two Rondes by launching attacks on the Bosberg, dropping small groups and staying away. Even in its last run, in 2011, the Bosberg was the scene of a major move by Philippe Gilbert which shattered the 12-man leading peloton, even if it didn't work out for Gilbert.

Now, of course, the Bosberg is nowhere to be found in Flanders Classics' plans. Another victim of the finale relocation; the Bosberg is simply headed in the opposite direction from Oudenaarde. If and when the Muur comes back at some point, so too would the Bosberg, you'd think. Don't hold your breath though.

Most resembles: Oude Kwaremont? Not in a physical way, more in spirit.

Take-Home Message: Memories... Flanders will never run out of purists, so the images of all the great 20th century cyclists huffing and puffing their way over the Bosberg will keep it semi-relevant. But without a place in de Ronde it can't keep its place on this list forever, unlike the Muur.

7.   Taaienberg

Stats: 530 meters long, 6% average grade, 15% max. Or if you count the runout all the way to the Bossenaarstraat, call it 800 meters and 5.6%. Sometimes called Boonenberg for the predictability of Tom Boonen's attacks launched there during the E3 Prijs Vlaanderen. Literal translation is "tough mountain."

Cobbles? Yes, on the difficult part of the course, the first 500 meters. The stones are pretty big, and in fact it was on the Taaienberg where I had my moment of clarity about using the gutters, although I jumped back on the stones when I realized there were people watching. But they aren't Class A *kinderkopje*, and there is some nice muddy pavement at the top to finish things off.

So How Bad Is It? 500 meters of climbing on the cobbles puts it squarely in the Koppenberg-Paterberg Greater Oudenaarde trilogy of awesome, but of the three it's the easiest for an amateur to survive. To the pros the length allows for more of a sustained attack and those guys might have more concerns about staying in contact over the Taaienberg than the Paterberg.

History: A ronde staple since 1973, the Taaienberg has also featured pretty often in the E3 Prijs, the Omloop Het Volk/Nieuwsblad, and even Driedaagse de Panne. Basically everything except the Scheldeprijs and Paris-Roubaix.

Strategic Importance: Evolving! Mostly, the Taaienberg has been where legs go to get tested, not to die. In de Ronde it traditionally figured about halfway through the last 100km, the bumpy part. Occurring within 4km of both the Steenbekdries and the Eikenberg, it makes for a nice package of climbs, the hardest of that set. Then things got worse for the Taaienbeerg after the Grand Reorganization when it was moved up to ascent #2, a thoroughly irrelevant spot. But its proximity to Oudenaarde kept alive the chance that it could figure in the end of the race at some point. [It's not overly VIP-friendly, boxed in by steep embankments and forest. So there's that.]

And sure enough, that's where it landed in 2014, fourth from the end, and the last in the Koppenberg-Steenbekdries triptych. It's got big potential going forward, and in 2016 it was the scene of an actual winning move, or the prelude to one, when Michal Kwiatkowski jumped, drew out Peter Sagan, and set the scene for the final card-shuffling that ended with the Slovakian soloing home to his iconic win.[50]

Most resembles: A kinder, gentler Koppenberg. Like several of the area ascents, the worst of it is close to the bottom, with the upper slope relaxing a bit, running on, an interminable runout waiting for the survivors. I think of these climbs like meeting a friendly-looking stranger who shakes your hand for about a second, then punches you in the face, leaving you semi-conscious for a while... but takes the time to call the paramedics, who slowly revive you and help you back on your feet. You're fine in the end, and in truth you were only briefly in jeopardy, but you don't remember enjoying anything after the first few moments.

Take-Home Message: Always do what the races do and toss it in with a few others. The headliners will remain further up this list, but the approach was memorable. Coming from the south, if you choose to approach it via the smaller road to the east, you spend about 30 seconds riding below the climb, in reverse direction, headed toward the entrance, looking up through the leafless trees (in early spring). It beckons you.

---

[50] So this book is going to be published like seconds after the 2016 race. My biggest problem in writing this has been knowing when to put the pen down (and having enough time to write it at all). Anyway, I guess it could be awkward to be adding this information about 2016 in almost real time, but there you have it.

8. Eikenberg

Stats: 1.2km long, 5% average grade, 9% max. The worst gradient, and cobbles, is at the beginning. The name means "oak mountain."

Cobbles? Yup — aren't they all? Nothing too dramatic though. They were refurbished in 2011 after a pronounced crown and some large gaps began developing.

So How Bad Is It? In a vacuum, it's a tough enough climb. In the midst of the Ronde you can look at it two ways: it's another hill, another chunk of energy spent from your dwindling reserves. And a long ride up as well — the third-longest of the cobbled slopes, after the Oude Kwaremont and the Kruisberg. On the other hand, if we're talking about the cyclosportive and you made it up the Koppenberg, Paterberg and Taaienberg, the Eikenberg won't be too demoralizing. Oh, and if the asphalt stretch in the middle isn't enough, there are asphalt gutters next to the cobbles at the bottom and the top. In other words, it's only as bad as you want it to be.

History: Debuted in the Tour of Flanders in 1956, then became a fixture in 1974, not unlike a lot of the climbs on this list. Not a coincidence, by the way: de Ronde changed character in the early 70s and became the race it is today, starting in Bruges and ending in Meerbeke with the Vlaamse Ardennen dominating the action. For decades it was basically a circuit around east and west Flanders starting and finishing in Gent, but like the rest of northern Europe the old cobblestone roads that defined de Ronde found themselves in increasingly short supply in modern Belgium. Progress demanded faster roads, paved ones, and Belgium had other priorities besides bike racing. The race reshaped itself not around the climbs so much as the stones, still found in plenty of places in this quaint part of Flanders. That they went uphill... bonus. But I do like thinking that the real story is the stones more than the ascents. Everybody has hills.

Strategic Importance: Starting in 2012, not much, as it's been relegated to the third rated climb of the day. It's a stone's throw from Oudenaarde, though, so as the new route shakes out the Eikenberg may yet have its day. But for most of the last 40 years the Eikenberg has found itself in the thickest of thickets, coming with some 50-60km to go but surrounded by hazards. Using the 2011 map for example, from the start of the Oude Kwaremont at km 171 to the transition off the cobbles at about km 204, no less than 11km are over the infernal stones, including the Paterberg, Koppenberg, Taaienberg and Eikenberg as well as the renowned Mariaborrestraat, Holleweg and Kerkgate cobbled tracks. Taken together, the Eikenberg may or may not be the place to launch a glorious attack, but it's definitely a place to get rid of the pretenders, and maybe send a message or two.

Most resembles: If the Taaienberg and Oude Kwaremont paired off and had a kid... it would be cobbled, start off hard and then level off some, and keep going interminably til your elbows turn to jello. Like the Eikenberg.

Take-Home Message: Just a great representative for the whole cobbled climbing thing. What it lacks in extremes it makes up for with the right mix of ingredients.

*****

The Ronde van Vlaanderen's place as *Vlaanderens mooiste* is as ingrained in Flemish culture as frites. Want proof? Just watch the sides of the road. As far back as the 1930s it was estimated that up to 500,000 fans came out to watch the race in person. In 2015, that number was around one million. [Estimates can be a tad... enthusiastic. But still.] More and more outsiders are catching on to this love, and are drawn to experiencing a culture in full-blown loving expression. From the long view, the numbers of fans keeps going up. The number of people signing up to ride the cyclosportive keeps going up (until they capped it this past year). The word is spreading, something is happening here, and people want to see, hear and feel it for themselves.

Sometimes this isn't such a great thing. I was recently rewatching the 2008 Ronde van Vlaanderen (shocking, I know) when I caught sight of riders doing something seemingly ridiculous. And professional cyclists, however sane, do ridiculous things sometimes, but this seemed to repeat itself a fair amount, and seemed almost impossibly silly.

The scene: as the holiest day in Flemish cycling entered its final 100km, the race was going through some preambulatory segments of secondary highway, these smooth, two-lane roads with wide shoulders that connect places like Oudenaarde to places like Ronse or Brakel. I don't recall exactly where -- maybe they were leaving Ronse after the Oude Kwaremont? -- but it was before the meaty stretch of climbs (Koppenberg, Taaienberg, etc.) that starts shaping the race. A small group was up the road, but they were losing time as the peloton surged. Suddenly the TV cameras focus on the outer edge of the peloton, as a few riders who had swung wide, off into the road shoulder, now realize that there are fans standing between the shoulder and the road... standing between these riders and the race.

In the ensuing seconds, which unfolded at high speed and were over before anyone had time to feel shock, nothing bad happened. Riders passed between the spectators who flinched and dodged the speeding projectiles. There were some very very close calls, and you could practically hear in your mind the whine of brake pads being slammed on, but the cyclists made it back onto the course and carnage was avoided. This time. In the Ronde van Vlaanderen's history, plenty of other people haven't been as lucky.[51]

Why does this happen? Why do riders hop sidewalks and do other things that put them behind the fans, in such obvious jeopardy? The answer is much less ridiculous than you'd think.

Part of it lies in a few brief statistics from the race. At this moment the breakaway started watching its advantage erode quickly, from two minutes to less than one in very little time. The break does not appear to have slowed, which means the

---

[51] See, e.g., "Langeveld, Sebastian," "2012," "spectator's left heel" and "broken collarbone." Also, it can end badly for spectators too. In 2014 it approached tragic proportions, as Johan Van Summeren collided with an elderly woman early in de Ronde, not through any particular risk-taking on his part but because she was seated with a few fans on a traffic island where the peloton couldn't see and didn't expect them. People along the course can and often do get shockingly close to the action, even darting across the street in front of riders like jackrabbits along a desert highway. Van Summeren was battered by the fall, but the woman took the brunt of the collision and sustained head injuries which left her in a coma for several weeks. Thankfully she pulled through and eventually recovered, to the relief of many and particularly to Van Summeren, who was distraught and both physically and emotionally unfit to ride Paris-Roubaix.

chase is ramping up. But strangely enough, no team seems like it's doing anything on the front of the peloton. It's simply a matter of a large group of guys deciding independently to pick up the pace.

From above the peloton looks like it's being slowly whipped by egg beaters: riders overlap from the left and right margins and accelerate to the front as quickly as possible, while at least some of the riders in the middle drift backward. Also, like the egg beater metaphor, there is a very small pocket of guys front and center who seem buffeted against the chaos, holding their ground.[52] These are the members of the royal family, the Boonens and Cancellaras, whom nobody dares nudge off of their position before the final hour or so.

The intense battles for position are commonplace in the sport, but Flanders is unique in certain ways. First, by Monument standards there are often BIG pelotons. In a sense the race is trickier and crazier than even Paris-Roubaix, but it's not as selective. You don't often see groups of 40 or more riders in contention late in the race in the Hell of the North. Not having experienced all of this I can only guess, and it seems odd that cobbled hills could be less selective than cobbled flats. But the answer lies in what comes after a lot of those hills: paved descents. After the Bernard Hinault *pavé secteur*, you've got nothing but windy flats on which to claw back that gap you let out -- but you let that gap out for a reason (pain) which hasn't gone away, and the wind might be making matters even worse. Whereas after the Paterberg, if you take a chance or two on the smooth, quick descent, you can get right back in the race. With each climb there are a few riders dropped for

---

[52] In baking circles this is called the "Boonen Effect." OK, maybe not, but it could be.

good, and the peloton continually shrinks as the race progresses. But after 150km it's still pretty large.

Another part of Flanders are the endless twists and turns, a maze of 90-degree corners and road furniture. When you aren't on cobbles or climbs or cobbled climbs, you may still be on roads as narrow as golf cart paths where it is hard to move up, or too busy stopping and starting around corners to launch a move. The opportunities to realistically go from 75th to the front are limited. But on the occasional wide highway stretch of Ronde parcours, suddenly that shoulder looks like a golden invitation.

This is a classic Tour of Flanders moment in the making. As the peloton approaches a key choke point, guys who don't want to get stuck in the back of the peloton have to force their way into the front, and 50 guys fighting for 10 positions is nasty, nasty business. And by fighting, we mean everyone. Cycling is a zero-sum game in such moments: if 50 guys want to be in the top ten, well, for every guy moving up, someone is moving down. If five guys overlap the group and race up to the front, that means the guy in 32nd is now sitting 37th. A steady stream of overlappers means your seemingly comfy placement is gone in about 30 seconds, and next thing you know you're the guy looking to sprint up from the back.

In de Ronde, all of this plays out in larger proportions than a typical race. The big group exacerbates the urgency of moving up on the highway, because you simply have no chance of moving up that far under any other circumstances. Not on the climbs, not on the cobbles, not on the tiny roads, not even on the medium-sized country tracks. On a shoulderless two-lane road, if you're sitting 75th, you can probably move up to 60th if you're lucky. Chances are, when you hit the highway, you've been stuck pretty far back for a while, and if that's the case, there's probably a team manager in your ear suggesting you might want to do something about it.

So the race turns on the highway. Suddenly, briefly, there isn't merely space but oodles of space. Go *vollgas* for thirty seconds and all your problems are solved. You don't see spectators standing in the bike lanes or shoulder space; it's just empty, inviting you, daring you NOT to make a move. Of course you jump; with a wet Koppenberg approaching you need to move up now or your day is over. It all makes sense. So you go.

And then, with your head down as you hammer out a full-on sprint, for nothing less will catapult you that far past an entire, hungry pack, only then do you see that up ahead, there are some fans by the roadside. In the road, actually, like soigneurs leaning into the travel lanes to hand up musette bags. They see the pack and inch forward just enough to give the pack space to pass. You are now coming up behind them, and need to dart between them to get back on the course. Will they flinch or stay still? Should you assume the latter and stay behind them? Or should you look for them to jump back instinctively (wouldn't you?) and veer back to the center through the space they just created?

There is no good answer besides hope.

*****

It's this and a thousand other little things that set the Tour of Flanders apart. Each race has its signature -- Paris-Roubaix, the long stretches of nasty cobbles; Milano-Sanremo, the distance and the Poggio; Liege-Bastogne-Liege, the incessant climbing; and so on. Flanders' signature is its many signatures. Yes, the climbs are the stars, but the flat cobble stretches hurt too. So do the pack dynamics. So do the skinny roads. And not mentioned before, so do all the little left- and right-hand turns that link all of these features together across a rolling, rural landscape.

Several riders have mentioned the constant turning as the decisive element of the race. Your typical 90-degree turn brings with it just enough squeezing effect to make everyone, even the guys at the front, slow down a bit. Each time this happens, momentum is lost, until the peloton starts collectively freaking out as the end draws near, in which case each time the peloton slows for a turn, it brakes hard and then stomps on the pedals, hammering back up to full-gas once the turn is executed.

Slow, hammer. Slow, hammer. Adios momentum. Bounce over some stones. More momentum lost. Slip on muddy patches. Remount and start again. Every feature of the course is another demand. Each climb another Station of the Cross. It's the little things that add up, when there are enough of them, but don't forget about the big things too.

Whereas Paris-Roubaix is shrouded in stories of hell and grim paths, Flanders is green, pretty, neat and impressive. But don't be fooled. This is a hard, hard day.

8: Flandriens – Stars of the Past, Present and Future

One of the deeper quagmires in sports fanhood is what happens when you fix labels to athletes, and this is as true of cycling as anything else. Setting aside the more obvious controversies -- anointing heroes and villains -- in cycling, even saying what a rider's job is can lead to trouble. Call someone a sprinter or a climber or a time trial specialist and you've got about a 50% chance of looking clueless inside the next week or so. Sure, sometimes a rider's obvious talents make labeling inevitable, but a fair chunk of the peloton consists of guys who do a little of this and a bit more of that. And then there's ambition, which causes riders to reject set roles labels as limitations on what they can accomplish.

But honorary titles are another matter. Nobody truly rejects being called a "contender," particularly if the words "Tour de France" appear somewhere in the sentence. Nobody argues with being called a "leader" even when their team passes the official duties around to a variety of riders. And nobody would demur at the suggestion that they were a *Flandrien*.

I think I can say that safely... because you don't get called a *Flandrien* if you haven't earned it, teeth gritted, legs pumping madly, as you speed for hours across a black-and-white landscape. You wouldn't be called a *Flandrien* if you didn't love floating over the cobbles, because if you don't love it you can't succeed. You can't even get noticed by the fans of Belgium, let alone celebrated above the rank of a mere champion. So yes, even if there's a slight pigeon-holing effect, I think it's safe to say that nobody would resist the term if they belonged to that select club of riders who have been deemed worthy.

As for the meaning of the term, supposedly Karel Van Wijnendaele described a *Flandrien*, back in the day, as strong in the legs and the will, probably from East or West Flanders, maybe escaping poverty. All of which fits nicely with the narrative promoted by Van Wijnendaele and his compatriots as the reason for starting *de Ronde*. This enduring stereotype, then, is of the Flemish rider striking out alone, heroically, from the pack as well as from his home, skating across the infernal stones. But these shared prejudices evolve over time, and nowadays there is occasional debate about how the term has changed with the times. Does it merely denote a Tour of Flanders winner? Or a noted/popular tough guy? Can a foreigner make the cut? Does the status even need to be achieved in Belgian races anymore?

And who exactly are the *Flandriens*? Again, no definitive list, but it wouldn't be hard to come up with some convincing names. Gather up a bunch of old photos of famous cyclists in bad weather, all in black and white of course. Run through the great champions of de Ronde and Paris-Roubaix, describing their feats of strength and perseverance, how they left their rivals behind when it seemed too much to ask. When I was in

Flanders, the national newspaper Het Nieuwsblad was doing exactly that. I didn't catch the entire series, but Eddy Merckx was listed second in the all-time Flandriens countdown, about the only thing Merckx hasn't won in his career.

The job of assembling an historic list of *Flandriens* is best left to experts like the Centrum Ronde van Vlaanderen in Oudenaarde.[53] But I have to mention one rider who, nearly all would agree, embodies the term. Alberic "Briek" Schotte. The Iron Briek. Twice Ronde winner, twice world champion, a rider who just hammered the bejeezus out of his rivals. No tricks, no finesse. He came from modest means, and when they went to make a monument of him, he allegedly insisted that it not be on a pedestal, above the people, but rather at a normal height. And so, in his village of Kanegem, an iron statue of the Iron Briek stands by the side of a cobbled road, life-sized, on his bike. Just as he would like to be remembered, no doubt.

Oh, and he was so *Flandrien* he died on the day of the 2004 Ronde. Actually, I'm not sure what to read into that — maybe it's a commentary on Leif Hoste's tactics? — but it must mean something.

---

[53] Undaunted by my lack of Belgianness or expertise, I did prompt the Podium Cafe to host a Tournament of Champions in 2013, four brackets of riders seeded 1-16 and going head-to-head to determine (by popular vote) the ultimate cobbled champion. The four brackets represented distinct categories: retired Belgians, retired foreigners, active Belgians and active foreigners. At least up to that point, we were making apples-to-apples comparisons.
For what it's worth, Tom Boonen and Fabian Cancellara cruised to victory in the active Belgian and foreigner brackets, while Sean Kelly emerged from the retired foreigners bracket. Perhaps most impressive was Rik Van Looy, the Emperor of the Herentals, who knocked out in succession Rik Van Steenbergen, Eddy Merckx and Roger De Vlaeminck to win the Retired Belgians region. But in the end both of the old blokes were no match in the Final Four for Boonen and Cancellara, with Tornado Tom taking the ultimate prize.

Briek's other nickname is the "Last Lion of Flanders," which may be a tad premature -- forever is a long time. But it says a couple things. First, in case you didn't know, there are *Flandriens* and then there are "Lions of Flanders." The latter is a most high, exalted form of the former, not merely a mascot designation connected to the ten zillion little Flemish flags you can find washed up along the entire route the day after the race.

By most accounts the first Lion of Flanders was a man named Cyrille Van Hauwaert, whose physical powers peaked about the time when some people back home were dreaming up a Flemish tour. Van Hauwaert won the 1908 running of Paris-Roubaix, the first Belgian to accomplish this task, while also scoring breakthroughs for his country in Bordeaux-Paris (all 570+ kilometers of it) and Milano-Sanremo. In six tries he never scored worse than sixth at Paris-Roubaix. Van Hauwaert's success didn't go on for long, but for this farmhand to ascend to leadership of the great French team Alcyon was undoubtedly a shocker back in the day. And if it in some way paved the path for Briek Schotte, all the better.

But Schotte, in being anointed the *Last Lion of Flanders*, broke the mold for Flemish cycling heroes. Legend has it that Schotte used to get up every morning at 3:30 to train before heading to work at the factory, prior to his turning pro. His glittering career, interrupted for six years by war, included classics greatness and second at the Tour de France (behind Bartali) in 1948. But he never had a better day than the '48 Worlds.

That afternoon, Schotte joined an early breakaway on the fourth of 26 laps in Dutch Limburg -- on a course that included the Cauberg[54] -- and made it stick. For perspective, each lap was 10km, which means Schotte attacked with some 220km to go. Coppi and Bartali quit when the lead reached eight minutes (supposedly because they refused to help each other). With seven laps remaining, Dutch star Gerrit Schulte bridged the gap, but he was gassed and Schotte countered immediately on the Cauberg, dropping everyone but Apo Lazarides, who clung to Schotte's wheel until the Iron Briek crushed him in the final sprint.

It's easy to see why Flemish fans wanted to declare an end to human history after that performance. How can you top it? Attack the Ronde while it's still rolling out of Bruges? Schotte's exploits made Fabian Cancellara look timid by comparison. Fortunately for those of us who were neither alive nor Belgian in 1948, human history has soldiered on, and if there hasn't been another Briek Schotte, there have certainly been riders who distinguished themselves as harder than the rest. *Flandriens* have not gone extinct.

*****

It's tempting to turn now to another ranking widget, like the Top Ten Awesomest Flandriens Ever! or some such thing. But a comprehensive treatment of the subject is an entire other book, preferably written by a Dutch speaker.[55] I can't fully tell you why Edwig Van Hooydonck won two Rondes and Eddy Planckaert -- of the Cycling Planckaerts -- only one. Every era

---

[54] The Cauberg is the centerpiece climb of the Amstel Gold Race, and is notorious enough to have been the prime feature at the 2013 World Championships as well. Its surface is smooth and it rises at a rate of 8%, with a max of 11% over its length of 1km.

[55] I'm gonna guess that the amount of information available in Dutch or Flemish on, say, Cyrille Van Hauwaert is approximately a thousand million times what's available in English.

has its own vast array of quirks, level of competition goes up and down, the races evolve, and to decipher these subtleties nothing more than a mastery of Dutch and some killer newspaper archives is required. By palmares we know that Merckx, Roger De Vlaeminck, Rik Van Looy and Rik Van Steenbergen lead the way. We know that Francesco Moser won three consecutive Paris-Roubaix editions and Fiorenzo Magni three straight Rondes. Jan Raas, Heiri Suter, Gilbert Duclos-LaSalle, Marc Madiot, Romain Gijssels, Achiel Buysse, Sean Kelly, Octave Lapize -- these are the names of men who evoke special memories of cobbled races gone by.

My hunch is that in places like Gent and Kortrijk there are entire libraries of books detailing the exploits of this crowd, albeit in Dutch. So rather than starting down that road, let's instead run through a more modern array of different types of Flandriens, the riders who have enlivened de Ronde over the last decade. It's been a fun ride, the races were actually available to watch, and this time cutoff enables me to ignore the forgettable 1990s. In rough order of quality...

10. The Flummoxing Flandrien: Stijn Devolder

Stijn Devolder, scion of Kortrijk, won the 2008 and 2009 editions of the Tour of Flanders, including the former while clad in the Belgian champion's jersey. Local kid, winning the biggest race, riding for the biggest Belgian team, in his back yard. Flandrien royalty, right?

Ah, not quite. Devolder presents a curious case, because his victories will always have everything to do with the fact that he was Tom Boonen's sidekick in those years. There can be plenty of debate as to whether he was the strongest man in those two races regardless -- both times Devolder attacked out of a small group in the vicinity of the Muur van Geraardsbergen and soloed home for the win, erasing any basic questions about his possessing the requisite abilities for the race. But circumstances muddy the picture, as there can be NO debate about what the favorites were up to while Devolder was sauntering home to glory. They were sticking to Boonen like *speculoos*[56] on toast.

Boonen came in to both editions as the prohibitive favorite, winner in 2005 and 2006, sitting on excellent form (confirmed in both 2008 and 2009 a week later with wins in Paris-Roubaix). To compound the matter, while both he and Devolder were then nationwide stars, only one was/is THE star, first among equals. For Devolder's entire career, Boonen has loomed over Belgian Cycling like the alien ships in Independence Day, blotting out the sky. As teammates they coexisted gracefully, and as long as Quick Step -- the New York Yankees of Belgium -- held a winning hand, the team had zero incentive to toss away an ace like Stijn. Two aces are better than one, as long as the aces themselves see it that way. Devolder's power worked decently on the climbs too, making him a valuable stage-race *domestique*, with the strength to ride on the front of the Tour de France and the climbing ability to help lift the pace on a critical ascent, for a while at least. In the Tour, Boonen and Devolder could be terrific teammates, chasing stage wins and points in ways that helped each other out.

---

[56] Belgium's answer to Nutella. I recommend peanut butter. Or Biscoff — it's made out of cookies.

At the 2008 Tour of Flanders Boonen was rebounding from the previous year's loss to Alessandro Ballan, and entered *Vlaamse Wielerweek* on cracking form. He won the Tour of Qatar with ease and bagged a stage in the Amgen Tour of California, back when it was still raced in February. He'd looked strong throughout the early spring. Everybody knew it, and the entire *Ronde* seemed to revolve around Boonen. There was little question about his strength, and even less question about whether anyone should try to tow him to Ninove for a sprint. *De Ronde* favors aggressive tactics, and with a very fit Devolder on his team, Quick Step manager Patrick Lefevre set out to punish everyone sitting on his ace. Devolder got into a small breakaway in the final 30km, while Boonen waited for another team to respond, counting down the climbs, right to the Muur. He's still waiting for that response. Devolder dropped his break-mates on the Eikenmolen, soloed up and over the Muur, and was never seen again.

Things at Quick Step seemed simpatico enough; Boonen regretted his fate but a good Fleming understands classics tactics, and he seemed genuinely happy for Devolder and the team. Moreover, the "loss" did little to diminish Tommeke's standing, thanks to his work in Paris-Roubaix, which he won a week later. Tornado Tom is not lacking in character; of course he wants to win, so there was some post-race lip-biting after de Ronde, but when he said nice things, he did so with the credibility of a guy who has often shown genuine, heartfelt support for his teammates.[57]

---

[57] Look at practically any photo of Filippo Pozzato winning Milano-Sanremo in 2006, during his Quick Step apprenticeship years, and you can't miss Tom Boonen sitting upright, clad in the world champion's rainbow kit, arms straining for the sky as he exalts in his teammate's theft of a monument which Boonen had hoped to win for himself. The list of world champions expressing spontaneous joy at someone else winning a monument is short indeed. But Boonen isn't that sort of Alpha dog.

And anyway, Devolder looked like a winner all day in 2008, animating the race at every turn. But when Devolder won a second *Ronde* in '09, under practically identical circumstances, nerves began to wear thin at Quick Step. Now Boonen was discussing Devolder as a competitor. By the following spring, it was getting noticeably uncomfortable around Quick Step, as Boonen's ability to disguise his feelings deteriorated and Devolder chatted openly about his hope of matching Fiorenzo Magni's record of three straight Flanders wins. Still, no sign of a split though, for two simple reasons: Devolder had another year on his contract, and Boonen just doesn't do the alpha dog thing.

In the end, the "problem" resolved itself in spring, 2010. Devolder was ineffective in all of the spring classics in 2010, and Lefevre hastened his departure by speaking a little too bluntly to the press. Lefevre, for his part, seemed to be riding Devolder in the media, either to victory or the door. Tensions frayed in the week before *de Ronde* as Lefevre hinted that Devolder hadn't prepared properly, while Devo insisted all was well. When his title defense went nowhere, the two spent the following week trading even more barbs, uncommon for a Belgian powerhouse in the middle of Holy Week, and three crashes later Devolder's cobbles season ended by the roadside in northern France.

Stijn Devollder in 2010. Photo by Chris Fontecchio

Devolder could have fought back against the PR tactics of his team manager, but instead he quietly took a deal for 2011 with the Dutch Vacansoleil squad. This seemed sensible enough, giving him a chance to operate somewhat outside of the spotlight -- gone, but certainly not forgotten. Fellow Fleming

Bjorn Leukemans certainly didn't go unnoticed in the Belgian press as the latter mounted two impressive near misses in the monuments while racing in Vacansoleil colors.[58] Better still, whatever Devolder did next could be fairly judged as the efforts of a team captain racing with no particular advantage, other than having mates like Leukemans to give him a fighting chance against Quick Step and the other powerhouses. If Devolder failed miserably enough (as he did in 2011 and 2012; by 2013 Devolder was a top domestique for Cancellara), we would ascribe his two Ronde wins as I do -- flukes of tactics in an era of Quick Step dominance. If he ever rides away from the Flanders peloton again, dropping Boonen in an act of hostility rather than triangulation, then no fan, however skeptical in years past, will block his entrance into the Cobbled Hall of Fame.

Take-away message: Having threatening teammates around your leader is an important part of team strategy. But you -- Director and team leader -- have to be willing and able to play all your cards.

Also see: Lammerts, Johan. The winner in 1984 was supposed to set up Eddy Planckaert or Eric Vanderaerden, two very successful (and Belgian) teammates on the famous Dutch Panasonic squad. But he had fantastic legs and the goings-on at the front of the race weren't enough to shake the Dutchman. Lammerts attacked with 3km to go and a dangerous Sean Kelly lurking. Like Devolder a quarter century later, if you're holding a winning hand, why not play it?

---

[58] Leukemans landed at upstart Vacansoleil after a year out of cycling for a testosterone doping case. Make of that what you will.

9. The Reluctant (ahem) Flandrien: Filippo Pozzato

There are a lot of ways to enter the realm of the Flandrien, but Italian riders don't have the smoothest path. As the stereotype of Italian cyclist goes, they often opt for cagey, wheel-grabbing tactics over glorious aggression -- as un-Flemish as it gets. Generalizations like that don't usually hold up forever (Magni? Tafi? See below...), but few years go by without someone pumping life back into it.

Enter Pippo. Initially raised by Patrick Lefevre at Quick Step as Tom Boonen's understudy, Filippo Pozzato spent most of the past decade playing the role of spoiler -- literally. Labeled a future star early on, an on-form Pozzato to this day still turns the pedals over as gracefully as an angel, and he's been lavished with prestigious contracts since turning pro at age 20, first at powerhouse Mapei, then with Mapei's quasi-successor Fassa Bortolo, before being taken under the Belgian wing. Nobody would call him a failure, but his lack of breakthrough wins (after 2006 Milano-Sanremo) is troubling to those who held such high expectations for him. Personally, I am always fooled by his smooth style, and until recently was regularly shocked to see him dropped from a leading pack -- just never saw it coming.[59] Apart from his pedalstroke Pozzato has long possessed a nice mix of skills for Flanders, the ability to power over short climbs and a pretty fair sprint at the end, along with

---

[59] Pozzato's last strong season was 2013, and he's currently languishing on the Southeast team as his career winds down. His last Cobbled Classics win was the 2009 E3 Prijs, though his run of form in 2013 saw him bag the prestigious summer classic GP Ouest France.

the requisite strength to maintain the long march across the cobbles. Sounds like a guy the crowd could appreciate at *de Ronde*, but most years nobody seems less liked than Pippo.

Pozzato's great sin has been his cagey, conservative style. He simply doesn't launch many aggressive attacks. After races he's been heard explaining that he figures out who the strongest rider is and takes his cues from that person. Lots of people do this, but almost nobody drew the criticism Pozzato did -- if they are criticized at all. Somehow the rest are forgiven for not being champions, or Flandriens, while Pozzato is not. Other riders accuse Pozzato of racing "negatively" -- refusing to attack -- or its second cousin, failing to share the work of a breakaway. Pozzato denies the charges, even goes on to claim that the complaining party (Boonen, Gilbert, etc.) retracted their criticisms to him. To the viewer it can be nearly impossible to tell when a rider is refusing to attack or pull, or is simply unable. With facts so fleeting and emotions running high, the Rashomon Effect settles in on the peloton very quickly at the finish line.

For his part, Pozzato has defiantly resisted the "wheel sucker" charge, even getting a massive back tattoo saying "Only God Can Judge Me," the ink that launched a thousand wisecracks. Personally I admit to having been a Pozzato apologist for a while.[60] I love watching him enough to believe what he says: that in '08 and '09 he couldn't beat all of Quick Step by himself (who could?); that following Boonen was the high-percentage play, only Boonen never cracked and Lefevre played his other cards. But I get the criticism too: for fans, he was simply too

---

[60] An admission I like less now that he has served a brief three-month ban in 2012 for working with notorious doping doctor Michele Ferrari back in his youth. Cycling isn't kind to fans who want to support it with all their heart.

good at his peak not to attack. The pedaling style is no mirage, Pozzato was clearly among the top five strongest classics riders from 2006-2012.

What of that "win or die trying" mentality, which is surprisingly rare in cycling? I am always astounded, even after so many years of watching, when a two man breakaway comes practically to a standstill in sight of the finish as riders say to each other "no, you go first" in hopes of grabbing one last draft before making the winning move. Numerous grand tour stages come to mind, where the spoils are occasionally left for riders who don't often get a shot at victory, and yet when the opportunity finally presents itself, perhaps even after years of waiting, it suddenly unravels in a fit of what looks like total madness. Riders in a small break will go so far as to lose a race entirely, even their second or third place, rather than tow a rival to victory, like a chump.[61]

In this way, though, the classics and the Belgians are different. Not to over-generalize, but in Flanders riders do rather often take the win-or-die-trying approach. Racers in Flanders are taught aggressive tactics throughout their development, so while people are people and Belgians don't all have aggression in their DNA, this coaching plus the urgency of a one-day classic tends to bring on the attacks. That Flemish fans root for the attacking riders is nothing new; fans worldwide loves action. That they would single out and condemn certain riders for not attacking... this is a bit more unique.

---

[61] American Chris Horner, participating in his first Tour de France at age 33, gave up on trying to win a stage when he and Sylvain Chavanel found themselves alone in the last kilometer of the 13th stage of the 2005 Tour. Even stranger than watching them stand still and let the pack swallow them up was the way Horner matter-of-factly dismissed the idea of taking the front and delivering Chavanel to the line, grabbing second in the process. It simply doesn't work like that... most of the time.

Filippo Pozzato and Alessandro Ballan. Photo by Chris Fontecchio

And so it goes with Pozzato. Like many a great athlete, he is punished for not living up to expectations, particularly well-founded expectations, when you see him and Boonen shoulder-to-shoulder at the front of a cobbled climb. The gifted style, the perfect position -- it's like fans are offended that he could have the ability to win the Tour of Flanders and not turn himself inside out in pursuit of that goal. You can almost hear their thoughts: "If that were me on the front, looking so good, I wouldn't stop attacking if I were bleeding from my eyes." Pozzato calculates his moves carefully... and the Belgian fans hate him for it.

Finally, though, in 2012, Pozzato took up the aggression in roughly the manner demanded of him by the rest of the world. As the race hit the Paterberg, making its debut as the final climb of de Ronde, it was Pozzato who went out front of the leading threesome, briefly putting Tom Boonen out the back and just barely taking Alessandro Ballan with him. This was Pozzato at his best, once again, turning over the pedals and looking as silky smooth as a dollop of marscapone. Only it wasn't just Pippo the talented; this was Pippo the aggressor, putting the hammer down on his decorated rivals, two former Flanders winners. It nearly worked -- and dropping Boonen would have made this change of tactics all the more notorious -- but Boonen closed the small gap on the descent, and the two Italians, while taking their pulls on the front, couldn't shed the Belgian champion. In the end Pozzato lost his best chance to win by half a wheel in a desperately tight sprint with Boonen. Damned if you do, damned if you don't. Since then, though, the negative commentary has calmed down, so maybe it wasn't all for naught?

Take-Away Message: Do you want to win or be loved? Some guys can do both; for everyone else, it's a choice.

See Also: Thor Hushovd, George Hincapie.

8. A Flandrien At Last: Steffen Wesemann

Want to form a generalized opinion of Flemish sports fans based on anecdotal evidence? The story of Steffen Wesemann's victory in the 2004 Ronde van Vlaanderen is a heart-warming place to start.

By the time the '04 race left Bruges, Wesemann, born in Saxony-Anhalt in East Germany, had spent twelve years plugging along as a pro, frequently winning the Peace Race, a stage race through former Iron Curtain nations, and threatening a big result on the cobbles. In 1995 he foreshadowed a career of classics fortitude with second in the E3 Prijs Harelbeke, and his second place in Paris-Roubaix in 2002 was confirmation of his ability over the hardest routes of the north. But apart from his share of sprint wins, mostly on German soil or further east, Wesemann lacked a signature victory heading into his thirteenth pro season.

The German rider was on a good day at the 2004 Ronde when he crashed 120km into the race, as the peloton headed into the Flemish Ardennes. It's hard to tell from recounts of the day whether he was hurt or disgusted, but with the race speeding off up the road Wesemann flirted with the idea of climbing into the team car, until his teammates insisted they could pace him back to the head of the race. Deutsche Telekom was still a powerhouse in 2004,[62] so Wesemann got a top-flite escort

---

[62] Wesemann's assistance that day came from stalwarts like Rolf Aldag, Mario Aerts, Serguei Ivanov and Andreas Klier. Strong squad, right? Maybe, until you look at Fassa Bortolo, who supported Belgian national icon Frank Vandenbroucke with young talents like, oh, Filippo Pozzato and Fabian Cancellara, plus a more established Juan Antonio Flecha. Which is impressive until you look in on Quick Step, who sent out Paolo Bettini, Tom Boonen, and Luca Paolini, to support captain Johan Museeuw. Bettini was actually the

back into position, and found himself thinking of the finale and the words of Walter Godefroot. The venerable T-Mobile director, a Belgian with two Flanders wins to his name, had always counseled Wesemann to get to the bottom of the Muur, go full gas to the top, then look around and see where things stand.

Two and a half hours later Wesemann attacked just like Godefroot drew it up, and after shedding all that was left of the heads of state, he found himself alone on the Muur with only Belgians Leif Hoste and Dave Bruylandts still in contact. With the skill of a Ronde warrior Wesemann unleashed a wicked descent of the Kapelmuur to solidify the trio's advantage, and they made it stick all the way to the finish.

As the trio steamrolled to the finish in Ninove with the help of a tailwind, Wesemann got on his radio to ask who these two young Belgians were. [Not sprinters, he was told.] Flemish fans, meanwhile, counted on two happy endings out of a possible three. But if the fans didn't care which of their two countrymen triumphed, the riders themselves certainly did. Shared national identity and even real friendships don't hold much water when personal ambitions and team rivalries[63] come to a head at the pointy end of a cycling Monument. So Bruylandts, the weakest

---

team's top finisher, ninth on the day, ahead of Museeuw (15th) and Boonen (25th). Flecha was Fassa Bortolo's man in 12th, while young Cancellara and Pozzato came in a forgettable 41st and 108th. Less forgettable? A start list that, when you add in Van Petegem, Ballan, Devolder, Bortolami and Bartoli, you have no less than 16 Ronde victories represented in that peloton, and more podium positions than I care to count. If it seems like a curiously quiet day, it could also be described as a moment between dominant generations, with the next one starting for real a year later.

[63] Bruylands rode for the Chocolade Jacques team, which evolved into the current Topsport Vlaanderen squad, the country's most prestigious pro-continental level proving ground for young Belgian talent. Hoste for Lotto-Domo, the team of Marc Sergeant which currently exists as Lotto-Soudal and has been the main foil to the Quick Step franchise for, well, ever.

of the three, attacked in the final kilometer, but rather than waiting for Wesemann to respond, on the grounds that Wesemann was clearly the fastest sprinter. Hoste saw the move as either a threat or an opportunity — they had to attack Wesemann eventually — so he reacted and reeled in his countryman. This created a massive opening which Wesemann neatly exploited for the easy sprint win.

Now, I'm not an expert in Flemish culture, but I'll venture a guess that after two horrifying invasions in the previous century, Germans don't qualify for "most favored neighbor" status in Flanders, so the sight of two Belgians negating each other and paving the way to a German victory is probably about as unpleasant a scenario as your average Flemish fan could conjure up. Which makes the story of Wesemann's reception pretty telling.

His wife Caroline was waiting in a bar near the Muur, and eventually the patrons realized who she was. Mrs. Wesemann says they were courteous but still told her a Belgian would win. When the riders hit the line, there was dead silence. A low moment, but nothing disrespectful.

But by the next day the German victor was celebrated. As he told it, "at the choice moment they think 'the Belgians have to win,' but then they were ALL happy with me – the next day… it was UNBELIEVABLE. Everyone was happy with me - they said 'you were the best on this day, and that is correct…' That's fair of them, they accept that if you win you are the best and they are happy for you."[64] That's class.

---

[64] Via Pez Cycling News, January 11, 2005 Link: http://www.pezcyclingnews.com/interviews/steffen-wesemann-pez-clusive-interview/#.VrLcnTZcLkE

Ultimately, while Flemish fans are fiercely loyal to their local heroes, national origin often seems to be a lesser consideration than what a guy can do on a bike. When a foreigner wins on the cobbles, he is treated like a cobbles winner first and a foreigner second. You get the sense that Saddam Hussein could have come around Bruylandts for the win in Ninove and still received polite applause and grudging respect along the lines of "he was the strongest today."

Take-Away Message: Just about everyone in Flanders respects the strongest rider. This isn't a nationalism thing. It's just what the race is truly about. [See the Honorary Flandrian category below.]

7.   The Frustrated Flandrien: Leif Hoste

The Classics are a tough thing to get obsessed with, offering few ways to win and a million ways to lose. You can be good -- really good -- at de Ronde every year for a decade or more and come away empty handed in the win department. If you're one of the many riders who plan their season around the Classics, well, frankly it's hard to picture how some of these guys maintain their sanity. "That's cycling" is the common refrain, an all-too-handy dismissal of the misery riders face every day, from crashes to illness to flat tires to botched sprints and so on.

And so we have the lonely quests, riders who fit the bill of the Flandrien not just for their ability to get around the course or their love of the stones, but for their willingness to accept the punishment that accompanies that love. This is most certainly a key characteristic of a true Flandrien. And in the last decade nobody has endured more punishment than Leif Hoste.

Born in Kortrijk, a veritable hub of Flemish cycling, Hoste took the dreamiest possible route to the peloton, turning pro with the Mapei juggernaut in1997 and spending a couple more years honing his craft alongside Museeuw, Tafi, Bettini and Bartoli. From there, Hoste slid over to Domo-Farm Frites with Museeuw, then Lotto-Domo in time for Peter Van Petegem's memorable spring in 2003. Throughout these years he showed ability, notching a win at the Belgian National Time Trial race and second in Kuurne-Brussels-Kuurne in '03, his first real classic palmare. A year later, it was time for his Ronde van Vlaanderen debut, and Hoste made his move.

On this beautiful, sunny April day, the big names of Museeuw, Van Petegem, Hincapie, Bettini, Erik Dekker, et al. couldn't react when Hoste joined the escape with only Bruylandts of the Belgian Chocolade Jacques team and Wesemann of T-Mobile on the climb of the Muur. I've already gone over that ending for Wesemann, but it's worth looking at the event from the perspective of Hoste. Here he was, in his first ever Tour of Flanders, living yet another Belgian cycling dream, earlier as the designated early breakaway rider up the road in service of his team, and now as the rider covering a winning move on the sacred Muur, suddenly taking over as the team's surviving threat to win.

Somewhere in this sequence of events, the dream faded. Maybe it was when a tiring Bruylandts -- himself on the attack at a few different junctures of the race -- tried his only big jump in the closing kilometers, knowing he couldn't beat Wesemann in a sprint, incredibly opening up a real gap... only to have his countryman Hoste react to the move and close it down with Wesemann sitting comfortably on Hoste's wheel. As recounted above, this scene shocked Belgian fans into silence, but Hoste pointed out what everyone knew -- that this wasn't national team duties and he had an obligation to try for the win. Worse, he entered the race as a domestique for Van Petegem and Leon van Bon, and had spent considerable time on the front of the race. So try he did, but as Wesemann's coach had predicted, Hoste was no match for the German in the sprint.

Hoste took the result well enough, acknowledging that he never expected to be anywhere near the podium when the day began, and nothing seemed too horribly amiss, even when a week later at Paris-Roubaix Hoste got briefly demoted from the leading group when a massive Flemish flag came loose and clogged up his rear wheel. [How did we misread these signs?]

After a nondescript 2005 Classics season and a move to join George Hincapie on the American Discovery Channel squad Hoste was back on top form for 2006. By now Tom Boonen had made the jump to sainthood, winning the cobbled double in '05 and sporting the world champion's rainbow jersey as he set out to defend his Flanders title. All eyes were on the new King of the Cobbles.

But if Boonen was an ace, Discovery had two kings to play, with Hincapie every bit as fit as Hoste coming into the day. The American's sprint was considered close enough to Boonen's to be worth a try, making Hincapie the designated leader. When the race hit the Valkenberg, shortly before Geraardsbergen,

Hoste attacked and found himself at the top of the climb with only one rider for company: Boonen. Cancellara briefly gave chase, and a coterie of other teams were left to close the gap, with Discovery hoping for Hincapie to get an armchair ride back to Boonen while everyone else burnt precious matches.

Hoste, his DS Dirk Demol later argued, had in fact attacked as a way of bluffing Boonen and his powerful team into defensiveness, for Hincapie's eventual benefit.[65] The flipside of this strategy is that Hincapie was a top favorite, and nobody was in a mood to help him, and anyway if Discovery wanted to take their chances against Boonen with Hoste... yeah, good luck with that. Once away, Discovery hedged and told Hoste to avoid working for a while to see if Hincapie could bridge up to the duo, but Quick Step's Bettini dogged Hincapie into oblivion, the two Belgians stayed away, and the sprint went exactly as everyone expected: to Boonen.[66]

Again Hoste seemed to accept his second place with justifiable pride. Nobody had outsprinted Boonen in anything of consequence lately, but the two countrymen had shared the title of strongest rider that day. If he didn't just hit the brakes and wait for Hincapie, well... riders of that stature always

---

[65] Self-serving post-hoc rationale? Dodgy coverup of a shameful conspiracy? Or honest confession of a failed strategy? It would scarcely be a bike race if we weren't left with these ambiguous, endlessly-arguable questions about what lurked in the hearts of riders and managers as a tense race played out. In Cycling, controversy is the other oxygen.

[66] Michael Barry, a teammate of Hoste and Hincapie at the time, later alleged that Hoste conspired to sell the victory to Boonen, as evidenced by the fact that Hoste cooperated with Boonen and that there were conversations with team cars. The idea is that, had Hoste not been paid, he would have just stuck on Boonen's wheel in the hopes that Hincapie would rejoin the group. And as an American fan, I can distinctly remember hoping that would be the case. But since the duo put 1.17 into the larger chasing group, it's hard to see the result as unjust in any way, nor does it seem suspicious for a Belgian to work in an attack with a shot to win Flanders from a two-man break. Except maybe this two-man break? I get it: helping Boonen get to the line in 2006 does not sound terribly credible. One more set of secrets that will probably be taken to everyone's grave.

believe they can win, and Hoste was no exception. In the end, public opinion seemed to say that Hincapie was too slow to react, playing too much of a waiting game. Boonen beat him (and the rest) by counterattacking, and from there Hoste was merely along for the ride.

Things went downhill for Hoste. A week later, Hoste finished another respectable second behind Fabian Cancellara in Paris-Roubaix, only to be disqualified with Peter Van Petegem and Vlad Gusev for crossing a train track when the gate was down. Maybe there is a superstition about this, like walking under paint ladders or breaking mirrors. Maybe tracking down Bruylandts was bad juju after all. Because what happened next spoke of nothing less than a curse.

Hoste, now with the Lotto boys again,[67] was his usual self in the 2007 Ronde, in with the leaders as the race entered Geraardsbergen. Quick Step had again dominated the day, with rainbow-clad Bettini patrolling the front for Boonen (maybe)[68] and sprinter Gert Steegmans shadowing a

---

[67] It's safe to say that the 2006 Ronde did not leave him in great standing with his mates at Discovery. But Boonen too was a former Discovery/Postal protégé, and when the time came to be a protected rider, he went home. Hoste got a nice raise and a captaincy in his return to Sergeant's Lotto team. Stijn Devolder left the Americans a year later to work for/with/against Boonen at Quick Step. It's what Belgian classics stars do: ride for Belgian teams. Money reinforces that, since Belgian teams will value classics acumen more than the typical foreign team.

[68] Bettini rode for some iteration of the Quick Step team from 1999 until his retirement in 2008, and in the final few years he made little secret of his desire to win the Tour of Flanders, even at the expense of his teammate Boonen. The justification was that the Cricket, as he was well known, had three other Monuments in his pocket — Milano-Sanremo, Lombardia and Liege-Bastogne-Liege — as well as an Olympic road race title and by the end two World Championship rainbow jerseys, the first of which he carried on his shoulders at the 2007 Ronde. With no realistic hope of winning Paris-Roubaix, a race he usually skipped altogether, Flanders represented the last jewel in his crown of possible one-day glory. In retrospect, however, Bettini never finished higher in Ninove than seventh (2006), and his cobbled dreams were more of the pipe variety — possibly even a Patrick Lefevre sleight of hand too. Also, to Bettini's credit, he never really acted on his ambitions or otherwise deviated from his role of helping Boonen.

dangerous attack from Cancellara, but with the peloton arriving intact at the foot of the Muur Lampre's Daniele Bennati moved up in front of Boonen and put in a devastating pull, igniting the action and setting up his teammate Alessandro Ballan for a blistering attack on the Muur's upper slope.[69] Boonen faltered for the first time in ages, and Hoste, sensing the danger, accelerated around his nemesis, caught up with Ballan after the descent, and the pair sped off for Ninove.

Surely this was his chance. Unlike 2004, this was a two-up situation, where the tactics are straightforward enough. Unlike 2006, his companion Ballan was less than a world-class sprinter, to put it kindly. Surely this was the dream sequence that he'd awakened from prematurely before. Things got even better when the cat-and-mouse games of "you first;" "no, after you;" "no, I insist" ensued in the last kilometer and ended with Ballan gamely taking the lead. This time the other guy was set up, and Hoste was ticketed to win. Hoste stuck to Ballan's wheel as the Italian accelerated for the line, and jumped with 100 meters to go, coming past Ballan with predictable success.

But somehow Ballan didn't let go, tucked himself into Hoste's slipstream, dug deep inside his lanky frame and located one last ounce of fighting spirit, kicking out a final desperate 50-meter burst. In one of the most improbable scenes of the decade, the beaten sprinter turned the tables at the last second, as Ballan came back around Hoste for the victory. By

[69] Bennati, a fair sprinter at the time, cemented his place in Flanders domestique lore with this pull. Both he and Ballan were on fire coming into the race, giving Lampre a chance at a solo attack in the latter and a sprint win from the former, if the race never broke apart. To their credit, they didn't hedge their bets, committing Bennati to setting up Ballan, and the rest is history. To some extent he became known as an all-round stud, and in an interview with BMC boss Jim Ochowicz, when I asked him to compare Davis Phinney to a current rider he admiringly cited Bennati. He still rides lead-out for Tinkoff-Saxo, as of this writing, and occasionally goes after sprint victories for himself.

about four inches. Hoste slammed his bars and roared in profane frustration.

From the moment Ballan raised his arms in shocked triumph, it was clear that Hoste was shattered in a way that he might never recover from. Hoste has since gone on to some solid results, finishing as high as fourth in Paris-Roubaix, claiming another national time trial title, and making his presence known in de Ronde (let's just say he waves his arms around a little too often). His Ronde finishes after 2007? 19th, 27th, 29th and 56th. In 2012 Hoste joined the Accent Jobs-Willems Verandas team, a second-division squad, all but signaling the end of his quest. De Ronde remains the dream from which he woke up an instant too soon.

Take-Away Message: The classics are cruel. Full stop.

See Also: About 99% of the peloton. OK, maybe Sylvain Chavanel. Definitely George Hincapie, Pozzato, and for the moment Sep Vanmarcke and Zdenek Stybar.

6. The Hopeful Imports: From Magni to Phinney

Throughout my time in Flanders the local press found itself chatting about the lack of Belgian success in the 2010 classics season, a subject that became more and more pointed until finally a Belgian victory happened on Belgian soil. Brabantse Pijl, the Brabant Arrow, was the occasion where the home country broke the duck. In 2010 Brabantse Pijl got re-slotted as a post-Paris-Roubaix changeover (hangover?) race where the peloton stops clanging about on the cobbles and starts to climb, and Sebastian Rosseler had delivered the nation from further embarrassment at the proverbial eleventh hour when he out-kicked two of his countrymen from an all-Belgian break, which the peloton mercifully never reeled in. After all, Flanders had been such a gracious host for going on three weeks now. It was only right.

While the story of de Ronde and the Classics season is rooted in provincial identities and loyalties, and the Belgians love their home-grown winners every bit as much as you would imagine, the race has long been a big draw to foreign riders. And by draw I don't mean that they show up there, looking for a win. I mean, they become embedded in the Belgian scene, professing their love for the infernal stones and orienting their season around the spring classics. In some cases it just all makes perfect sense. Italians and Spaniards and Brits are not exactly strangers to cobblestones, if not perhaps at the same dosage level.

Then there are body types. Hincapie was frequently called "Big George" on TV, Ballan often towered over his climber teammates, and Cancellara, Peter Sagan, Alexander Kristoff... these guys are more solid than spritely. These are riders with more than enough wattage for the pro peloton, but they'll never match the watts-per-kilogram output that is a prerequisite to winning a race up a mountain. People of all body types fall in love with cycling, so rather than turning the clydesdales away, cycling has simply created events (a hundred years ago) to celebrate the best athletes over 160 pounds.

Still, having the body type for the cobbled classics is just a start; winning in Flanders requires that you love them too.

Fiorenzo Magni did. The Tuscan won three consecutive editions of the Ronde van Vlaanderen from 1949-51, the only rider ever to do so. All three editions were raced in dreary weather, but overcoming hardship would become Magni's trademark. Magni's first win came in a sprint from an 18-rider peloton, in the last edition of de Ronde before the discovery of the Muur van Geraardsbergen. The following yeah, Magni escaped for the final 75km with Dutchman Win van Est and Frenchman André Mahé,[70] whereupon Magni claimed the honor of becoming the first rider in Flanders history to launch a successful solo attack on the Muur. Briek Schotte, 2.15 back, was the only finisher within nine minutes of Magni.

But his real stamp on the race was imprinted in 1951. Bidding to become the first treble winner, Magni again winnowed down the pack to nine riders, and attacked the race in Strijpen, just as he'd done the previous year, only this time nobody could answer. For 75km Magni soldiered on through the rain alone, earning enough intermediate bonus prizes, it is said, to purchase a house. His final advantage was 5.35 over Frenchman Bernard Gauthier. Nobody else was within ten minutes. The top Belgian finisher was former double-winner Rik Van Steenbergen, sixth, over twelve minutes in arrears.[71]

---

[70] Mahé is best known as the winner of Paris-Roubaix in 1949. Or one of them. Mahé was in great shape entering Roubaix that day, all alone and cruising to a solo victory, when he found his entrance to the velodrome obstructed by crowds who, back then, were allowed to roam the streets more freely than nowadays. In the chaos and confusion, Mahé was guided away from the crowds... and the velodrome entrance, to somewhere just outside the track. A journalist on a moto caught the error and sped up to him, telling him what had gone wrong. Mahé found a media entrance that led him into the track, on the wrong side, and completed the race, whereupon he was declared the winner. Then came the pack, and a sprint, won by Serse Coppi, and the Coppi brothers began to argue that Mahé had not completed the course and should be disqualified, leaving Serse the winner. After a few months of protests flying around, the race declared both victors.

[71] It's probably safe to say Magni wasn't 12 minutes better than Van Steenbergen, though Rik I was getting into his mid-30s by then. Cycling has a binary element to it — winners and everyone else — and once Magni got far enough away, the pack stopped

His historic third consecutive win earned him the nickname "Il leone delle Fiandre," or the Lion of Flanders, from (rather presumptuous) Italian journalists. Back in Flanders they called him "de Toscaan van Vlaanderen," or the Tuscan of Flanders.[72] The "Lion of Flanders" had been loaned out once already (Cyrillle Van Hauwaert) but for a foreign cyclist to be called the anything "of Flanders" by the Flemish fans and media was a truly high honor.

Magni did nothing to diminish this stature, though he never raced de Ronde again. Magni went on to win the Giro d'Italia in 1951 and from that point became focused on Italian races of all stripes, plus the Tour de France. But even a second Giro victory in 1955 was lost to history's dustbin after his final Giro performance in 1956. That year an aging Magni crashed and broke his clavicle on stage 12, shunning a doctor's urging to quit and soldiering on. Magni subsequently refused x-rays, not wanting to know how bad his injuries were, but was having trouble gripping the bars from the pain in his left shoulder. So his mechanic attached a piece of inner tube to the left side of his bars, which Magni famously held in his teeth to reclaim some of his lost leverage. This worked OK until four days later when he crashed again, this time breaking the dome-like head on his humerus (upper arm bone) where it met his still-broken shoulder. Magni supposedly was put in an ambulance, but when he realized this he forced the driver to stop so he could keep riding.

---

bothering to chase. Probably the same goes for Gauthier, whose second place was worth chasing until it too was out of reach. If you lose by one minute or ten, what difference is there?

[72] Magni collected about as many nicknames as victories. After a quick search I found, in addition to the two above, "the White Wolf," "the Biscuit" (for his premature baldness), and "the Third Man," anointing him Italy's other champion alongside (or in rivalry with) Coppi and Bartali.

Then things got bad.

Five days later, the Giro entered the Dolomites under forbidding skies. On tap for stage 21 were climbs of the Costalunga, Passo Rolle, Gobbera and Brocon climbs, with a finish at Monte Bondone. Rain soaked the peloton early on, and eventually turned to snow on the final climb as temperatures plummeted, and riders began to abandon the Giro. With Charly Gaul on the attack and about to write his name into Giro history, overnight leader Pasquale Fornara climbed off his bike. So too did virtual maglia rosa Nino DeFilippis. And Miguel Poblet, Federico Bahamontes, Gastone Nencini -- in all 45 riders failed to finish, with 43 retiring and two missing the time cut. Gaul won the nine-hour stage and was taken off his bike in a delirious state to thaw out in a hotel bathtub. Alessandro Fantini toughed out the conditions for second, seven minutes back. Magni, inner tube still in his teeth, finished third. His final place on GC, two days later, was second, 3.27 away from victory.

So Belgians can rest comfortably knowing the powerful Italian cobbles master holds their most sacred record, for now. I'd say it's in good hands.

Regardless, Magni paved the way for foreigners who have since come to Flanders with a cobbled dream of their own. By the early 1960s, British riders were coming to Flanders ready to catch the bug, culminating in a Ronde victory in 1966 by the great Tom Simpson (still the only Anglo winner). More recently, American riders like Hincapie and Farrar have joined the scene, speaking openly of their long-standing ambitions to win de Ronde. The number of guys increases every year.

Of the most recent foreigners, one stands above all (literally), but I'll get to him in a moment. Guys like Hincapie and Ballan and Pozzato have been true Flanders warriors, but only Ballan broke through, and all come with the taint of their era which will prevent them from truly being honored.[73] Peter Sagan is another example of a foreign rider about whom much was already being said as of 2012, though at first, while he had a Gent-Wevelgem and E3 Prijs on his shelf, he was winning races all over the world, including a shot at the record for Green Jersey wins at the Tour. We wondered whether he would evolve into a "Cobbles Guy." With his glorious 2016 Ronde van Vlaanderen victory, in the Rainbow Jersey no less, we wonder no more.

Take-Away Message: Flanders is a secret to nobody anymore. The idea of kids growing up dreaming of winning the classics is no longer just a Belgian or Italian thing. The gospel of Flanders is no longer spread by elusive French magazines and sporadic TV clips. Video, photos and stories of life on the infernal stones proliferate worldwide. Big, strong kids like Taylor Phinney grow up (and up, and up) picturing themselves enduring, even enjoying, the punishment dealt out by the cobbles. Young

---

[73] How much do you want me to say about doping in this book? The short version is that it hangs over the sport, now only slightly less so than, say, 10 years ago, and the lack of scandals in the Cobbled Classics doesn't really change the state of affairs. It suggests, rather, that riders have an easier time staying out of trouble in Flanders. One long-standing hunch is that classics riders are more likely to engage in off-season doping to ramp up their winter form and ride it all the way through the spring. It's low-risk and less sure to help than loading up on whatever the week before the race. But it's not nothing. I don't think it's worth engaging in speculation, for a lot of reasons, but have tried to at least footnote the known infractions attached to the riders discussed here. In my opinion, that's enough for now. This book is more about the races and the experience of riding in Flanders than the particular athletes involved.

foreign riders don't emerge with just dreams of winning but a healthy respect for what the race is, what it has been, and what it represents -- a cycling tradition of embracing hardship. The "mondialisation" of the Tour of Flanders can't be stopped, and except for the purely partisan, this is good news. But actually winning? Well, Belgium will never run out of riders determined to stop them.

See Also: Zdenek Stybar, John Degenkolb, Kristoff, Sagan, Geraint Thomas, Ian Stannard and too many others to name here.[74] Also Dutch guys, barely foreign, like Lars Boom and Niki Terpstra here.[75]

5.   The Honorary Flandrien: Andrea Tafi

So yeah, foreigners have been breaking through and fulfilling the Flandrien dream for some time now, and especially of late. But I'm not sure there's a better example (pre-Cancellara) of a foreign rider who is not merely successful there but truly fits the bill than *il Gladiatore*, Andrea Tafi.

Mind you, I have some trepidations about praising anything that happened in the drug-washed 1990s, but the Mapei team

---

[74] Watch out for the Brits. Thomas, winner of the E3 Prijs Harelbeke in 2015, has already arrived, as has Stannard, winner of the 2014 and '15 Omloops. Then there is Sir Bradley Wiggins, iconic Tour de France champion and holder of the Hour Record, along with numerous time trial and track victories. Wiggins ended his Team Sky career after the 2015 edition of Paris-Roubaix, his second stab at cobbles glory following an unexpected and very inspiring ninth place in 2014. Wiggins' appreciation for cycling history drove him to pursue the Hell of the North one final time, and he managed to attack the leaders with 30km to go before settling for 18th place. Still, his focus on the meaning of these races was telling, as was his application of pure-power track acumen to Paris-Roubaix. The UK cranks out strong track guys. Expect plenty more of them on the cobbles.

[75] Boom is only technically an outsider, hailing from Noord Brabant, just across the border from Antwerp. I probably have more trouble fitting in at a coffee house in Vancouver, BC than Boom does on a ride through the Vlaamse Ardennen. Terpstra is from North Holland.

was one of the sport's more fascinating experiments in blurring the Flandrien/foreigner lines. Founded by Giorgio Squinzi, president of the Mapei industrial materials manufacturer, Mapei amassed a spectacular collection of classics talent, helping them to a ten-year run of dominance not easily matched anywhere in the sport, even by Belgian teams.

Of course, Mapei was arguably a Belgian team, at least for its last five years, if you go by registration. Numbers-wise, they employed more Italian athletes than Belgian, but among the latter were no less than Johan Museeuw, Frank Vandenbroucke, Leif Hoste, Wilf Peeters, Tom Steels, Stijn Devolder and Fabian Cancellara — OK, not Belgian, but close enough.

Anyway, cycling is rarely dominated by any single entity in modern times, thanks to the variety of disciplines and packed racing calendar, control of which is beyond the physical powers of a mere 25 humans no matter how strong. You simply can't *be* everywhere at once, let alone winning. But at times during the Mapei years it must have felt otherwise. Most years, a team total of 50 victories, counting all stage race general classifications, stages, and one-day wins, is enough to all but guarantee you the #1 team ranking in the world. Twenty-five wins is likely good enough for a spot in the top ten.

So when Mapei won 95 times in 1997, they were more or less shattering the mold. Over nine years, their 651 victories -- an average of 72 per year -- is enough to bring one's mind to a complete halt. Needless to say, Mapei got used to being ranked #1, holding that spot for eight of their nine full seasons.

Three times they swept the podium at Paris-Roubaix, including the famous 1997 approach to the velodrome where the trio of Mapeis carried on like riders on a Saturday club ride, before celebrating around the track and paving the way for a pre-arranged "sprint" that was "won" by Johan Museeuw.[76]

By the new millenium the Mapei project was winding down, with the Belgian clique and their sponsor Quick Step splintering into a new team as Squinzi and the Italian management slowly withdrew from cycling. But in 2002, the end hadn't yet arrived. Quick Step were moving up in the world on the strength of Museeuw, but Mapei still had an ace to play. Andrea Tafi, one of the team's most respected warhorses, had been around since 1989, and had one card to play: raw power. Tafi had won Paris-Roubaix by attacking the leaders no less than six times in the final 50km. He thundered away from the competition in the 1996 Giro di Lombardia -- a climbers' race -- to win by over two minutes.

And his victory in the 2002 Tour of Flanders was scarcely any different. On a beautiful, sunny day in Flanders, Tafi rode his usual aggressive style, launching numerous attacks in the final 50km, in what was shaping up to be a real slugfest of a race. With him in the last hour were champions like Johan Museeuw and Peter Van Petegem, both former Ronde winners. So too was a tip-top George Hincapie. Not that Tafi just ground them all to dust; it's Flanders, and on the hellingen Tafi relied on teammate Daniele Nardello to help him play defense on a couple occasions, most notably as Museeuw attacked on the Muur. But on the run-in to Meerbeke, Tafi launched his final

---

[76] Again... doping... the podium consisted of Museeuw, Gianluca Bortolami and Tafi, each of whom was connected to doping at some point during their career.

attack of the day, at the 4km mark, when his rivals were becoming discouraged and/or inattentive. Five seconds became ten, then fifteen, and the race was his.

Summing up, that's a career Flanders-Roubaix Double, won by hammering people from the front of the race. Oh, and his accomplishment places him in special company, as the only Italian rider to win both races. By national victory tallies, Italians rank second in Flanders wins and third in Roubaix, making Tafi's lone feat even more remarkable.

Take-Away Message: Not much different than #6, except that foreigners have made significant careers, entire careers, out of the classics, and earned a special place in Flemish hearts as a result.[77]

4. The Biggest of the Big: All In for Paris-Roubaix

If the Cobblestoned Classics are a season with in a season, one race in that subgrouping stands truly alone, a season within a season within a season. The Hell of the North, Paris-Roubaix. The character of the race we will get into in a bit, but suffice to

---

[77] A while back Tafi and Francesco Moser (3x Paris-Roubaix winner) spoke to La Gazzetta Dello Sport about the lack of recent results by young Italian riders on the cobbles. Their answer? Start em young. Tafi in particular pointed out that foreign riders needed to start on the cobbles as teens, and to spend several years fighting, even in vain, in order to fully appreciate what it takes to win. Oddly enough, American riders might be in a better position than their teenaged counterparts. While every European cycling nation of consequence has plenty for its young riders to do at home, the more distant foreigners like the Americans need to pack a suitcase and head over to Europe. USA Cycling has set up shop in Izegem, owing to Belgium's endless opportunities for high-quality racing, meaning the Americans are more likely to show up for the junior cobbled races than the Italians or Spanish. For example, in the 2013 Ronde van Vlaanderen for Juniors (held in June), the 93 finishers included 80 Belgians, 7 Dutch kids (including the winner), three Americans, and one rider each from France, Australia and Estonia. Tafi is right, Italian teens apparently aren't showing up in Flanders. Just dreaming of de Ronde is not enough to carry a rider to the winner's circle, but not dreaming of it is a pretty good way to get eliminated.

say that the lack of any significant hills, besides rolling farmland, reshuffles the deck for the classics peloton. To the front come the biggest, most powerful riders in the sport, the guys who stand out even among the cobblestone peloton already containing bigger and stronger guys than the average race. These are guys who are big enough to be at a disadvantage to the Flanders aces (some of whom are under six feet tall and 150 pounds, large enough to withstand the pounding but small enough to zip up the climbs).[78] To these XL cobblestone studs, Paris-Roubaix is the day they get their revenge. Here are just a few of the recent standouts in this category.

* **Magnus Bäckstedt**, the only Swede to lift a cobble overhead in Roubaix, won the race in 2004 in a four-man sprint over Tristan Hoffman, Roger Hammond and a precocious Fabian Cancellara. At 6-foot-4 and around 200 pounds, Bäckstedt didn't resemble too many of his rivals, and exemplifies the split between cobbled riders and Paris-Roubaix studs. His highest finish in the Tour of Flanders was 43rd. His first try at Paris-Roubaix, Bäckstedt finished 7th. Roger Legeay, longtime manager from the Peugeot system, once said of Bäckstedt, "He's not a flahute. He's not especially the fastest, but after 260km on the cobbles, it's often the rider who feels freshest who wins."

* **Johan Van Summeren**, all of 6'6" and some 170 pounds, also earned an engraved cobble on the Avenue Alfred Motte

---

[78] Supposed heights and weights of some recent Flanders winners: Nick Nuyens, 5'10", 150 pounds; Stijn Devolder, 6', 165; Peter Van Petegem, 5'9", 150; Michele Bartoli, 5'10", 143. Paris-Roubaix winners include Van Petegem, but also Magnus Backstedt, 6'4" and 204 pounds; Johan Van Summeren, 6'6", 168; and so on. Not a dramatic difference, but there are definitely riders who ride Flanders and skip Roubaix, for lack of size, and riders who relish Roubaix more than they ever would Flanders, for lack of lack of size.

(the race's final section of ceremonial cobbles) with his Paris-Roubaix victory in 2011, when he utilized the presence of his teammate Thor Hushovd -- himself a Paris-Roubaix specialist -- back in the peloton, shadowing Fabian Cancellara, to join the winning threesome, and then mercilessly powering away from his break-mates Marten Tjallingii, Gregory Rast and Lars Bak to make it home alone. Van Summeren's win was the cause of much rejoicing and teeth-gnashing. Summie was a popular rider who spent most of his very useful career in the service of his smaller teammates. Whether it was in the classics, where his brute strength was always a major asset, or in the Tour de France, where he soldiered away at the front of the race for his team in hopes of setting up the climbers (Cadel Evans, for a couple years with Lotto), Van Summeren was highly regarded and seemingly well liked. So for a guy like that, who cheerfully pays his dues again and again, to win the biggest race possible for his skillset, well, who could be upset about that?

Fabian Cancellara, for one. The Swiss Bear came into 2011 in his usual fantastic shape, but after his dominating 2010 performance he was a heavily marked man. The Garmin (nee Slipstream) project had steadily been upping its ante on the classics, with boss Jonathan Vaughters investing pretty heavily on guys who could ride the infernal stones. Neither of the two biggest stars -- Boonen or Cancellara -- were for hire (though rumors say he tried to sign the latter one winter), so instead Vaughters went with the roster-packing route, a task that came to fruition when the Cervelo Test Team folded and left Thor Hushovd and Heinrich Haussler available to Garmin in late 2010.

Two weeks earlier, Garmin could do nothing to stop Cancellara from winning the E3 Prijs in a familiar-looking 30km solo break, and Vaughters lamented to the press that while he had the strongest team, he didn't have the strongest rider. In France, however, he had a couple of the strongest guys, particularly Hushovd and Van Summeren, and when the latter made it into a breakaway as the race reached its final hour, the plans went into motion.

Hushovd followed the expected acceleration by Cancellara, with Ballan for company, but with 30km to go and Cancellara having done all the work, the Swiss Bear sat up and began bickering with his companions, insisting that they share in the duties. Hushovd took the front but with no great ambition, and Cancellara began barking at the Garmin crew in the support car for holding back the Norwegian, clad in rainbow, from attacking. Shortly thereafter they were joined by a third group of riders, and the gap to the front grew to over a minute as they reached the Carrefour de l'Arbe. There, down to four leaders, Van Summeren launched his winning move, and while Cancellara indignantly ditched Hushovd with four km remaining, he was too late to catch Van Summeren.

* Gilbert Duclos-Lassalle was another true Paris-Roubaix warrior. A bit tall and powerfully built by cycling standards, "Duclos" hung around the sport for 14 years before he achieved his greatest triumph, victory in the 1992 edition of Paris-Roubaix. Prior to his 37th birthday, the Frenchman had achieved his share of wins but few of any consequence apart from the 1980 Paris-Nice and two editions of the GP Ouest France-Plouay. In Paris-Roubaix, however, he was locked into a lifelong pursuit which saw him take second on two occasions --

1980 and '83 -- before falling back. So when, at 37, Duclos-Lassalle stole away from the peloton and won the Hell of the North, it was the culmination of many years' effort. And if anyone doubted whether 37 is too old to win a major classic, Duclos came back and won again in 1993. This time he had company, in the person of Franco Ballerini, who spent the first two minutes after the race waving his arms in triumph, thinking he'd pipped the Frenchman for the win. But replays showed Duclos-Lassalle clearly winning by about six inches, and a loud roar went up over the velodrome when the announcer confirmed the result. In doing so Duclos achieved the record as the oldest winner in the race's history, at 38 years and eight months, a record that stands today.

* **Marc Madiot** was a pretty good model of perseverance himself, and another of France's great one-trick Paris-Roubaix ponies. Actually Madiot made a strong impression across the northern races, from Liege-Bastogne-Liege (6th and 7th in 1984 and '87) to cyclocross (French champion in 1982). He came third in Lombardia in 1987... and eighth in the Tour de France in 1983, an edition remarkably heavy on time trials (six of them). But only in Paris-Roubaix did Madiot achieve great success, with a powerful win in 1985 by more than two minutes over teammate Bruno Wojtiek and a starry chasing group of Greg LeMond, Sean Kelly, Eddy Planckaert and others. A year before he closed out his career at age 33, Madiot again rode away from the pack in a hard edition of Paris-Roubaix, once again choosing the Carrefour de l'Arbre as the spot to make his winning move. Seven riders pursued him but got no closer than 1.07 by the time they reached the velodrome. Madiot's fiery nature was undoubtedly a factor in his success, and something for which he has become even better known of late,

maniacally cheering on Thibaut Pinot from his driver's seat as the Directeur of the Francais des Jeux team during a stage victory in the 2012 Tour de France. An iconic road racing champion of France on three occasions (and once in cyclocross), Madiot is on a short list of the great home-grown French cobbled champions.

*****

All American eyes are currently on BMC's Taylor Phinney, all of 6'5" and racing at something in the 190-pound range. I spoke with Phinney by phone shortly before the 2013 Paris-Roubaix, when he came in with high hopes of making a strong impression, as well as high expectations following his 15th place in his debut the previous year -- plus two victories in the U23 version prior to turning professional. Phinney, son of two great athletes -- Davis Phinney, a sprinter and Tour de France stage winner and Connie Carpenter-Phinney, a ground-breaking Olympian in both cycling (gold medal) and speed-skating, as well as a 12-time national cycling champion -- noticed Paris-Roubaix early on as family friend George Hincapie took aim at the race each year.

Before the turn of the century, Paris-Roubaix was the only race besides the Tour de France which received adequate attention in the US, and as Phinney grew into a cycling star... and grew... and grew, Paris-Roubaix remained in his thoughts. He mastered the track, winning multiple world and national championships, then signed with the Trek-Livestrong team, where his apprenticeship included the two U23 Roubaix wins. Next he moved on to BMC for his first top-level pro adventure, and success came ahead of schedule. After some injuries limited his role in 2011 and kept him out of the cobbled classics, Phinney truly arrived the following year, taking two bittersweet and impressive 4th place finishes in the Olympic road race and time trial to cap a brilliant season. In his Paris-Roubaix debut, he worked for teammate Hushovd, running bottles and assisting with positioning, but despite this he never ran out of gas and kept pedaling to his highly respectable result.

The following year he continued to show his class, grabbing 7th in brutal conditions at a snow-shortened Milano-Sanremo, mere days after an even more heroic effort that left him sobbing on the team bus. As nearly-freezing rain lashed the peloton on the penultimate day of Tirreno-Adriatico, a 209-km death march over several horrendous low-altitude climbs, Phinney struck out alone from the shivering hordes hoping to stave off elimination and stay eligible for the final stage, a short time trial where he would be among the favorites to win. Few of the riders in his wake had any incentive to finish, and happily climbed off their bikes to escape the misery, but not Phinney. By his account he gripped the bars, thought of his dad's determination (as a rider and as someone battling Parkinson's disease), and poured out the wattage in desperation. He failed in his immediate objective, missing the time cutoff by several minutes and taking the DNF. But he showed his true colors, a depth of character and desire that, combined with his natural ability as a biggest of the big riders to "float across the cobbles," as he says, to be a winner in the Hell of the North before long.

By 2013 Phinney showed his enthusiasm, if not his experience, joining a powerful early breakaway including former winner

Stuart O'Grady, as well as talents Geraint Thomas (Sky) and John Degenkolb (then Argos-Shimano) on a long breakaway attempt, even holding the honor of leading the race into the Forest of Arenberg. A thrill, no doubt, but in the end Phinney ran out of gas when the race hit high gear with 50km to go. Things looked far different the following spring, when Phinney could be seen calmly waiting among the leaders for the race to develop, and develop it did... but without Phinney, victim of a flat tire in the Carrefour de l'Arbe. In more than one way, though, he'd arrived. That sort of bad luck is part of life in this race, and only memorable if you were strong enough to ride with the very best. Which he was.

Oh, and Phinney's perspective on Flanders versus Roubaix? "For me Roubaix has always been the best race because I'm typically bigger than a lot of my coworkers, and it's that one race where I get to stick it to them, because they get to stick it to me on every climb (in Flanders)."

The last chapter remains unwritten, and when you can expect to see it is anyone's guess, particularly after a horror crash in 2014 put Phinney out of the sport for more than a year. But by the following summer he was sort of back, and as 2016 approaches there are reasons to hope that he will pick up right where he left off. Stay tuned.

3. The Local Flandrien Hero: Peter Van Petegem

Like the Paris-Roubaix specialists, so too does the Tour of Flanders cultivate its own subspecies of pure specialists, riders who are so attached to the race that they can scarcely be seen outside of March and April. Riders so identified with the race in the minds of fans that they only belong in one type of competition. Peter Van Petegem typifies this group.

Born and raised in Brakel, about halfway between the Taaienberg and the Muur, Van Petegem spent his career chasing success in the cobbled classics, isolating himself from the rest of cycling more and more as his career went on. Van Petegem achieved the hallowed Flanders-Roubaix Double in 2003, joining Heiri Suter, Raymond Impanis, Rik Van Looy and Roger De Vlaeminck amont the shortest of short-lists of Cobbled Splendor. Van Petegem was the eighth rider in history to achieve the Double, and the seventh Belgian. [The total is up to ten now.]

In the 2003 Flanders, *De Peet* took deeply troubled star Franck Vandenbroucke at the finish line, just as he had done four years earlier for his other Ronde win. The race featured a dozen or so riders reaching the Tenbosse together, after an early breakaway had been chased down by an eight-rider group consisting entirely of Italians. Van Petegem made the juncture, dropped everyone but Vandenbroeck on the Muur, and won the two-up sprint.

A week later Van Petegem still had plenty of fight left in his legs. Waiting until the Camphin-en-Pevele secteur to make his decisive move, Van Petegem launched a powerful thrust away from the chasing pack, weaving through officials and support vehicles, and curtains of dust billowing in their wake on this dry day through Hell, before latching on to the wheel of race leaders Dario Pieri and Vyatcheslav Ekimov. This phenomenal show of both strength and nerve earned him a place in the finale, which consisted of a few half-hearted attacks and a brilliant duel in the velodrome. Ekimov, every bit the hard man that Van Petegem was, also shared Van Petegem's deep experience with track racing -- Van Petegem was a regular at the famed Six Days of Gent, the highlight of the Six-Day racing scene in northern Europe. Entering the velodrome Van Petegem took the lead, but quickly maneuvered the out-classed Pieri into the dreaded first position as the trio circled the upper edge of the track . Ekimov, sitting third, made his move down the boards in the final turn, but Van Petegem was ready and shot past the exhausted Russian for the win. Pieri, drafting his way into second, pedaled up to the jubilant Belgian and the two gladiators completed about quarter of a victory lap in a respectful, exhausted embrace.

It never got better than this for Van Petegem. Winning the Double -- clad in the UCI Leader's jersey -- was the high point for *de Zwarte van Brakel* ("the black from Brakel," so named for his dark hair, olive skin and permanent five o'clock shadow). At 33, his window was closing and a new crop of classics champions was coming of age. The following year Van Petegem fought his way to sixth despite a late flat, and a nullified third in the crazy 2006 edition, before slipping at last from the favorites' crowd and climbing off the bike in 2007. That final burst in the Roubaix Velodrome marked his last victory as a professional. His final competition was at the GP Briek Schotte, in honor of the Iron Briek and at the urging of Quick Step director Patrick Lefevre. Because that's how cobbles champions go out: at a modest race in Desselgem, paying homage to their fellow champions.

More than just a guy who scored three huge wins, Van Petegem is widely seen as a cobbles ambassador, more so even than Johan Museeuw, whose retirement was muddled by doping allegations. Van Petegem has consulted with pro teams aiming to step up their performance, most notably a year directing the Garmin-Cervelo squad in the classics. His main post-cycling gig is running a bed and breakfast called Le Pave with his wife, located around the corner from the Haaghoek cobbles. He also consults with the organizers of de Ronde van Vlaanderen and Omloop Het Nieuwsblad (which he won in 2002). In short, he's pretty much everywhere in the classics scene. I passed him on the street in Oudenaarde the day after de Ronde. Just hanging around Oudenaarde, PVP and I. Where else was there to be?

Van Petegem's local connection is hardly unique; plenty of cobbled classics studs grow up along the course. A more recent example of a rider who seems born to win a cobble is Sep Vanmarcke, currently riding for the remnants of the Rabobank project, now called ~~Blanco~~ ~~Belkin~~ LottoNL-Jumbo, after two years at Garmin. Vanmarcke was born and raised in Wortegem-Petegem, a short ride from the Koppenberg, and idolized the races as his older brothers pursued their cycling dreams. Before long it was Sep's turn, and in a short time he left his brothers' accomplishments behind. Riding for Topsport Vlaanderen, he gained international notice with his second place at Gent-Wevelgem in 2010, appearing as the mystery guest in the otherwise well-decorated sprint I described above. From there Garmin manager Jonathan Vaughters scooped him up, adding Sep to an international classics team led by Hushovd, Van Summeren and Tyler Farrar. After a developmental season in 2011, Vanmarcke shot to the front of the cobbled peloton with a sprint victory over no less than Tom Boonen to win the 2012 Omloop Het Nieuwsblad. Vanmarcke stayed strong into the cobbles season, forcing the action at the E3 Prijs with some daring attacks, before settling for fifth place in the bunch sprint, and finally running out of gas in the longer monumental races.

Following the season he jumped ship, citing Garmin's lack of clear roles for him, and eventually landed at Blanco -- teaming up in 2013 with Lars Boom and a strong supporting cast. After some nagging knee issues and a forgettable Tour of Flanders, it was Vanmarcke (and Stijn Vandenbergh) who jumped away for the winning move of Paris-Roubaix, with about 30km to go. Unluckily, he eventually drew out Cancellara and Zdenek Stybar for company, and after Vandenbergh and Stybar came a-cropper in the Carrefour de l'Arbe secteur, the Swiss Bear saved enough strength to sneak around Vanmarcke on the home stretch of the Roubaix velodrome for the win. Vanmarcke was visibly upset at his narrow miss, but simply staying with a dominant rider like Cancellara on top form showed the kind of class Vanmarcke possesses, confirmed in 2014 by another winning move, lost again to Cancellara on the line in de Ronde. Vanmarcke, still only 26, keeps getting closer, and his supporters can all see where this is eventually headed.[79]

---

[79] Though, if his supporters only knew… Vanmarcke suffered through a less notable 2015 campaign, losing touch with the winning move at Flanders with just under 30km to go — and vainly chasing before giving up. A week later he was 11th in Paris-Roubaix, with the first large chase group, as punctures interrupted his efforts at key moments, and we all sort of wrote it off to the Classics being hard to sustain attacks at year after year. By winter, though, Vanmarcke revealed that his performance left him wondering what the point of even continuing as a cyclist was. Retirement? Thankfully he only mentioned it as something he considered and dismissed. Vanmarcke also had wrist surgery, to alleviate another limiting factor in recent years. But there is no mistaking the difficulty of staying sane while chasing the classics — an all-or-nothing proposition that can blow up on you for a hundred reasons. And it's only worse when you're a homegrown Belgian star.

2.   The Invading Flandrien: Fabian Cancellara

Fabian Cancellara has probably had more nicknames hung on him than the entire Omega Pharma team: Tony Montana, Spartacus, the Swiss Bear, Tony Spartabear, and Shiva the Destroyer. OK, the last two haven't caught on yet, but nicknames are a pretty good sign that people are interested in you, and almost no rider of the last decade has piqued the interest of fans as much as Cancellara.

I wouldn't go so far as to say that he is universally loved, but only because his dominance in time trials and eventually the spring Classics has made lovable underdogs of hundreds of his competitors. That said, Cancellara is probably the most consistently popular rider, and continues to come up with new ways to impress his fans. When he won Paris-Roubaix in 2006, it was a watershed moment but not quite a total shock. When he won Milano-Sanremo in 2008, stealing away from the sprinters winding up behind him... *that* was a total shock. When he won a sprinters' stage of the 2007 Tour de France while wearing the yellow jersey, using the same tactic of launching himself into a blistering solo effort from farther out than most mortals ever could, that was unbelievable.

Cancellara capped it all off by doing the Double in 2010.[80] In de Ronde, he shattered the field on the Molenberg, drew out only Boonen, and cracked him on the Muur. A week later, everyone expected him to attack the Paris-Roubaix field from 30km out. Maybe even 40km out. So what does he do? Attack

---

[80] Well, the Triple, if you want to count E3 Prijs, which I highly recommend you do. But the Double is thus far the universally accepted standard.

at 50km, and solo home again. A year later, Cancellara again exited the peloton in Flanders with some 50km to go, picking up only Boonen's teammate Sylvain Chavanel for company, Chava having been up the road at the time of the attack in a failed five-man escape. Cancellara powered the pair all the way to Geraardsbergen, with confusion reigning in his wake, only to suffer cramps and let a dozen guys, including eventual winner Nick Nuyens, back into contention.

Such scenes -- featuring the Cancellara diesel powering the winning move -- have been repeated enough by now that Cancellara has gone looking for a fairer fight, one where he doesn't do all the work, with varying success.[81] Except that he keeps winning. So yeah, success.

---

[81] And of course, Cancellara won in slightly less mythical fashion in 2013, attacking from the final climb, the Paterberg, to drop Jurgen Roelands and Peter Sagan with a mere 13km to go. Even less mystical was his 2014 win, a four-up sprint over Greg Van Avermaet and Sep Vanmarcke. Clearly he doesn't value mysticism above winning.

Oh, and speaking of fair fights, the flipside of him maneuvering others into helping him would be the 2011 Paris-Roubaix, when after his daring but unsuccessful attack on de Ronde, expectations were through the roof that Cancellara would launch himself again, successfully, a week later in France. When expectations become cast in stone, you can count on the riders to sit on the wheel of the projected winner, all day long, not lifting a finger to help seal their collective doom. "Fair play" becomes wishful thinking for the favorite. So when a threatening group reached the Carrefour de l'Arbe a couple minutes before Cancellara, and when Johan Van Summeren of Garmin-Cervelo launched his race-winning solo attack, the entire world coalesced around a plan to do nothing but follow Cancellara and let him sort it all out. One of the followers was Thor Hushovd, who was known to sit on a wheel on occasion (we'll get to that shortly), and who was a teammate of Van Summeren's that year. Cancellara began barking at Hushovd and his Directeur Sportif, Jonathan Vaughters, bemoaning their negative tactics… which was a little weird since their guy was up the road winning the race, and Garmin were in no mood to chase him down. But Cancellara's frustration that day was more properly directed at everyone else, and he said as much afterward when he congratulated Garmin for their tactics but said of everyone else, "If I had stopped for coffee, they would have stopped too."

Fabian Cancellara. Photo by Elizabeth Freer

Great times, but what makes Cancellara a Flandrien is his focus on the race, along with what he can do on the bike. Cancellara's first Paris-Roubaix win had fueled talk of him going for Flanders for a couple years, challenging a conventional wisdom that maybe the climbs weren't great for him, since he's more of a steady grinder than a flashy accelerator. But power is power, and Cancellara can thunder up a climb for a while, like he did in winning the Olympic bronze medal in Beijing over a hilly circuit, and by winning the overall title at a somewhat tempered Tour de Suisse in 2009. So it's fairer to look back at his Flanders performances and say that while he messed up strategically in 2007 (attacking too early) and had bad luck for the next two years, he was a Flanders winner-in-waiting, once he worked out all the kinks.

Of course, the perfect race for a large(ish), strong rider who can sustain unbelievably powerful efforts for a fairly long time is Paris-Roubaix, and as long as the race isn't won in a sprint, featuring actual sprinters, Cancellara is otherwise the perfect weapon. His resume currently reads three victories in the Roubaix velodrome, a pair of second places — the first of which came from 2008's iconic sprint with Boonen and Ballan, making for something of an all-decade podium moment — and a third in 2014. But did Paris-Roubaix make him a Flandrien? A foreigner winning a French race? Not bloody likely.

Which makes his 2010 Ronde win all the more important -- a day later he was in an Antwerp pub drawing a massive beer from the tap and receiving the accolades of his fans in their newly-christened official Tony Spartabear supporters bar. Welcome to Flandrien status. His failed epic a year later only adds to the legend. And when he did the second double in 2013? Well, the Spartacus Fan Club had a whale of a celebration in their new headquarters -- in a building in Oudenaarde which houses the Ronde van Vlaanderen museum. Ground Zero for *Vlaanderens mooiste*, and it's the Swiss Bear who gets the VIP treatment. Cancellara has called it "a great honor," but you'll never hear him call it a coincidence. This is a confident man, who grew up watching Tafi, Museeuw and Van Petegem contesting Flanders and Roubaix on TV, thinking that perhaps this was his calling. But for the matter of about 400 miles between Zurich and the Vlaamse Ardennen, Cancellara was every bit the future Cobbles beast we've had the pleasure of watching for the last decade, about as Belgian a racer as anyone else on this list.

1. The Lions of Flanders: Tom Boonen and Johan Museeuw

Nobody exemplifies the roller-coaster of a career facing the cobbles master more than Tom Boonen. A once-in-a-generation talent with great instincts and an indomitable team, Boonen surged to the top of the classics world in 2005 at the rather sprightly age of 24, when he registered his first victories in both Flanders and Roubaix.[82] His cobbled monument streak hit three in the 2006 Ronde, until Cancellara snapped it in France a week later, but no matter -- Tommeke, reigning Flanders winner and World Champion, was tops.

Fast forward a bit to when he rolled out of Bruges in 2011, which marked the fifth year of his Flanders drought, which reached six later that day when Nuyens led home a trio of riders who had beaten Boonen (and eight others) in, of all things, a sprint. For a variety of reasons, people began to doubt him and speak of his earlier achievements in the past tense. Nobody doubted that Cancellara was the better of the two in the classics at this point, as unthinkable as that had been half a decade earlier.

---

[82] Another view of his arrival might be that Boonen was tabbed the next great Flandrien when he was still a pup, riding for the US Postal Service team in 2002. At age 21, Boonen made his debut at the cobbled monuments, and a week after a notable 24th in Flanders, he found himself squarely in the middle of the drama of a classic edition of Paris-Roubaix. With the peloton caked in mud, Boonen sat in the lead group until eventual winner Johan Museeuw made his race-winning move, 41km from the line — itself an unforgettable moment in Belgian cycling lore as that Lion's third and last win. Boonen was working for teammate George Hincapie, and powered away with the American classics ace in tow. But while Hincapie was expected to be where he was, with three top-ten finishes to his name by then, Boonen was the surprise, and it was the young Belgian who survived all the way to Roubaix, after Hincapie slid into a ditch. Boonen yielded his second place to Stefen Wesemann in the velodrome, but third at that age, and in such a display of raw power, foretold where things were headed.

Tom Boonen at the 2015 World Championships. Photo by Chris Fontecchio

But in 2012 he delivered a magnificent classics campaign that might never be topped. With Cancellara stalking him, Boonen won the E3 Prijs and Gent-Wevelgem, both from mass sprints. In de Ronde, Cancellara tragically crashed out with a broken collarbone, leaving Boonen to regain his Flanders glory in a three-up finish over usual suspects Pippo Pozzato and Alessandro Ballan, Boonen holding off Pozzato by barely half a bike-length. And to cap it all off, Boonen preempted any criticism about the nature of his sprint wins by dropping the entire peloton of Paris-Roubaix with 56km remaining (save briefly for his teammate Terpstra) en route to a thunderous conclusion to his historic rampage.

And a year later, it was Boonen's turn to crash out of Flanders, holding his cracked ribs. That's cycling. No, really -- that's exactly how it goes, especially in the ficklest of the fickle classics.

All through this topsy-turvy period Boonen steadily dominated one race, Paris-Roubaix, winning in 2008 and '09, and a fourth edition in 2012, tying the all-time record of Mr. Paris-Roubaix, Roger De Vlaeminck. But he hasn't had the field to himself. Cancellara struck back at Boonen's legacy in 2013 with a second double that took his Paris-Roubaix total to three, and nearly missed a third Double in 2014 that would have elevated Cancellara firmly into the top spot. And the Swiss Bear has bagged three titles at the E3 Prijs in four years, which was on the verge of being named after Boonen following four straight wins (and a record total of five).

The roller coaster has wrenched Tommeke's reputation around even more violently at the Tour de France. Since winning the points competition, somewhat against the prognostications, in 2006, he has twice been sidelined after testing positive for recreational cocaine use, a drug which has little to do with cycling apart from ruining a few promising careers along the way.[83] On the second occasion, the Tour relented and allowed him to race, but on a week's notice, enough to kill his preparations. Boonen rode anonymously in 2009, unable or unwilling to insert himself into even the top ten of a single stage sprint. In 2010 he sat out with a knee problem incurred two weeks earlier in the Tour de Suisse. By 2011, Boonen

---

[83] Cocaine has been featured in drug mixtures, such as the infamous "pot Belge" mix of amphetamines, heroin, cocaine, caffeine and other nonsense. But by itself it is considered to be of no benefit to endurance athletes, and a potential cause of dangerously elevated heartbeats. Plenty of riders have gotten into trouble with the drug, but generally on their own time. These include riders like Marco Pantani, who died from cocaine poisoning, and Frank Vandenbroucke, who also died tragically shortly after his career ended, and who was alleged to have a cocaine addiction.

seemed to have lost interest in the green jersey he secured in his last full Tour, saying he had had enough of dangerous big-bunch sprints, and was only hunting for a stage somewhere.

But roller coasters eventually slow down, just like this metaphor, and when fans step back to take in his whole career, that's where it becomes impossible to believe he once went six years between Flanders wins. When you look at his palmares, they scream "Classics God." He holds at least a share of the record for most wins in Flanders (three), Gent-Wevelgem (three); Paris-Roubaix (four), and E3 Harelbeke (five). At de Ronde, it's less surprising that he's tied the all-time career record of three wins than that he hasn't broken it.[84]

But the fickleness of fate and cobbles aside, if he never wins again Boonen will still be remembered as one of the most successful cyclists of his generation. His career includes every type of win you could imagine from a guy his size, with the exception of Milano-Sanremo. Like a lot of tall riders with excess power, he was cast as a sprinter in the easier events, and he racked up prestigious victories (e.g. Champs-Elysees, 2004) while honing his strength for the long cobbled classics. By 2004 he was winning races by the bushel, and by 2005 he joined the greats with the double win in Flanders and Roubaix.

That magical '05 season saw him take the world championship road race, again in a sprint against pure sprinters, putting Boonen as high atop the cycling world as you can get without

---

[84] What does it say about a major race that it's been around for 100 years and nobody has won more than three editions? Of the five Monuments, de Ronde is unique. The record at Paris-Roubaix is four (Boonen and others); Lombardia and Liege-Bastogne-Liege is five (Coppi and Merckx, respectively); and at Milano-Sanremo a lucky seven (Merckx). Here's a guess: it says you should work hard every day and say a little prayer to the Cycling Gods before bed. Every night.

a yellow jersey. There were stories of him putting out 1600 watts of power in a sprint, and snapping seemingly unbreakable carbon cranks with a flex of his powerful thighs. Boonen rode the wave into the following spring, bagging wins at will and gifting victories to loyal teammates when not keeping them for himself. The wave crested in Ninove, when Boonen raised his arms on the line in salute of his second Ronde win, no other rider crowding the picture frame, and Boonen flashing the rainbow colors to the adoring crowd. If there is an entry in the dictionary for Flemish Nirvana, it comes with a picture of this triumph.

De Ronde is a race for which Tornado Tom seems to have been lovingly crafted by the Cobble Gods. His tall frame and long thighbones enable him to exert the power bursts of crank-snapping legend. That may or may not be true, depending on how reliable you think internet forums are, but his ability to blast up the *hellingen* of his native Flanders in wicked accelerations is not in doubt. While Cancellara's solo strikes are more feared at the moment, an in-form Boonen is still plenty strong enough to make an attack stick, particularly if he has any worthwhile company. Another weapon would be that sprint -- after all his evolution as a sprinter, Boonen can still take 99% of the field in the kind of small-group sprint typical of the classics. If you haven't beaten him before you see the 1km banner, it's probably over for you.

But what really makes him the ultimate Flandrien is aggressive riding, hallmark of the region's cyclists, sort of the barley in this Flandrien brew. In 2005, Boonen won de Ronde with nobody else in the picture, just like he was taught to. The following year, Boonen made the race a two-man affair by launching his attack on the Valkenberg, shortly before Geraardsbergen, and dragged only countryman Leif Hoste to the line, where he mercilessly used Hoste as a prop in his iconic pose, winning de Ronde in the World Champion's jersey. Of the next four fallow years, Boonen owns the second from 2010, the also-ran finishes behind Devolder, and one subpar effort during that stretch, in 2007.

Even the two Devolder years say more about Tommeke than about Stijn. Sure, it's easy to recognize greatness when a guy crosses the line first, but how many riders have dominated a race -- a *monument* -- by doing nothing? Boonen cast such a large and intimidating shadow over the peloton in the 2008 and '09 Rondes that his rivals, upon watching Boonen pedal smoothly all the way to Geraardsbergen, basically committed suicide as soon as Devolder attacked them. I know this sounds like an exaggeration, but picture the situation in the second of these two, 2009: knowing full well that they had gambled poorly on Devolder imploding the previous year, knowing full well that he could sustain an attack from the Muur to the line, they let him go anyway. Faced with the choice of chasing Devolder and escorting Boonen to a likely win, guys like Filippo Pozzato, Thor Hushovd, George Hincapie, Juan Flecha and Alessandro Ballan decided they would just lose to Devolder and spare themselves the trouble.

This kind of hopelessness is not unheard-of in some corners of the sport, like a long breakaway in a grand tour stage, where three unheralded domestiques find themselves working with a B-list sprinter whom they know will eat their lunch in the last 50 meters. But that's a far cry from a race featuring the cream of the classics crop, truly elite riders racing in an all-or-nothing format for one of the sport's biggest prizes. And even those stage-race domestiques will pull some tricks out of their sleeve to ditch the sprinter, if possible, before accepting their fate. Boonen on the other hand broke the spirit of the ultra-elite crew simply by sitting in amongst them. That's greatness. And if anyone thought this was a mirage, Boonen reinforced their image of him a week later by winning Paris-Roubaix. Both years.[85]

Johan Museeuw is the other Lion of Flanders, of recent vintage. I'm not sure I can do him justice, nor that I want to. For starters, Museeuw's heyday wasn't one in which I participated as a fan. His three Flanders wins spanned from 1993 to '98, years in which it was probably best not to watch. Sure enough, Museeuw confessed to a variety of doping offenses four years after his retirement in 1994, and received a suspended jail sentence plus a rather pathetic EUR 2500 fine.

Still, he had undeniable qualities that probably would have made him a winner on some level had the sport been on the up-and-up in his time. The best -- and best-known -- story about the man came in 1998, when he crashed in the Forest of Arenberg on mud-slicked cobbles and shattered his left kneecap. Worse, inept care led to his wound becoming

---

[85] The Specter of Boonen was alive and well in 2014. He endured a strange spring in which he seemed fit until struck with the sadness of his partner's loss of a pregnancy, just as the classics were about to begin. But his team held its usual lion's share of the cards, with a beastly strong Vandenbergh and very threatening Stybar in tow, as well as co-captain Niki Terpstra. With Boonen drawing his share of attention, Terpstra attacked the entire peloton on the Paterberg in Dwars door Vlaanderen and was never seen again. Two weeks later, Boonen was on the move in Paris-Roubaix, unable to shed his main competitors but presenting a show of strength that was undoubtedly on the minds of his fellow leading riders when Terpstra was allowed once again to escape and take the win alone. These were power plays, by Terpstra of course, but assisted in no small part by the Specter of Boonen and the unwillingness of rival teams to escort a four-time winner to the Roubaix Velodrome so he can break the record.

gangrenous, and there was discussion about the possibility of having to amputate the leg. His life was even briefly at risk. But Museeuw and his trusty left leg recovered, well enough to win Paris-Roubaix in 2000, when he ditched his rivals and crossed the line solo, pointing at his left leg, extended outward, for all the world to see what was on his mind. That was his second victory in Hell, and a third win followed in 2002, itself a major comeback after a terrible car wreck in late 2000. A fourth win eluded him in the final month of his career, in 2004, thanks to an inopportune puncture with seven kilometers to go, as Museeuw sat in the lead group licking his chops and plotting out what he regarded as an inevitable triumph. Museeuw finished his last cobblestone classic by heading to his team bus and sobbing for a half-hour. Perhaps this is the perfect ending for a Flandrien, rather than the one he had in mind.

The determination to overcome these kinds of horrific injuries says that Museeuw had the heart of a Flandrien. Probably the legs too. But the tragedy of the 1990s doping heyday is that it's impossible to say much of anything definitive at all.

Eddy Merckx impersonator on the Muur. Photo by Chris Fontecchio

9: The People Come Out To Ride de Ronde

Friday started out perfectly enough... in Amsterdam, at the luxury hotel where my friend Joel was staying, on a business trip. Joel lives a block away from me in Seattle, travels with a frequency that I can hardly comprehend, and was as excited as I was about meeting up halfway across the world from our cozy neighborhood, in one of the more intriguing cities. Nothing about the logistics was easy, including getting there Thursday after waking up in Gent, biking to where the Europcar office had once been, biking another 15km or so to where it now was, moving out of my b&b in Gent, trekking down to Oudenaarde to drop off my stuff (which itself consisted of some helpless wandering in search of street that I couldn't pronounce), and driving to Amsterdam with just in time for dinner. My brother was arriving in Brussels Friday afternoon, so at no point did I develop any illusions about seeing Amsterdam in any meaningful way. But after a quick breakfast we managed to squeeze in enough time at the Rijksmuseum to see a few master works -- including several minutes staring in wonder at Rembrandt's *De Staalmeesters* (Syndics of the Drapers' Guild), a favorite of mine -- and depart the Netherlands with some satisfaction.

The plan was drawn up where I would pick up my brother Pete arriving at the Brussels airport, drop down to Oudenaarde, unload his stuff, and get to Gent in time for a 5pm press conference with the Garmin-Transitions team. Reality was more like, start driving, slow down, crawl along for three hours, talk to Pete on the phone, pick him up two hours late, and go to Oudenaarde for the night. Not that Pete was complaining; he was too busy chatting up Fabian Cancellara in the baggage claim area after taking a connection from Zurich with the Swiss star. Nice way to touch down in the World of Cycling.

Upon arriving in Oudenaarde we did manage to zip over to the Koppenberg, five minutes from our apartment by car. I had built up Joel's expectations enough that he opted to spend the extra hour he had available before hopping on a train back north walking up the hallowed stones, and for Pete's part he had waited too many years to see the stones and wasn't interested in delaying another day. The highlight of that exercise was when, near the top, a box truck had gotten in a spot of bother, blocking a few cars who for some reason were trying to drive the infernal slope. Last in that short line was an HTC-Columbia team car, and as we walked by the window lowered and Mark Cavendish, then the world's best sprinter and future World Champion, asked if we knew what the holdup was. Did I mention my brother was having a good time in Belgium?

All this and dinner with some friends from the Podium Cafe had my brother, coming off an overnight flight, desperate for sleep... no small matter since the next morning, Saturday, it was our turn to ride the Tour of Flanders for ourselves. Or, not exactly: the Ronde van Vlaanderen for Wielertouristes comes in three sizes: a 75km sampler, a 150km heart-of-the-matter version, and the official, entire 250km course, from Bruges to Ninove.[86] We split the baby. A course of 150km, including all

---

[86] Exact distances change and certainly the entire format has been altered since de Ronde moved its finish to Oudenaarde. But last I checked there were still three basic options:

the *hellingen*, promised a long enough day in the saddle, an early start, and a lot of mysterious logistics to trip us up.[87]

Me, my bro, Mark Cavendish's car and the Koppenberg.

Out of mercy I let Pete sleep til 7:30, which put us rolling out in the intermittent rain and cold of a classic Flemish spring day around 9am. We departed from Ninove, the finish line of the

---

ride the entire route, ride the entire Vlaamse Ardennen portion, or ride a selection of climbs squeezed into about half that latter distance, e.g. 75km.

[87] Why am I whining about logistics? Only as a warning to Americans coming to Flanders and expecting to find their way around with no trouble. It doesn't work that way. But while you're spinning your wheels, you'll probably encounter enough pro cyclists to make you stop caring.

Ronde van Vlaanderen as well as our adventure -- a logistical necessity since nobody relishes doubling back to the car via a train ride across Belgium in their freezing, wet bike clothes.[88] The 150km version was exactly right for us, purist inclinations aside. This version replaces the opening 150km of the actual race course -- the flat, ceremonial portion that mostly isn't deemed worthy of TV coverage -- with a 50km reverse loop that joins the course with 100km and all of the famous *kasseien* and *hellingen* still left to go.

The purpose of riding the cyclosportive is to experience what cycling permits like no other sport: a real connection between us regular folks and the rarified action we love. Cyclosportives are a European phenomenon where a famous race course is closed an extra day ahead (or so), and opened up to anyone interested in riding... in this case (and probably many others) for a fee, in exchange for all the forms of support you need, like food, water and mechanical assistance.[89] A handful of the 19,000 starters on this day, generally the ones rolling out as early as the organizers allow, will actually compete in a race to the finish, but the thousands of less driven participants will concentrate more on surviving and soaking in the experience.[90]

---

[88] Also, while very friendly to cyclists, I'm not sure the Belgian Railway relishes the idea of hundreds of mud-covered wielertourists descending on them at once.

[89] And apparently it's a growing trend. There was no Paris-Roubaix sportif in 2010, but there is now. The Skoda Challenge version is run the day before the actual race, with a longer-running Paris-Roubaix sportive taking place in June. Sportives have existed for many years around the Tour de France and other great events. There are even extreme sportives such as Paris-Brest-Paris imitating races that no longer exist. Sportives such as the Maratona delgli Dolomiti also race or ride over the famous locales of the Grand Tours without being strict imitations of pro events. In sum, if you want to imitate what you've seen on TV, chances are there is an organized event to hook you up.

[90] In the US, the slightly Italianized version — the Gran Fondo — has firmly taken hold. Since we lack legendary race courses, a typical gran fondo is organized around a particularly beautiful and difficult ride, of which we have an endless supply, especially in the West. They sound like plenty of fun, but the European version of riding stages of the races we love are on another level.

And what an experience it is. Name another sport where you are allowed to even touch the surface where the champions do battle, let alone take up your own version of the event? Sure, a few lucky folks walk gingerly onto the field at Yankee Stadium or the Super Bowl or Old Trafford, but even that minimal contact is way outside the norm. The people who get to really use the famous sports facilities are even more limited. You know who gets to tee it up at Augusta National? The members of Augusta National. I recently spent a morning at Seattle's Safeco Field, attending Fan Fest with a friend who has season tickets. The Mariners, like a lot of other sports franchises, have unearthed a revenue stream in tours and events like this party, and they do a nice enough job impressing the kids. We were allowed to play catch in the outfield under watchful eyes. The kids skid into second base before ushers moved us out to the next limited station. The infield grass was not to be touched. It was still certainly fun enough. But the overriding message was that the hallowed grounds of Safeco Field were being heroically defended from the invading hordes.

Cycling could not be more different. You can cycle up the Koppenberg any day of the year. Even on race day[91] casual riders and fans need only clear the course for a few hours prior to the women's race, and it's open for business as soon as the last men's rider and his escorting course vehicle go past. Cycling lets fans in closer than many, many sports -- the scene at the start line is a close-quarters parade of greetings and autographs. Cyclists aren't hard to talk to, and on the days before a race they're not hard at all to spot, riding the open

---

[91] Of which there are several. De Ronde and KoppenbergCross on November 1 are the two I can name, but apparently there are some local races that run up the thing as well. Because… if you had a Koppenberg, you'd race on it as often as you could, right?

roads in their kits (though good luck catching up to say hello). There's a prevailing sense of tolerance among the riders toward their fans, like you would hope to find in a sport which needs all the support it can get.[92]

What's really going on, however, isn't so much Cycling letting fans into their cloistered world -- it's them venturing out into our world. The hallowed grounds of the sport are 99.9% public property, save for the odd velodrome or ski resort road. The definition of a racer is someone who can surmount whatever the road and weather conditions of the real world throw at them. Alpe d'Huez is a mountain road in France, open to traffic every day. The Gavia and Stelvio and Mortirolo passes are ancient routes connecting adjoining valleys and populations. The Madonna del Ghisallo is a public road, along with the Angliru, the Mur de Huy, the Poggio di San Remo, the Champs-Elysees (though mind the traffic), the Cauberg and the Cote de la Redoute. Even the Paterberg, built by a farmer to attract cyclists, is publicly available.

Cycling these pathways gives anyone who takes up the challenge a chance to get even more of a taste of what the great races are like. What they do and what I do is the same basic experience, albeit under vastly different conditions and speeds. Maybe a pedestrian can't feel it, but any conditioned

---

[92] This is an evolving matter, to be fair. The two biggest changes in terms of fan attention in the last decade are the rising popularity of the classics and the explosion in media outlets. At some point the most famous riders need to take greater measures to protect themselves and their sanity from the rising tide of interview requests and fan interactions off the bike. Such measures already exist around the *maillot jaune* at the Tour de France, and Lance Armstrong's last forays into Europe, including this 2010 Tour of Flanders, came with his praetorian guard. Still, they aren't likely to trickle down very far, very soon. There will always be a large number of *domestiques* going about their business in an untroubled manner. And at any given race the contenders are a different lot than the last given race, which should mean that, apart from a chosen few, most riders should remain pretty accessible to fans for the foreseeable future.

cyclist can. You feel the varying road surfaces, the climbs, the winds, the broken rhythms of the course, and the way a section of rough cobbles takes the starch out of your legs so the subsequent climb can deliver the *coup de grace*.

This was what my brother and I paid 40 Euros for the privilege of experiencing at the Ronde van Vlaanderen Sportive, along with the weather conditions that have helped make the spring classics famous(ly miserable). But it wouldn't be the full experience without a long, slow march before the real action got going. As I said, we opted for the 150km version, which started at the finish line and circled back 50km before joining the course.[93] This still left us with two hours of getting acclimated before the real work began. Rain and hints of snow came down in ten to fifteen minute waves, varying in intensity but often heavy enough for a good soaking. The intervening sunbursts did little to warm up frozen extremities, though on that score the temps were manageable if you didn't stop exerting yourself for too long.

Prior to joining the heart of the Ronde parcours, we stopped twice at the designated pit stops, which were either open-air tents or warehouses decked out to feed and hydrate the masses. Croissants, honey-waffle cookies, bread, fruit and drinks were in long supply, but the key to the stops was to fight any rational impulses and get back on the bike as quickly as humanly possible. Before your core temperature could plummet and rigor mortis could set in on your ambition.

---

[93] Like I said above, the design of the 150km route has also completely changed since 2011. Because de Ronde itself now turns in loops around the Vlaamse Ardennen, so too does the mid-distance sportive roll out of Oudenaarde and join the course pretty quickly. The first climb of the 2016 edition, the Wolvenberg, comes at the 9km mark. I suppose I can applaud one element of the course change then — the aligning of the Wielertourist event more closely with the race. Yippee.

*****

Those opening 50km, delivering the Cyclosportive from Ninove to the real Ronde course, were spent largely on forgettable roads, places like two or four-lane tarmac strips where you can settle down and start building your anticipation of the hallowed cobbles and climbs. Such roads give the day a certain rhythm: dull grind -- excited burst -- dull grind -- food stop -- dull grind -- excited burst.. and so on. Not unlike the actual Tour of Flanders.[94]

Luckily for us, in addition to the lack of wayward pedestrians we were in no particular hurry on the open stretches, no battles in advance of the cobbles and skinny roads, at least not early in the day. Position meant nothing to us, and time didn't either, for a while. But we did need to finish up in under nine hours, which seemed like forever to Pete and me, having done 110 miles in Vermont a few years back in about five hours. This would be harder and slower, for sure, but a four-hour buffer seemed ample... until about the halfway mark of our bumpy journey.

Immediately after we joined the actual race course, the cobbles began. Honestly, I don't remember all of the climbs as well as I remember the stones. Sections like the Paddestraat, Holleweg and Haaghoek that seemed to go on forever. The locals passed by me on these sections with seemingly little

---

[94] Actually the opening phase of de Ronde is usually dripping with significance, finding villages which merit an up-close look at the race, and lined with excited spectators. Compared to a great many races, it's very exciting and emotional, at least for fans. It's only overshadowed in excitement by the latter half of the race, and if most of the riders aren't keyed up about the opening stanza, it's because nobody can afford to be excited about all seven hours in the saddle.

effort, and even Pete, coming off a brutal New England winter where outdoor training was often a distant dream, would pull away from me. I had heard enough people say that keeping the pace high would diminish the effect some, but for at least the first few long passages I simply couldn't manage.[95]

This plus the rain increased the need to stop at every food station, to get warm and get blood sugar stores replenished. The stations didn't offer much warmth -- if anything, they made life colder. The first one or two were in warehouse spaces, open on both ends, and crammed, wet and chaotic in between. Food choices were mostly unheated too, the message being get back on your bike if you want to warm up.[96] Later stations were outdoor affairs, though thankfully we were beyond caring by then.

Still, as improbable as it seemed, time was actually becoming an issue. Our 3pm finish target became 4, then 5, then half past get me the hell out of here. The only true solution was to stop thinking about it, which wasn't hard -- all it took was a sign saying "Paterberg 3km" or something along those lines.

*****

The flat cobbled streets of Flanders remain one of the sport's under-appreciated elements... for now.[97] Most casual fans can name the Muur or the Koppenberg, and maybe another dozen famous cobbled climbs. The organizers of Paris-Roubaix have

---

[95] [Insert chicken noises.]

[96] The correct message, by the way. This isn't luxury travel. Or worse, cricket.

[97] The notable exception is during Omloop Het Nieuwsblad week, which typically features three long stretches of "flat" cobbles in the finale after the last *helling* has been climbed.

instituted a cobble rating system whereby people from 185 different countries can describe to you why the Forest of Arenberg is more treacherous than the stretch at Quievy. Those are the headliners. In that arena, the flat cobbled stretches in Flanders struggle to compete for the public eye.

And yet we underestimate them at our peril. The worst stretches of cobblestones north of the French border might look tidy compared to the legendary *pave* of Paris-Roubaix, but to an American cyclist unaccustomed to Roman-era road-building technologies I can assure you, they leave their mark. And make no mistake, de Ronde would be nothing without them. I've hunted around for English descriptions of the big flat sections tearing the race apart, but the history of de Ronde is too cluttered with hills. So does that mean they aren't decisive? Not even close.

First, even if nobody attacked on the flat cobbles, they would still play a major role in the outcome, simply by draining the precious energy reserves of the peloton. Cobbles demand that you apply more power to get over them, obviously, but the position battles leading into the cobbles, described above, are equally exhausting. Worse, when the line stretches out on the cobbles and the wind hits from the side, gaps open up quickly, and some real urgency is required to close them. The peloton has already spent half a day battling the wind, rain, constant twists and turns, and funneling effects from skinny roads. The long, flat stretches of cobbles apply the coup de grace to the energy reserves of many, many riders.

In fact, the Ronde van Vlaanderen planners have been including clear mention of the handful of named cobble stretches in the official maps since the turn of the millenium, if not earlier. The earlier ones I found, you had to scan closely to see "Mariaborrestraat," but starting in 2002 the official race maps have included graphics mentioning certain notorious stretches by name and showing other flat, unnamed stretches with the ubiquitous cobble graphic and a sector length in meters. The locals know them, the racers know them, and so, obviously, does the race organization. The only people who sometimes don't give them their due would be the media, and the fans who depend on it.

Well, peel away those blinders... here are the eleven stretches of flat cobbles notorious enough to be named and rated by the race (one to five stars, though nobody warrants more than four at present):

Lippenhovestraat
Locale: Velzeke-Ruddershove, just north of Zottegem
Stats: 1300 meters, three stars.

Pretty chunky rocks but as I have no personal experience here I can only guess that this wide, tidy stretch doesn't have any other hidden treachery. At least in the Omloop, where it features late in the race, riders can be seen using the vertically aligned cobbles on the margins, to save a few jostles.

Huisepontweg
Locale: About 5km north of Oudenaarde
Stats: 1500 meters, three stars.

The Huisepontweg was banned from de Ronde when it fell into disrepair, though as of 2008 it's been cleaned up.

Distinguishing character would be a rather large windmill alongside the road. Older pictures show a definite crown in the center of the lane, with muddy, disorganized stones sloping away to the margins -- very Paris-Roubaix-looking. Another old photo shows the dry crown framed by deep puddles. It's no shock to find that the race organizers wanted it out, and less of a shock that nearby residents would have preferred something tidier.

Funnily enough, the repair of the Huisepontweg has its own forty-year saga, with locals in Wannegem-Lede calling for the route to be paved smooth back in 1969. But as often happens in these parts, cycling intervened. First the route was designated as an historic monument, not unlike the Koppenberg, which threw a spanner into the plans.[98]

Worse, some local bigwigs, including Guy Verhofstadt, who served as Prime Minister of Belgium from 1999-2008, used to ride on these stones, and refused to let them be removed. Former president of the Flanders regional government Kris Peeters[99] eventually shook loose a million euros for the route to be redone in cobbles. Now the crown is gone and the stones are remarkably orderly, lacking the old charm, but narrow, and overall probably making for a more realistic host to a bike race.

---

[98] The Mayor of Bruges, no stranger to the presence of protected sites, suggested the entire Ronde van Vlaanderen be a UNESCO World Heritage Site. Appealing on a certain level, though even Belgium, owners of the world's most incomprehensible system of government, might balk at a process that would require checking with the UN before changing the route. Hm, unless it prevents the exclusion of the Muur....

[99] Peeters, who is my brother's age, is now Deputy Prime Minister of Belgium, a man on the move.

Varentstraat

Locale: The Kaster district of Anzegem, between Kortrijk and Oudenaarde.

Stats: 2km, three stars

Redeveloped in 2009 after falling into disrepair, this old Roman road[100] is a nice, uniform stretch of cobbles, with a 90-degree bend in the middle. Anything over that 2km length is gonna hurt, but as the first cobbles of the day, they... hurt a little bit. Only because I wasn't really ready for what lay in store. Now, if I doubled back to Varentstraat, I'd probably find these stones somewhat quaint. And I might even jump on the dirt footpath that runs alongside, and that the riders use without a second thought during the race.

Paddestraat

Locale: Velzeke-Ruddershove, just north of Zottegem. Practically adjacent to the Lippenhovestraat.

Stats: 2400 meters, three stars

The Paddestraat is among the longest sectors, on par with Mariaborrestraat and slightly shorter than the Kerkgate. For some reason it only warrants three stars; as it lies north of Oudenaarde, our route missed out on it. Anyway, the margins of the road consist of packed dirt, a relief valve for anyone sick of cruising over the big bumps, as long as it's dry. It winds

---

[100] Apparently Roman roads still exist throughout the former Empire, and including a few in Belgium. The classic Roman road outside Italy would be a long-distance stretch connecting two cities of some significance. Varentstraat, for example, was part of the Roman road connecting Bavie in northern France to Oudeberg in West Flanders, and was recorded by Joseph de Ferraris in his maps dating back to the 1770s (more on them in a sec). Anyway, Roman roads are known also for having a center crown to promote drainage, as well as a footpath alongside. This is a whole separate book topic. I'll stop now.

back and forth and has a slight tilt to it — uphill in the race, which makes for good control. The road supposedly traces part of the old Roman Via Belgica road from Boulogne to Cologne. Today, it's home to a monument to the Tour of Flanders: a cobble suspended inside a wheel, set on a pillar which lists all the race winners since 1973.

Mariaborrestraat

Locale: Etikhove, south of Oudenaarde a few km, in the shadow of the Koppenberg, albeit on the opposite side.
Stats: The official statistics list the Mariaborrestraat at 2.4km, including the Steenbekdries and the descent of the Stationsberg. So I guess you could break the Mariaborrestraat into three parcels:

* the first 800 meters: turning off the N60, a secondary highway connecting Oudenaarde to Ronse, the road dips slightly and the cobbles are very rough. This was actually the first serious stretch of flat cobbles I encountered on the whole trip. On my first big riding day I had gone first to the Koppenberg and the Korte Keer, which summits on the N60. From there I descended the Koppenberg on the highway heading back toward Oudenaarde, then noticed the Ronde van Vlaanderen signs pointing to the next right turn. So I turned, rode about another 50 meters -- and started bouncing around like I'd stepped into the 1906 San Francisco Earthquake. These are hard, hard cobbles.
* The Steenbekdries comprises the next 700 meters of cobbles at a manageable 5%, frankly the easiest stretch of Mariaborrestraat.
* Lastly, the Stationsberg descent is another 900 meters at 3.2%, and is really as bad as it gets. Rarely if ever does de

Ronde descend on cobbles at any sort of pitch, and maybe those guys wouldn't mind if it did, but to anyone not used to the sensation of getting rocked on the stones, having to fight gravity really adds a layer of nastiness to it. By the time the street made its semicircle around the train crossing and past the iconic Maarkedal station, my wrists were atrophying from the death grip I had on my brakes.

Doorn

Locale: Oudenaarde, on the northwestern edge of town.
Stats: 1,650 meters, four stars.
Doorn means "thorn," not a bad name for this straight, narrow stretch of old-style cobbles. They rate four stars, which is what they'd get from Paris-Roubaix too, thanks to the road shape and the cobbles themselves. The shape is pure farm track: barely wide enough for three bikes across, with mud framing the road and deep ditches running parallel on both sides awaiting anyone who comes unglued. The stones are big, albeit not rounded like the classic kinderkopje (baby heads) but flatter and maybe manageable at times. Still, it's an old road, no two stones are alike, and there are sneaky little gaps all along the way. In wet weather those gaps hide under puddles, waiting for any tire unlucky enough to come rolling through. The sign at the entrance reads "weg in schlechte staat," i.e. road in a bad way. Don't say you weren't warned.

Holleweg

Locale: Volkegem, a few km east of Oudenaarde.
Stats: 1500 meters, four stars

Another patch of very rough cobbles, sandwiched in among several difficult challenges. The Holleweg rides along the crest of a hill, which is climbed via the Kattenberg from the north (cobbled), the Boigneberg from the south (paved), and two more routes from the west, the Wolvenberg and the Volkegemberg. Neither approach is all that difficult, but the Holleweg is. Stones are large, come in a variety of patterns, and get pretty rough, particularly on the margins. Like the Doorn, this is an old stone path in the process of slowly disintegrating. Plenty of ways to get in trouble... especially when wet.

How old is the Holleweg? It appears on one of the famous Ferraris Maps, a 1770s-era charting of streets in what was then the Austrian Netherlands. The Ferraris Maps, created by Joseph De Ferraris, are a collection of 275 detailed and beautifully drawn maps comprising the earliest-known mapping of Belgium. Drawn mostly in lavish green, brown and red, the maps show roads, houses and other buildings, castles, canals, redoubts, forests, and numerous other details of 18th century Belgium. Apart from sitting in three separate museums, the maps are known to have guided Napoleon's forces through the country during his campaigns. That's the first known charting of the Holleweg. How long it was there before De Ferraris discovered it is anyone's guess.

Kerkgate
Locale: Mater, barely 1km east of the Holleweg.
Stats: 2,500 meters, four stars.

The Kerkgate is really as bad as it gets. Coming in the race (or the cyclosportive) on the heels of the Holleweg, there is almost no letup with the infernal stones. The road goes up gently for much of the stretch, which takes away the relief anyone might have felt at the sight of cobbles that don't quite meet the "baby's head" or 'disrepair" descriptions. The stones aren't as slow as their illustrious neighboring kasseien, but toss in a 2-3% grade and you won't be setting any speed records. The road itself only dates back to the mid-19th century, making it one of the more modern stretches of cobbles.

Donderij

Locale: Nukerke, between Oudenaarde and Ronse.
Stats: 1500 meters, four stars.

Some of these ratings are a bit perplexing. Yes, the Donderij is a 1500-meter segment, but newer cobbles, nothing to get anguished about. The difference between new and old, if you haven't already grasped, is the difference between easy and hard. Toss in a hill and you've got another story, but even on the Koppenberg the new stones are nothing like the old ones. Fortunately, for entertainment's sake at least, there are plenty of the latter on hand at the Kopp.

Anyway, perhaps the 50-meter rise in the road is what warrants the rating. At race pace, in the midst of a long day, the incline probably hurts a bit extra.

Ruiterstraat

Locale: Mater, almost connecting the Holleweg to the Kerkgate.
Stats: 800 meters, one star

How does a one-star stretch of cobbles rate a name and a listing in the Ronde Hall of Cobbles? Beats me. Maybe the 800 meter length. Any time you're spending more than a couple minutes bouncing around, you notice it.

Haaghoek

Locale: Sint-Konelis-Horebeke, further east from the Kerkgate closer to Brakel.
Stats: 1,700 meters, four stars

Legendary cobbles, really one of the signature roads in all of Flanders, and another entry in the Ferraris Maps. Cobbles are cobbles sometimes, at least over the 90% of the country that's flat. But this stretch has some real character. The cobbles themselves are very rough, particularly at the beginning; of a piece with the Holleweg and Doorn stones. They change patterns; they vary in states of decline; and at times they threaten to toss you into a ditch. What separates the road in character is how it sinks in the middle, causing a slight descent at the start and rise at the end, not unlike the Forest of Arenberg in France. And anytime you're making that comparison, you're onto something.

*****

To underline the importance of the "flat" cobblestone sectors, look no further than the Omloop Het Nieuwsblad, the late February race that features them like no other. In the 2012 edition, an initial selection was made on the Taaienberg, started by Boonen and including Thor Hushovd, Sep Vanmarcke, Matti Breschel and Juan Antonio Flecha among the big names. Boonen and Flecha had teammates in Dries Devenyns and Matt Hayman, making the former two even more dangerous. But Vanmarcke, already a protagonist, had ideas. First he used the Molenberg's short but wicked slope to crack Breschel and Hushovd a bit. They used the descent to catch back on, but next was the Paddestraat, and the two Scandinavians cracked again, never to return. Finally, on the Lange Munte, a long, wind-bitten stretch of bouncy stones found on the run-in to Gent (and not usually occurring in de Ronde), Vanmarcke attacked once more, cracking the two lieutenants and putting himself back on level terms with the two remaining rivals, Boonen and Flecha. Deprived of Devenyns' help, Boonen started his sprint too early and got smoked by a wide-eyed Vanmarcke, who was stunned to have beaten a guy who towered over the sport when Vanmarcke was a teenager.[101]

Nice story, but in truth Vanmarcke, who grew up riding these very roads, used the cobbles like they were an extension of his body. Each acceleration, on the hilly stones or the flat ones, diminished his rivals, be it the fatal double blow he landed on Hushovd and Breschel or the more subtle effect of putting the older stars under pressure. He didn't crack Boonen or Flecha on the Lange Munte, but in burning some of his matches he burned several of theirs too. Against a superior sprinter in Boonen, Vanmarcke usually loses, but the more exhausted everyone was in the final meters, the greater the chance that victory goes to the guy with a little bit of gas in the tank, not the fastest sprinter. By this measure, Vanmarcke had a chance. A great chance, as it turned out.

*****

---

[101] Boonen went on to have a season for the ages, so don't weep for him. If anything, he was wisely managing his form at this point, five weeks before de Ronde.

Back to my own tale of cobbled woe, after the Paddestraat burnt matches weren't nearly as big an issue for me as banged brain cells. My first long pass on the cobbles left me feeling slightly punch-drunk. On subsequent passages I relaxed my shoulders slightly so I didn't jar my brain as much, but I couldn't let go of the death-grip on my bars, and my frozen claw-hand became tough to unravel at the end of, say, six or seven cold, brutal minutes. My rear tire was on the skinny side (stupid, I know) and would occasionally slip between stones that my wider front tire had bounced over, giving me the sensation that someone was ever so briefly grabbing my rear wheel. Anything resembling a descent was far worse, as I struggled to contain the forces of gravity from pulling me where I wasn't psychologically ready to go.

And not without reason. I saw only a few low-speed spills, but I did see some debris which gave me pause: pumps, bottles, pieces of derailleurs and whatnot. They say anything not bolted down can shake loose, and it often did. In prioritizing staying upright I may have been a bit timid, but I wasn't crazy.

I was fit, however, so when we started climbing, I managed to recoup at least a share of my dignity. Going up the cobbles was unbridled joy, as long as it didn't hurt too much, and it basically never hurt too much. Over slopes like the Oude Kwaremont and Taaienberg I ground my way to the summit. And on the three occasions when I didn't simply ride up and over the hills, it was not without a little "help" from some of my neighbors. There was the guy who swerved left and stopped, pinning me against the grassy embankment of the Paterberg. There was the guy who swerved right as I was coming past him on the Koppenberg, though in fairness my rear tire was acquiring a nice coat of mud·by then, so I wasn't long for that ascent. And then, of course, there was the particularly tall chap in front of me who splayed himself across the entire width of the Kapelmuur (right at the spot from which we would spectate from the next afternoon), his body going right and his bike left, momentarily shutting down all traffic on the hill.

This last one interrupted what was shaping up to be the day's most triumphant moment, the part described in the prologue, where the aura of the Kapelmuur put me in a higher state of being. As iconic as the other climbs may be in their own right, it's the Kapelmuur which, to me, symbolized the apex of the race itself, where champions don't merely survive as they do on the earlier ascents but where they are transformed into the legends hanging on the walls of every sports pub within 100 miles or more. Unlike any other section of the course, my never having been there before did nothing to dent sensation of something very familiar, not to mention utterly unique and remarkably beautiful. Also, unlike any other section of the course, spectators lined the roadside in more than the odd grouping standing gamely in the rain and urging on the tourists. Here you saw them, lots of them. You heard them cheering "courage" (the French version of the same spelling) and whatever other Flemish encouragements they could offer.

I was also feeling strong, having gotten over the first 600 meters of climbing with little trouble, so when my human landslide of a companion fulfilled his destiny, I paused for only a moment. Within seconds he had gathered himself and cleared the path, I had skirted around him and remounted, and the climb was back on, before the experience could slip away.

The reward for this was not only getting over the 19% gradient section on my bike, but turning left and skirting along the walls of the pub which framed the penultimate slope -- packed air-tight on race day with bodies on the patio and hanging out of the windows, and maybe half-full today. Across from the end of the pub was the right turn up the round, grassy hilltop to the chapel, where trees give way to sky (now showing a bit of blue again) and where fences were replaced by the tiny church's dome.

In the thirty years since the Vesten/Kapelmuur version replaced the old Abdijstraat Muur, thousands of racers -- including most of the greats -- have surely felt the same sense of relief in seeing the top of the last really hard climb, knowing as we did that nothing could stop us from finishing what we'd started, be it a tourist jaunt or a winning ride into Flemish Heaven.[102] And while I know it's a job for the professionals, every one I've asked has expressed some sense of awe. I'm sure they would understand my utter exhilaration of getting having made it that far, worked that hard, all over this dreamscape of cycling history. While gathering my wits at the top alongside at least a couple dozen other stopped riders -- because everyone stops at the top of the Muur, for at least a moment -- the weight of the ride evaporated from my mind instantly. Tired legs and

---

[102] Yes, I was referring to the race, but it's worth pointing out that the experience of climbing the Muur recreationally should also be referred to as Flemish Heaven. I ran through the details before, and maybe the old Muur was tougher (maybe), but there is no way it was more moving. A gritty, urban(ish) cobbled climb is a good thing, but can't hold a candle to the recent Muur, where the narrow city streets pass by shops and a public square, then rise through a dark, dense forest, then climax at an exquisite little chapel often painted against green grass and a blue sky. In a country known for grey weather and unspectacular vistas, there is a lot -- a LOT -- to be said for the aesthetics of this wonderful climb.

cold feet meant nothing anymore. It was almost all downhill and downwind to the finish.[103]

Waiting there at the finish in Ninove, nearly nine hours after we set out, was a drab festival of wet riders and muddy bikes, sponsor tents, impromptu pubs, disco music, and of course a frituur. We'd grabbed finishers' tee shirts, had our hands full of gear, but no way were we leaving the scene without a celebratory cone of frietes. In Belgium, the frietes rarely ever disappoint, but these had to be the sweetest ones I'd tasted all week. Intense physical activity and junk food are strangely compatible bedfellows.

We drifted out past a sparse crowd of cyclists and loiterers hanging around the parking lot, past the vendors and the disco tent. We had our own engagement and a few complications to deal with as well. The next day wasn't merely the biggest day of the cycling calendar, it was also Easter, to be followed by a bank holiday Monday. We needed a few provisions, for starters, and a tank of gas. Earlier in the morning, all of this seemed like something worth putting off, when we figured to be done riding by no later than 4pm. Only now it was well after six, the country was shutting down, and people were waiting for us in Oudenaarde.

****

---

[103] Ahem, except for the Bosberg, another favorite climb of many Flemish fans, though I have to say I had stopped caring by then. Between exhaustion and needing to get back to Oudenaarde, and above all the anticlimax associated with anything that came after the Muur, I can't say I recall much about that climb besides knowing that we were almost done when we got over it.

This was the night of the official Podium Cafe gathering. The Podium Cafe, the website I started in 2006, had grown well beyond its original purpose of giving me, Pete, our friend Drew and a few other folks a place to chat about cycling, in place of the cumbersome email chains we had been relying on (and clogging our employers' servers with). Now it was a virtual cafe frequented by cycling fans from every continent -- well-known regulars, semi-regulars, passers-by and people lurking from a distance,[104] all there to consume a pretty good daily supply of news articles, interviews, analytical exercises, race predictions, interactive features, fantasy games, fashion critiques, and jokes. Lots of jokes.

But the lifeblood of the Cafe is perhaps the live threads, where on race day people log in to the site while watching the action

---

[104] There are over 6,100 registered members at present.

and chat with each other about anything from what's happening to what might happen next to, oh, beer, food, geology, rodents, and so on. [That's a series of inside jokes, sorry.] As unbelievable as this concept would have seemed a decade or so ago, it really is like gathering in the local pub to watch the race with fellow zealots, drifting back and forth between the action and whatever else people care to chat about.

One tradition says it all. Starting in maybe 2008, someone came up with the idea that you couldn't (or shouldn't) celebrate the greatness of the Tour of Flanders without beer.[105] More than a few threads have devolved into a true night at the pub experience, and there is nothing outrageous for fans of the Tour of Flanders to crack open a beer at whatever hour feels right. [The race coverage starts at 6:30am Eastern time, a/k/a the middle of the bloody night in Seattle.] Inevitably this led to the designation of the Koppenberg as the official toasting time, for reasons I can't remember, but it makes perfect sense. The more poignant moments later in the race are too engrossing to stop and do something as ridiculous as saying cheers to your computer, but things are still pretty casual when the race reaches the Kopp. And nobody misses the climb of the Kopp.

In subsequent years the Tour of Flanders has carved out a niche in our community, not unlike in the rest of the world, whereby a significant number of people will swear that it is the pinnacle of the sport. Those folks (OK, us folks) will insist that this race, thoroughly obscure to most American minds, in a

---

[105] This isn't a frat house -- by no means is it expected that everyone consumes alcohol. But beer is pretty ubiquitous to begin with, and the Belgians have made sure to create a strong linkage between the suds and cycling. Make of it what you will.

somewhat overlooked corner of Europe, represents the totality of suffering, wits, beauty and suspense, while catering to a pretty wide variety of skills so as to make the outcome extremely difficult to predict. Never mind whether that opinion is shared widely — as it increasingly is, particularly among American fans — love of Flanders has become one of the Podium Cafe's trademarks, and quite a lot of us wear it proudly.

Whether or not de Ronde rules the Classics is beside the point. The true message of Ronde worship is that cycling should be loved for its full character -- a mix of the race, the landscape, the history and the passion that goes into it. Whether Flanders or Paris-Roubaix is the *best race* is a matter of taste. But in the US and many other countries, the popular perception, if it exists at all, has generally been that Paris-Roubaix is the most famous, therefore the best of the Classics. Flanders, for seemingly ever, was woefully underrated. The perfect fit, then, for defiantly proud die-hard fans of this brutal sport.

So it was fitting that the biggest in-person celebration to date of internet cycling fanhood[106] would take place half a block away from the Centrum Ronde van Vlaanderen museum in Oudenaarde. In the week leading up to our gathering, the Podium Cafe had been a veritable hog wallow of Flanders love. I posted exhaustively detailed pictures of *hellingen*. I live-blogged the consumption of a particularly large bowl of

---

[106] Internet cycling fanhood has expanded a bit in the last six years, to say the least. Meanwhile, the Podium Cafe has hosted a couple large gatherings in the US, associated with first the 2013 Cyclocross World Championships in Louisville, then the 2015 road World Championships in Richmond. Next on the docket: a return to Flanders in 2017.

mussels.[107] I devoured and passed on tidbits of Flemish cycling media with nearly the same gusto, including my favorite: a picture of Tom Boonen's girlfriend walking a small dog with Boonen's face cropped in. That one of the nation's largest magazines was still goofing around with digital photo cropping on its cover was Flanders in a nutshell. Fun, sure, but we're a long way from Milan or Madison Avenue.

Writing up every detail finally came to a halt by the meetup, however. I'd gone offline for much of Thursday and Friday during a side-trip to Amsterdam, Friday night my brother arrived, and Saturday was spent entirely in the saddle. And as we finished up the cyclosportive, we were already due back in Oudenaarde.

Waiting for us was a bright orange banner hung in the front window of the Pub and a dozen or so unfamiliar faces of very familiar people. We made introductions: a couple from San Francisco, two dudes from Montreal, another couple from Australia and New Zealand, friends from DC and London and Utrecht and Malmo. We shared a night in the pub, not remarkable in any way that is worth recounting except for the fact that it happened. The internet doesn't just imitate real life, it sometimes leads us to it. Thanks to so many hours of time online with these fine people (and so many others), I was at a pub talking cycling with familiar, friendly cycling-mad people, something that would almost never happen organically back home.

---

[107] OK, post-blogged, since eating mussels requires two hands. But between the jet lag and the alcohol I forgot the entire concept of time, and 158 comments later the meal was history.

This is really what we toast when we're watching at home in the American pre-dawn hours and the Tour of Flanders peloton hits the Koppenberg. Community. More specifically the community that unites around an almost secret, visceral, spectacular passion. For decades I longed for the chance to experience this great monument like the true fans, packed inside supporters clubs with the race blaring over the conversation. And now, from the comfort of my own living room, I can.

10: Ronde van Vlaanderen Day

It's about as close to Christmas (for cycling fans) as you can get. I mean, think about the parallels:

* It's not a day, it's a "season";
* People spend weeks leading up to the day rehearsing for it;
* Stores are closed;
* The party starts unusually early;
* You're expected to eat and drink with abandon, and group singing is part of the fun;
* There's even a church where people gather on the actual day, albeit without going inside. Of course, by many accounts the church is actually 260km long, and everyone is inside, paying their respects. So yeah.

Finally, the day of *de Ronde* had arrived. All the days spent with the racers tuning their game and poring over the course, the fans milling around or riding the cobbles for themselves, the endless previews, blog posts, bets, arguments, organizing and so forth... there was nothing more to do but run the race itself.

The specifics of how people celebrate this high holiday are its own chapter. A majority of the population will stay home, but on this day in 2010 an estimated 1.2 million people will turn out in person to watch at least some part of the race -- slightly more than the 1.1 million Belgians said to have watched on

TV.[108] The choices are initially between picking one spot or several, attempting the start, finish, or places in between, and as we woke up the critical decision-making began.

The first choice involved seeing the start. It happens so long before the key points in the race that you can definitely get there and some other prime race-watching location. But with my brother still lagging on US time and having rallied painfully early the previous day, we'd decided on Flanders Eve not to try to make the start in Bruges. Working backward, the start happens around 9:30, which means the fun starts about 8:30 and is over by 9:15, save for the starting gun. Adding in the challenge of parking in a small, very old (and completely unfamiliar) city on a day where a few hundred thousand others have the same idea, and you're talking about an 8am arrival. Bruges is maybe an hour from Oudenaarde, which means waking up and eating breakfast at the crack of absolutely not. On to plan B, camping out on the Muur and waiting for the race to come to us.[109]

Our reward for being sensible was access to the start of the women's race, which was due to kick off at 11am in the Oudenaarde central square ("Grote Markt"). Women's cycling is evolving and growing even more fitfully than the men's side,

---

[108] These numbers are in no way verifiable, but hey, if the race organization says they were there, it must be true.

[109] Some of our people made it to two spots, the Molenberg and the Muur. That was probably the most ambitious plan that still made sense. You couldn't do the Muur and the finish, since they were a mere 16km apart; by the time we could get to our car the race would be over. You could pick an earlier point and the finish, e.g. the Koppenberg, but that meant no Muur, and since when is anything won on the Koppenberg? Given the logistics of getting into Geraardsbergen on Ronde van Vlaanderen day, there weren't many ways to see the race multiple times and get to the Muur, particularly if you didn't really know how to get around Flanders. Imagine trying to go from one point to another, only to find that critical roads were closed by the race, and you missed everything. This was our one day. Failure to pick a great spot was not an option.

but no matter, this was a big day for the elite women pros. The teams and races are largely separate from the men, but in the past decade several organizations have run both men's and women's team. As to events, in 2010 a few large races ran both men's and women's events — a trend that has spiked upward since. This shared course format brings some massive benefits to women's cycling. The costly infrastructure that poses such barriers to the sport are all taken care of: same barriers along the road, same police forces keeping an eye out, even the same media caravan which gets to double its coverage, with motos and helicopters available (maybe) to check in on both races to some degree. It doesn't always lead to live TV coverage, but it can, or at least a highlight show might appear later. And then there are the fans.

That day, the seventh edition of the Ronde van Vlaanderen voor Vrouwen was 120 km, a bit less than half the men's distance, and consisted of some early warmup miles before joining the men's route for the punishing last 70km. Some 180km of the men's route were omitted, but the women's route on this day still featured nine climbs (including the Eikenberg, Molenberg and the Muur) as well as nine cobbled stretches marked on the course.[110] The vast majority of fans in place for the men's event are ready (drunk) and waiting (drinking) when the women come by. Since the men's race passed through Oudenaarde that year without much fanfare, and locals had the choice of several famous cobbled hills within 15km to watch the suffering, the town square wasn't likely to attract much of a crowd if not for the women's event

---

[110] The 2014 version, to update things, ran 135 km, starting and finishing in Oudenaarde, featuring ten *hellingen* including the Oude Kwaremont-Paterberg finish, as well as the Haaghoek, Lippenhovestraat, Paddestraat and Ruiterstraat cobblestone stretches.

and their fans. Which at that point didn't really include me --
not yet anyway, until I'd had more time to learn who's who.

But several of the Podium Cafe crew were big fans. Ed had
climbed part way up a utility pole to improve the angle on his
photos. Jens had gone his own way to catch some early action
on the road, stopping by the Molenberg, and Jim and
Elizabeth were wandering around the square when we'd
arrived. The riders were pretty accessible until it came time to
sign in and head for the starting line. The scale of it all was
different than a men's event, fewer riders, fewer fans, less in
the way of tricked out team buses. But there were plenty of
each, a nice buzz building in the crowd, and the caravan
forming behind looked no different from the other classics.

Riders milling around near the starting area chatted in a
relaxed way, not much of an edge to them, in a way that
seems typical of long days. I'd seen plenty of backstage shots
at short events (e.g. time trials) where riders are getting in the
zone. And my own racing experience consists of desperately
searching for the right balance of calm and nerves prior to the
start. But when you've got several hours in the saddle and the
major moves are at least 50km away, this is no time to wind up
your energy or emotions. With the sun peeking out now and
again, there was nothing to dampen anyone's spirits (for
another 60km anyway). Eventually the announcers called up
the star riders, lined them up in starting order, asked the rest
of the riders to fall in behind, and sent the race and caravan
away.

The anticlimactic nature of race starts is a bit jarring to me.
Nothing was going to happen in the race for several hours,

and even when it did, it wouldn't be in downtown Oudenaarde, so after all this buildup the best thing to do was to go home, or to a pub, or to somewhere else along the course. Once the last motorcycle in the caravan departed, the one signaling the end of the rolling enclosure that surrounded the race, the square emptied in minutes. Imagine if you had a ticket to the Super Bowl, cheered through the introductions for an hour or so, then the game kicked off... and everyone went back to their hotels for lunch and a nap. That's big-time cycling.

The men's race was already in its third hour by the time we got out of Oudenaarde, so we wasted little time getting to our appointment with the Muur. Flanders can be tough to get around on race day, with the closed course forming a diagonal blockage across half the region. But from Oudenaarde we needed to just stay a bit north of the action on some of the bigger roads and we wouldn't hit any closures until Geraardsbergen, our destination. Once there, we had no idea what parking would be like and feared the worst -- from our previous day's ride we'd seen how small Geraardsbergen was, and who knew how many other people had the same idea? But it turned out that the N-route, also known as Zonnebloemstraat (Sunflower Street), ran parallel to the Muur and had grassy shoulders on which people were parking their cars. Rules weren't clear, but the prevailing logic was, and it was a short, unburdening walk to the Muur.

Our luck didn't stop at Sunflower Street either. The Muur isn't exactly a stadium, as far as accommodating the crowds is concerned. The lower slopes down in the town proper ascend broad boulevards where fans can line up ten rows deep, easily, assuming you'd want to. But at the top of the town, the leg-snapping Kapelmuur section leaves the busy village behind and snakes through a dense forest on a narrow lane, with a single pathway on the right side barely a meter in width from the road to the chain-link fence separating the action from the adjoining ravine. On a quiet evening, it must be a lovely place for Les Grammontiens to take a peaceful stroll.[111] On Ronde Day, it looks like a terrible place to shoehorn in several thousand people.

Muur this way. Photo by Elizabeth Freer

---

[111] Geraardsbergen, or Grammont in French, is one of several towns located just north of the linguistic border in Flemish territory, but nonetheless culturally French. An island of Frenchness inside Flanders. Because Belgian language boundaries aren't complicated enough.

What we call the Kapelmuur is actually a detour off of Oudebergstraat, the main route up the Oudeberg or Old Mountain.[112] At the point where Oudebergstraat narrows to a foot path, the Kapelmuur detours off the road, turning right onto an initial cobbled ramp as the race heads into the forest. Doing so launches the peloton into the teeth of the steep, rough Kapelmuur, which then turns left onto a second viciously hard ramp of nasty cobbles. All along this way is the aforementioned narrow sidewalk on the right side and a steep embankment on the left. Once the former got packed -- and I do mean packed, between the road and the fence -- people began filling in the latter, lurking in the trees and hopefully staying sober enough not to fall off the bank and onto the race some ten feet below.

't Hemelrick. Photo by Chris Fontecchio

---

[112] See chapter 7 for the longer version of this discussion.

This second ramp tops out at a flat left-hand turn where the road grazes a corner of the 't Hemelrijck ("the Kingdom of Heaven") pub, itself an icon of the pre-2012 race with people hanging out the windows and crammed into its narrow patio on Ronde Day. At this corner you could cross over and find porta-potties and mobile stalls selling beer, sausage and frietes on the lawn behind the pub, a critical development, because buying from the pub itself was not an option. Access to the pub and its patio was limited to the connected folks seated at tables inside, watching the race on TV, or standing behind a temporary barrier forming the key outdoor viewing angle. You could walk through -- because on the opposite side the sidewalk gives way at the corner to an impassable tangle of fencing and shrubs -- but don't expect to stay.

Not that you would want to anyway, because across from pub's VIP section is the famous right turn to the Chapel, where Oudebergstraat resumes and the Kapelmuur goes over the summit. Technically named the Chapel of Our Lady of Oudeberg, or Kapel van Onze-Lieve-Vrouw van Oudeberg, the race's most famous structure is better known simply enough as "The Chapel." The Chapel sits on a gumdrop-shaped dot of a hill surrounded by steep, rounded slopes, but the landscaping is all lawn, and arriving fans emerging from the dark, narrow forest path were finally free to stretch their arms, lay out a blanket, and luxuriate in the open-air mini-stadium of the Muur's summit. The race climbed right to the Chapel, close enough for riders to touch its east wall from the saddle, before plummeting with shocking suddenness down to the N-route in the valley, disappearing up the road. That's cycling, gone before you know it, but not before a few thousand voices can sing in unified approval.

Photo by Chris Fontecchio

Our timing was still good as the sidewalk of the second cobbled ramp was just beginning to get packed, and some early risers have already staked out Podium Cafe Ronde van Vlaanderen Headquarters. The two Canadians, two Antipodeans, and two Americans had fastened the \o/ banner to the fence halfway up this stretch, probably the nastiest part of the Muur. From our spot, we could see the riders turn left from the first ramp to ours, then watch them suffer to the corner by the pub. From an action standpoint, this appeared ideal, and until the race came by, we could walk across the hallowed road and be in line for food or beer in about 30 seconds. It was not as sunny as the Chapel lawn, but we were basically guaranteed a front row seat.

I wandered around for a while with my recorder, chatting with fans of various origin about why they were here. Italy, Spain, Holland and the US were well represented among the people I spoke with. The Marco Bandiera fan club drove up from Milan to cheer on their man (who I'd barely ever heard of before, or since). A family in Rabobank shirts and hats sat soberly on lawn chairs.[113] A group of American moms and daughters climbed to the summit to mingle with some boisterous local boys and cheer on George Hincapie. The large contingent of Spaniards next to our group were eager to chat and mug for pictures. Across the way, the ever-present Norwegians in their viking helmets began congregating in the woods above the road, killing the time with boyish drunken reverie.

As the race drew closer, the crowd filled out in smaller groups, mostly Belgians (as far as I could tell). Or at least, it would stand to reason that the outsiders would err on the side of arriving way too early, while the savvier locals would know when and how to show up efficiently. At some point access is closed off, so anyone flirting with that deadline either knows how not to get caught or hasn't come thousands of miles in hopes of standing on the Kapelmuur, or both.

Falling into the latter category, we arrived three hours before the fireworks, but there was plenty to keep us entertained, besides beer. Mingling with the happy fans. Framing photos of the sacred grounds. Watching the Eddy Merckx imitator, complete with 1970s clothing and bike, do lap after lap on the

---

[113] I can't speak with great authority on the nature of being Dutch at a Belgian race, but by all appearances it's like walking into Yankee Stadium with your Red Sox hat on. Not dangerous, and you might not even be mistreated — this is a polite part of the world — but I'm sure the Dutch fans can tell in some subtle way that nobody is on their side.

stones. And following the latest developments in the race, as my brother's blackberry conveyed regular text updates.[114]

After nearly two hours' wait the women's peloton drew near. The race caravan began with some police motorcycles signaling the closure of the road. Then more motorcycles, and a few more, undoubtedly to make very, very certain that everybody and everything was off the road, or at least that the police got to watch the finish in Ninove. After nearly ten minutes of sporadic vehicular traffic, a rising tide of voices signaled that the riders were here. I was up by the chapel at the time, positioned across the road from the chapel lawn so as to capture the riders and the iconic Chapel image together.

Grace Verbeek and Colnago Sweater Guy. Photo by Chris Fontecchio

---

[114] This was an innocent time, when you couldn't necessarily expect your phone to work at all, let alone connect to the precise information you wanted and deliver it to you in an effective way. Twitter was home to some 70,000 users (now 100 million). Facebook hadn't really taken over. Certainly video streams on mobile devices were a distant dream to your average smartphone user. Pete travels to Europe for work, and had ponied up for full-on data access. From there, the CyclingNews ticker gave us race status in the form of who was in the lead group and gaps to chasing groups. That got us through.

A solo rider was the first to arrive: Grace Verbeke, from the Lotto Ladies team, not a clear favorite to win but a contender. Being Belgian, her appearance on the attack, alone on the Muur at the front of the Tour of Flanders, sent the crowd into a frenzy. For the next several minutes riders chased Verbeke in twos and threes, with the other heads of state not terribly far back. Verbeke looked good, but hardly had the race in hand.

Being where I was exposed me to two recognizable faces in the Tour of Flanders crowd: Screaming Guy and Colnago Sweater Guy. I wish I'd talked to them because at the time I wasn't aware of their ubiquity (possibly an internet sensation only), but since then it's become apparent that these were two of the better known fans-who-stand-in-the-same-place-and-maybe-in-the-same-clothes-every-year, of which there are surely others.

Alyona Andruk and Screaming Guy. Photo by Chris Fontecchio

The race is all about tradition, and individual fans are bound to come up with their own mini-traditions over time. Screaming Guy is a thin, young-looking man with longish straight brown hair who stands on the low wall at the bottom of the Chapel Lawn, hunched over and screaming his support in full-bodied emphasis as the favorites pass by. Colnago Sweater Guy is an older man, round and balding, in a bright white-as-fresh-snow sweater with the Colnago bicycles brand name stitched across the front and a matching cap. He isn't quite as, um, screamy as Screaming Guy, offering more graceful exhortations to the passing riders. As far as I can tell he stood no more than ten feet uphill from Screaming Guy, either on the same low wall or just in front of it on the road. And as far as I can tell, they could be found playing their part every year. What they have done the last few years is a bit of a mystery at press time. My guess is Paterberg. Or perhaps they sit atop the Muur, bewildered by the lack of action. Or watching it on their iPhone.

Our gang on the Muur. Photo by Chris Fontecchio

Back at PdC Central, the gang was trading Jupiler runs and watching Pete's texts for updates. Jupiler is the ubiquitous Belgian Budweiser, i.e. a beer with no great distinction, but tolerable and inexpensive. For all the intricacies of Belgian beer, the roadside brew scene is about what you'd expect from a college tailgater. Not that there is anything wrong or even unjust about it; Belgium's finer beers maintain their image of superiority by making themselves available in decent establishments, where they pour it by hand and in matching glasses, not into plastic cups in the middle of a field. If you *are* in the middle of a field drinking from a plastic cup, Jupiler makes an acceptable substitute for the Belgian beer experience that beer lovers travel the world to sample.

Belgian ales are the envy of the brewing world. Not that they have a monopoly on great beer; as far as I can tell practically every country not living under a religious code hostile to alcohol makes beer. And nowadays, if you can make beer, chances are you or someone within 100 miles of you can do it well. Ingredients and information, once largely unobtainable to all but the most serious brewers, can now be found at strip malls and bought/downloaded from websites. So yeah, tasty beer is everywhere.

For the highly refined ales of little old Belgium to stand out above the crowd, then, there needs to be an extra ingredient: mythology. And here's where Belgian beer is without peer. Yeah, the breweries are old, dating back to the 1830s or the Crusades (depending on what you call the beginning), but so do Germany's. It's the presence of monasteries in the brewing business that helps Belgium drop its rivals in Cancellara-esque fashion in the Great World Beer Race. Think about it: who even knew monasteries still existed? OK, I did, but just barely, in the way that I know condors still exist: not unknown in their native habitat (Tibet for monks, the Andes for condors), but largely absent from their former range, as well as the public eye. So driving the production of its best brews indoors, into the haunting quiet of a monastery, even at only a handful of Belgium's 180 or so breweries, is mystique enough.

But monks bring more than just old-world aesthetics and recipes. Belgian breweries include a couple dozen "Abbey" beers, the certified ones being related to some sort of monastery, but the Trappists are a category of their own. Trappist monasteries, originating in France and spread throughout Europe, are of the Order of Cistercians of the Strict Observance which, like the name suggests, split off from the Cistercian Catholic order when they thought their brothers and sisters were becoming too lax. Trappists are hardcore. The kind of people who aren't going to mess around when it comes to observing their faith, or the brewing process.

They also don't seem to care terribly about commercial success.[115] Only eleven trappist monasteries meet the rules of the International Trappist Association for brewing -- six in Belgium, two in the Netherlands, and one each in Austria, Italy and (huzzah!) in Spencer, Massachusetts. Some like Chimay and Westmalle can be found easily in American pubs and grocery stores,[116] all are highly regarded, but in at least one respect St-Sixtus Abbey, brewers of the Westvletern family of three ales, stands alone.

First, the Westvleteren XII is highly acclaimed, winning competitions for best ale on more than one occasion, meaning at least some people consider it the #1 beer on the planet, amidst the debates that rage on about such matters. Doubling down on mystique, the ales are sold only at the Abbey, in quantities of one or two 24-bottle crates, only to people who make phone reservations and who haven't purchased any "Westy" in the previous sixty days (mass production doesn't fit in with monastic life, and the monks want to give everyone a fair chance of trying their ales). They produce 66,000 cases a year -- the same total output they've maintained since 1946.[117] All sales contain the admonition *niet verder verkopen*, "do not resell," and if you put some for sale on the internet, chances

---

[115] The internet tells me that Trappist ale makers tend to have a "patersbier," a special "father's beer" intended only for the monks, and occasionally served at their on-site cafe, if they have one.

[116] These two and La Trappe make more than three million gallons of beer annually, enough to supply a pretty fair portion of the western world's beer snob population. By contrast, St. Sixtus, only makes about 125,000 gallons, and a few others make under 100,000.

[117] The world population has increased by about a billion people (33%) since 1946.

are you'll get a call or email from a monk asking you to stand down.

Think about it: a Belgian ale which is rare and beloved enough that people will take part in a worldwide scheme to defraud monks, just for a sip. Good stuff. You could sell it at a premium in 150 countries, as fast as you could produce it. But the monks are doing everything they can to restrict it severely in Belgium and exclude it from the remaining 149 countries entirely. *That*'s mystique. In fact, mystique barely begins to cover it. Paul McCartney's fatal 1964 car accident has less mystique than St-Sixtus' ale.

While I was in Belgium I did not come into contact with Westvleteren Ale, not having known about its fame then, and even if I had, it probably wasn't for sale anywhere I went. Except maybe the convenience store next to the Gravensteen castle in Gent, which had a thousand million different beers and a thrillingly shady atmosphere. If I knew what the right words to say were, I bet the clerk would have disappeared for a minute and come back with a bottle. Anyway, the scarcity has resulted in a worldwide hoarding mentality so bizarre that, as of this writing, you can buy a six-pack of Westvleteren XII bottles on eBay, along with two matching glass goblets, for $200.00. That's a six pack of bottles. *Empty* bottles. [Full bottles run at about $250 or so, and aren't often listed.]

Briefly in 2011 some 7700 gift packs of Westvleteren XII made their way around North America for sale to certain lucky establishments, including a restaurant in Vancouver, BC where I dined one night, largely because they had Westy on their beer list. The actual ale was long gone, leaving behind the manager who described the sensation of having it on the premises, and his hopes for more someday. Which are probably dashed; the Abbey says they only let out some product to raise money for renovations to the monastery roof, and they have no plans to ship their prized ale overseas again. If you want it, you have to go there, or find someone on eBay willing to defy the monks.[118]

The story has a happy ending, because Jens, who has run the Podium Cafe with me for several years now, bought a couple crates of Westvleteren XII a couple years ago, brought them home to Sweden, lovingly cared for them (often by drinking them), and transported roughly a dozen or so full, perfect bottles of the stuff to Richmond, Virginia for our gathering at the 2015 UCI World Championships. I drank several of them over that week, brought two more home for sharing, and now have those empty bottles on display in my kitchen. And I will not be selling them on eBay.
★★★★★★★★★★★★

Anyway, back to the race. To our delight, reports were that Fabian Cancellara and Tom Boonen had opened up a thirty second gap on the rest of the elite field in an attack on the Molenberg. We didn't know then that Cancellara had initiated

---

[118] Or better yet, find Sint-Bernardus ales, which are sold in at least three locations I know of within walking distance of my house, along with presumably another thousand or so shops and pubs in America. Their Abt 12 is considered a very close match to the Westvleteren XII in recipe and style. Why? Because the two were one and the same, as of 1945 when the Sint-Sixtus monks decided to stop selling beer outside their monastery (and a nearby pub) and licensed the extra production to the Trappist monks of Mont des Cats, who had moved to Watou to make cheese. The Watou operation brewed and sold Sint-Sixtus beer outside the neighborhood, using the same recipes and yeast from the original Sint-Sixtus strain. In 1992, the powers that be ruled that "trappist ales" only included beer brewed within the walls of the monastery, and the joint arrangement ended. But the Mont des Cats folks carried on brewing under the name of their Watou farm, Sint-Bernardus. And the results, I am pleased to say, are spectacular.

the attack, a clue to what lay in store for the rest of Spring; just that the race was probably down to a star-studded two-man duel. This development meant that Quick Step and Saxo Bank wouldn't be involved in any chasing, of course, and most of the remaining teams were lacking in the kind of pursuit mojo that would be required to catch two giants of Flanders, *if* they were at full strength. In all likelihood, teams would spend more time squabbling about whose turn it was to lead the chase than banding together to make it happen,[119] all while Quick Step and Saxo lieutenants -- several of whom were capable of winning if you were foolish enough to tow them up to the leaders -- would be doing what they could to disrupt the effort.

The only real issue was whether the two were strong enough to finish off what would amount to a two-man, 45-km effort, the Molenberg coming at km 217 of 262. That kind of distance is typically reserved for desperate or daring attacks, or team maneuvers meant not so much to win but to make someone else do something they don't want to do (i.e. work). The big names typically wait just a bit longer — on the old course, maybe the Berendries or Tenbosse with 34/26km to go if not the Muur, 16km from the line.[120] Or so goes the conventional wisdom. But long attacks are hardly unheard-of, especially in decent weather and with a tailwind minimizing the pain of the final segment to Ninove. Notably, this same duo, along with Juan Antonio Flecha, had left the field behind at about the same point in the E3 Prijs eight days earlier, with no tailwind

---

[119] Following the race George Hincapie, regretting his hesitation on the Molenberg, said that this is exactly what happened: the rest of the field just watched each other to see if anyone would take up the chase.

[120] On the new course, it's quickly becoming standard practice to attack on the final climb of the day, the Paterberg, or the Oude Kwaremont ascent immediately preceding. Standard practices don't tend to last, so hopefully, if we are truly stuck with the new route, things will open up as racers become accustomed to it.

assistance. The early attack might have surprised their rivals, but not shocked them.

Not that anyone *wanted* to question these tactics. As far as the fans were concerned (with the exception of the Spaniards next to us), a Cancellara-Boonen duel was exactly what the occasion called for. Pozzato and Ballan were the only two, besides Flecha, in this class of Ronde riders, and the two Italians were both missing their top form -- Pozzato actually went home with the flu. Few would have complained if the chasing duo of Bjorn Leukemans and Philippe Gilbert had made the juncture, and Hincapie would not have seemed out of place in the front, but twice-winner and perennial favorite Boonen versus all-round superhero Cancellara, pounding away at each other for an hour or so, was more or less the kind of duel you'd draw up in a comic book.

As the buzz of helicopters drew closer, we readied ourselves for the moment. Last Jupiler runs were made; frietes were finished off; positions were discussed (I was going low for photos, Elizabeth next to me shot at eye level). Fake Eddy Merckx made his final laps as the fans grew less and less interested in pre-race theatrics. The Norwegians up on the hill stopped threatening to push each other down the slope, and leaned in closer, vastly increasing the chances of one of them falling onto the road. The front row along the rope line became positively packed.

A few vehicles started trickling past -- motos officially closing the road, official and police vehicles ready to enforce matters if anyone missed the point, which nobody did. At the lower corner a marshal manned the rope opening where people could still cross from the woods to our side, but only in theory, since our side was a suffocating wall of human flesh by now. More cars, more motos, surely the next one is the sign that the riders were here.

The real signal came from the crowd. As Boonen and Cancellara turned onto the first slope of the Kapelmuur 200 meters below, just out of our view, the crowd there burst into pandemonium, an unmistakeable cue to those of us around the corner and within earshot. Cycling can be a disappointment in person if you stand on a flat surface and the race appears and disappears in the time it takes you to reach for your camera, but standing on an ascent is another matter entirely. The race approaches slowly, as does the noise announcing its arrival. The riders go by at a pace that lets you drink in the action. If it's a serious enough climb (such as this one), the shattered pack passes in dribs and drabs, giving you time to shout out dozens of names. The slow build-up of anticipation to the long, lingering crescendo is perfect.

And when it arrived, it was everything we had hoped for. Boonen and then Cancellara appeared around the corner, onto our ramp, riding more or less in unison, Boonen visible first only because he was taking the outside line. Both riders looked like the picture of cycling heroism: Cancellara bearing the white cross on red field of the Champion of Switzerland; Boonen in his Belgian flag color scheme, wide vertical bands of red, yellow and black *driekleur* that match so well with the brooding spring landscape. Two giants wrapped in their colorful flags, symbols of excellence and pride, digging deep as they swung into view, shoulder to shoulder, gliding up the stones with uncommon dignity.

Our view. One moment, dead even; the next, Cancellara pulls away. Photos by Elizabeth Freer

Then it happened. Watching them approach us they really were in a dead heat, but inside their respective quadriceps the Tour of Flanders was being won and lost in this very instant. With no chasers in range, we turned to watch them climb the rest of our section of stones, and with each pedal stroke it became clear that Cancellara was inching ahead.

We screamed instinctively, god knows what -- I can't recall practically anything I would have yelled. One of their names? "GO!"? "OMIGOD!"? A stream of profanity? I have no idea, because primal excitement was in complete possession of my brain. Through the fog of this war, though, we saw it: at the top of the road, where the riders turn left to go past the pub, Cancellara disappeared. And Boonen... well, Boonen wobbled just a bit. It was a good five seconds after we lost sight of the Swiss Bear before Boonen too was gone. There was no mistaking what we were witnessing. Cancellara had won the Muur, and maybe the entire race.

Later Boonen would say that he suffered a cramp, right in front of us. Undoubtedly true, but there was more to it than a mere misstep inside his circulatory system. He was weakening, if ever so slightly. By the time the duo descended the other side of the Muur, Cancellara was 30 seconds ahead, and Boonen would never see him again.

Back on the Muur we screamed various versions of "Cancellara just dropped Boonen!" at each other until the message settled into our brains. By this time Gilbert and Leukemans swung into view and the screaming rose back up again. If I can recall (and that's a big "if" considering the scrambling effect the race was having on my brain) the noise simply kept going with no break.

Gilbert and Leukemans. Photo by Chris Fontecchio

As we finished screaming at Gilbert and Leukemans, our neighbors on the lower slope were already starting to scream for the next group, Brit David Millar, followed by four riders led by American George Hincapie. As this foursome climbed out of view, a larger group came up, including Lance Armstrong and... er, who cares? Lance was in the house![121] Stijn Devolder was in the same mix: strong, but not strong enough to secure his place in history.

The parade was on: rider after rider who are household names in the cycling world, if not necessarily for winning in Ninove. This is partly the monument effect, where the sport's greatest riders all come to the greatest races, whether they are suited for them or not. This is also partly de Ronde. Ask any Tour de France hero what he's doing on the cobbles in April, and he'll almost certainly tell you, this race is special. The history, the fans, the difficulty, the technical nature, it's all a draw to anyone who rides a bike for a living. Standing in the middle of it, watching the ashen faces go by on bikes bouncing magically up the brutal slopes, in a deafening roar of humanity, you get it. You totally get it.

It was a good ten minutes before the last riders came through -- a mix of spent helpers, outgunned newcomers or second-division guys, and skinny climbers out of their element. Even on this holy day of cycling, there was no shortage of guys just along for the ride. Cycling's rules require that the very best races, making up the UCI Pro Tour (now "World Tour") calendar, invite all the Pro Tour teams, including Spanish and

---

[121] A few centuries ago, seeing Lance still evoked positive feelings. Also, American fans probably should care, because behind Lance was Tyler Farrar, who would go on to finish fifth on the day, a high point of his career to date.

Italian squads for whom Flanders is no great priority. Even here you'll find competent guys, but consider the (now defunct) Euskaltel-Euskadi squad of Basque climbing specialists. No disrespect intended, but statistically speaking, the ninth guy on their Flanders startlist had as much chance of winning that day as I did.

Same went for some of the second-division riders, guys from Pro Continental-level teams not included in the Pro Tour. An invite to the Tour of Flanders means more to a less heralded Belgian team than anything short of a start in the Tour de France. On this day the peloton included Belgian squads Topsport Vlaanderen and Landbouwkrediet, Dutch teams Vacansoleil and Skil-Shimano, as well as the ubiquitous Cervelo Test Team. Collectively, these squads could be counted on to produce a rider or three whose impact on the race wouldn't go unnoticed. One or two top-ten placings is not unusual for the Pro-Conti set. But their depth is another matter, and the bottom-rung additions to their roster are guys who won't be in sight of the helicopters by the race's last hour, either having lost their way or spent themselves running bottles.

After everyone had filed past, Pete's Blackberry kept us up on the main event, as we began walking down to the upper square of Geraardsbergen, the top of the old Muur, where a giant TV screen broadcast the finish. Cancellara's lead was going out steadily, and having seen this film before, we knew how it would end. The local hero had no chance of slaying the foreign dragon.

This is not literally true, I suppose, but almost. Cancellara on his own was at this point the best in the world, a guy whose technique and position and cornering were all so precise as to make pursuit nearly pointless. If Boonen could match him pedalstroke for pedalstroke, he would probably lose a good 2-3 seconds per kilometer on technique alone (and Boonen's technique is pretty solid). To bridge the gap, Boonen would have to be just that much stronger, or Cancellara would have to crack. Given what we witnessed on the Muur, neither of these outcomes seemed a remote possibility.

This is not to diminish what Boonen did on this day. As a former winner and all-round uber-champion, Boonen would not be seen by anybody in Belgium in any sort of realistic light, but cramps and all Tommeke was putting the wood to the entire rest of the sport on this day. Gilbert, moments away from beginning his ascent to the very top of cycling,[122] never saw Boonen after the Molenberg. Stijn Devolder, owner of the previous two wins largely by sneaking out of the shadow of his illustrious teammate, was nowhere near Boonen's class today. Ballan, Flecha, Hincapie, the other cobbled heroes, Lance freaking Armstrong -- none of them could do anything to contain Boonen.

Boonen himself was closer to victory than it seemed. What if he didn't cramp? Could he have clung to Cancellara's wheel over the top, back down the Muur, and over the Bosberg? Because if he did, he was a pretty good bet to win. In light of his performance it's clear the difference in strength wasn't

---

[122] In 2010 Gilbert was coming off a historic accomplishment the previous fall, winning the "Autumn Double" of Paris-Tours and the Giro di Lombardia, two very prestigious and completely different races which had only been won by the same rider once before (Jo de Roo, 1962). In 2011 Gilbert would top that feat, and then some, becoming the first rider to win the quartet of Brabantse Pijl, Amstel Gold, La Flèche Wallonne and Liège-Bastogne-Liège in the span of two weeks. Sixteen months and a few million dollars later, he won the 2013 road world championship. If the quality of a win is as good as the people you beat, then this was one heck of a victory.

great, and sitting on Cancellara's wheel was well within Boonen's ability. If it came to the last 100 meters, it almost certainly would have fallen to Boonen. Cancellara doesn't have a sprinter's closing speed, so his sprinting technique consists of going full-bore from 300 or so meters out from the line — more of an attack than a traditional sprint — forcing the faster guys into the uncomfortable position of raising their speed too early or watching Cancellara finish off the attack. But Boonen's strengths are pretty similar to Cancellara's. If he could stay close, avoid the mishap he committed in Harelbeke, the sprint would have been his to win.

But a terrible win it would be. Even the home crowd would be challenged to celebrate a win where their rider, in Flanders of all places, wheel-sucks his way to glory. To the purist fans, Boonen's cramp was a painfully righteous gift from above, sparing us of any ambiguity in the outcome of this race. Cancellara was the strongest guy in Flanders that day, to the doubt of nobody, not even Boonen. The final gap was over a minute (+1.15), and the only drama on the finishing straight of the race was Cancellara's victory celebration, where he produced an angel pendant from his back pocket that his daughter had given him. He held the pendant out for the cameras and fans, kissed it, grabbed a Swiss flag from the VIP crowd along the finish, and soft-pedaled across the line in delirium, to applause that exceeded merely polite levels.

Back at the Muur, we drank in the scene, literally. Which is to say, we descended from our spot to the square along the broad-boulevard reach of the old Muur and commenced drinking at a make-shift cafe. If beer constituted our "effort" today, this was a cool-down Jupiler. Some of the locals were

drunk, including one older guy who clung vainly to consciousness and his seat, but I personally felt little effect. For whatever reason, I rarely feel drunk, as my brain tends to skip the fun part and head straight for hung over. And 20 minutes of screaming kept my body processing toxins faster than I could replace them. Pete, Jens, Mark, Jim, Elizabeth, Ewoud, the Antipodeans... we mostly just chatted calmly and exchanged looks of disbelief at what we had just experienced. Of 262km of racing, we stood at the exact spot on the course where the race was decided. The setting was the one you hope for, the iconic Kapelmuur, the most beautiful slope the great race has to offer. You couldn't make up a better outcome for us. In 2011 the race came down to a home-stretch sprint and by 2012 the Muur was removed from the reconfigured Ronde -- which made our experience the last great moment on the Muur, for now.
*****

Cancellara's feat had one amusing sidebar to it. When riders dominate other dominant riders like never before, it can be a bit of a struggle to accept the reality of it. Nowadays the usual response would consist of fans openly questioning whether the winner rode without performance enhancing substances. It's an ugly thought, even under the most tempting conditions (i.e. a guy you never heard of suddenly rocketing up Alpe d'Huez), but cycling has made its bed here.

In Cancellara's case, however, a rider of his stature couldn't be torn down in this way. He was already too great and too well-liked for all but the most hardened cynics to go there. Instead, the whisper campaign focused on whether Cancellara had hidden a motor in the down-tube of his bike, flicking it on as he rounded the corner below us and using it to propel him past his helplessly non-motorized rival. Apart from being theoretically possible, the entire affair seemed pretty tongue-in-cheek from the start.

Quickly a Zapruder-esque video began making the Youtube rounds. You can see his finger flex… *right there*! Websites (like mine) debated not so much whether the rumor was true but whether to dignify it with a response. The story reached its apex when Jered Gruber, reporting and shooting photos for Pez Cycling News, got a chance to probe Cancellara's bike just hours after the race as part of a photo shoot. [By some massive coincidence, the rumor swirled around the so-called Gruber Assist, a battery-operated mini-motor that could fit inside a seat tube, and no relation to the writer.] Gruber argued rather convincingly that if there was a motor that weighed as much as a rather clunky third wheel concealed inside the down-tube of an ultra-light professional racing steed, it would have been hard for him to miss. I also liked the part about how the Gruber Assist requires a 31.6mm opening, but the seat tube of the Specialized Tarmac Cancellara rode that day had 27.2mm of space. In the world of cycling conspiracies, it's the little things that matter.

Anyway, most people laughed it off for a while, but six weeks later when people were still discussing it, disgust set in. Boonen's manager Patrick Lefevre called the possibility "outright theft" if true and called for the UCI to investigate, which they refused to do in this case, though they spoke cryptically of future bike screenings to combat "motorized doping," and claimed to have met with the manufacturer to investigate further. I wish I could say I were joking.[123]

Apart from this sideshow, Cancellara's victory was greeted warmly in Flanders. A supporters bar was located in Antwerp, and the Swiss winner could be seen on TV Monday sipping a beer the size of Lake Geneva amidst his Belgian fans. The scene caused me to do a double-take -- Antwerp is in the direction of Boonen's hometown of Balen, 50 kilometers to the east, and the idea of Boonen's neighbors convening to celebrate his conqueror was jarring to me. Does this happen in sports? Would the Red Sox stop off in Brooklyn to hang with a pub full of locals and celebrate a milestone victory over the Yankees? Not if anyone, including the locals, valued their life. In the entire universe of stick-and-ball sports, it's hard to conjure up a plausible parallel occurrence.

But cycling is different from baseball, or football, or soccer, or cricket, or any of the other sports people follow passionately and occasionally riot over. In cycling, the riders don't represent a geographic locale *per se*. They can expect a lot of support from their home town or region, like anyone else in popular culture. And some teams work to cultivate a geographic identity, like the former Basque Euskaltel team or the Russian Katusha team or the Topsport Vlaanderen squad of emerging young Belgians. Most top teams, however, are melting pots, and often their sponsors and licenses are equally lacking in a clear geographic link. Moreover, riders go where their best chances to win or get paid lie, not where they can hang with

---

[123] Such small motors do exist, and in 2016 one was found in the frame of a bike belonging to a woman riding for the Belgian national team in the 2016 Cyclocross Women's World Championship. Femke Van Den Driessche was disqualified and retired before she could receive a lifetime or lesser ban for this episode.

their *paesani*. Even if you're Dutch and you prefer Dutch riders, chances are there are at least three or four teams which interest you. The supporters' bond to a single team that happens in practically every other sport isn't really there in cycling. The bond to a single rider isn't there either; you could love Tom Boonen more than life itself, but when the Giro d'Italia or Liege-Bastogne-Liege is on and Tom's home resting, you'll probably find someone else to root for just as passionately.

At the risk of psychoanalyzing the entire population of a country where I don't live, I suspect something else is going on that explains Cancellara's warm welcome. The locals aren't just friendly folk (though that's certainly one defining characteristic); their celebration of the Swiss Bear is tied to the fact that he is, in essence, celebrating them. If teams are increasingly international, then the one element of cycling for local fans to truly identify with are the roads. The passion that Cancellara and so many of the other foreign riders bring to Flanders is a deep appreciation for the physical shape of *de Ronde*. Ask practically any classics rider you meet what they think of the race, and I'm nearly certain they will gush with adoration about the course and the fans, in either order. This is especially true of the top contenders, who dedicate themselves to being adapted to the cobbles. The result is kind of a love-in, by traditionally bitter sporting standards. Instead of fans celebrating their town by rooting for the athletes, it's the athletes who are celebrating the fans' town, and the fans' task is to just enjoy it. So when a rider honors the race as Cancellara did by winning in grand style, what's not for the Belgian fans to like?

2010 Tour of Flanders

Men's Results:

1. Fabian Cancellara, Team Saxo Bank, 262.3km in 6:25.56
2. Tom Boonen, Quick Step, at 1.15
3. Philippe Gilbert, Omega Pharma-Lotto, at 2.11
4. Bjorn Leukemans, Vacansoleil, at 2.15
5. Tyler Farrar, Garmin-Transitions, at 2.35
6. George Hincapie, BMC, s.t.
7. Roger Hammond, Cervelo Test Team, s.t.
8. Maxim Iglinsky, Astana, s.t.
9. Danilo Hondo, Lampre-Farnese Vini, s.t.
10. William Bonnet, Bbox Bouygues Telecom, s.t.

Women's Results:

1. Grace Verbeke, Lotto Ladies Team, 119km in 3:09.27
2. Marianne Vos, Nederland Bloeit, at 0.03
3. Kirsten Wild, Cervelo Test Team, s.t.
4. Emma Johansson, Redsun Cycling Team, s.t.
5. Adrie Visser, HTC Columbia Women, s.t.
6. Chantal Blaak, Leontien.nl, s.t.
7. Noemi Cantele, HTC Columbia Women, s.t.
8. Judith Arndt, HTC Columbia Women, s.t.
9. Regina Bruins, Cervelo Test Team. at 0.08
10. Annemiek Van Vleuten, Nederland Bloeit, at 0.51

11: Dottignies, and the Women Take Charge

The great exhale came the day after the Tour of Flanders. Now in country for nearly two weeks, almost none of it standing still, I took the opportunity to hang around the flat for a few hours blogging and doing nothing much, while Pete and Mark went for a ride. It was a national holiday in Belgium, the day after Easter, or perhaps the day after De Ronde, but in any event few shops were open, and food wasn't happening except at a pub, a hotel or maybe a random truck.

Cycling was happening, however. We had ourselves an afternoon date, across the language border in a francophone town called Dottignies, tucked into Hainault province just steps from where Flanders and Wallonia meet France. The elite women's peloton was reassembling itself (for the most part) to attack the gentle, rolling terrain of Hainault. In short, it was time to go a-racin'.

Let's back up. Women's cycling, if I may be permitted a few gross generalizations, is a rather small but growing counterpart to the men's world. Cash, sponsorship and races are often in a state of crisis, and comprehensive, stabilizing solutions seem forever just out of reach. But for the most part there exists an exciting, growing calendar of events and a serviceable slate of teams to contest them. The sport has a handful of megastars, enough to drive the narrative, and the racing is, well, it's racing. What's not to love?

The calendar has a full dose of Italian and Belgian events, a particularly strong Dutch influence, and important races in places like Sweden and Germany that are poorly served by the dudes' scene. France is also important, while Spain has much less of a presence than its men's version. And the English-speaking countries are gaining steam.

I suppose you could broadly put the women's events into four categories:

1.   The Grand Tours

The biggest race on the women's calendar is the Giro d'Italia Femminile, or the Giro Rosa (formerly Giro Donne, the Tour of Italy for women). Sponsored by the Epinike Sports Club and the Region of Lombardia government, the Giro Rosa has been going strong since 1993 -- forever in women's cycling. Every year the race covers up to ten stages, generally ending up north after coming from, well, almost any direction. In a week and a half the race can't cover the entire boot, but it's stable, it includes serious alpine climbing (Mortirolo Pass in 2016), and draws the best field in the world. TV coverage, the lifeline of women's cycling, is hard to get live, but RAI, Italy's national broadcast network, shows extensive highlights.

The Tour de France Féminine existed for a while, until the Tour de France told them to stop using their name. Then it became the Grand Boucle, before losing its sponsorship and disappearing in 2010. Since then the race has been revived, or a race anyway, as La Route de France Féminine, which made its debut in August, 2012. With the demise of the prestigious and long-running Tour de l'Aude, France is struggling to sustain a "grand tour." The Route de France has run four editions since the 2011 race was canceled, including a mountainous 2012 version with the final three stages held in the Vosges region, and a return to the fearsome Planche des Belles Filles, a steep 6km ascent averaging 8.5% gradient in 2015.

For 2014, the Tour de France's organizers, ASO, began hosting a women's race in Paris called La Course by Le Tour de France, hours before the Tour de France itself rolls into town -- a first crack in the wall that has stood between the women's peloton and cycling's mega-companies. The format was repeated in 2015, either a good sign that 2014's edition worked, or a bad sign that ASO didn't see fit to expand beyond a single day. Still, ASO taking up the sport's mantle in France is a game-changer. But on what level is to be determined.

Germany, meanwhile, fills the void with the Thuringen Rundfahrt der Frauen, a week-long trip through the Free State of Thuringia. Less mountainous than the Giro Donne, the Thuringen Rundfahrt is more of an all-rounders Tour, featuring plenty of climbing if not anything made famous by the men's field. It too has been on shaky ground, with the 2014 schedule placing it a day after the start of the Giro Donne, forcing riders to choose one or the other, though in 2016 it comes comfortably five days later, leads into the Olympics in August, and should continue to attract a very strong field.

2. Major Races Associated with Men's Races

One regular suggestion on the endless forums concerning "how to save women's cycling" is "by running it with the men." The thinking is that if you're running a men's race, it only serves the cause of equality to run a women's race. Women's cycling could use the support, and tapping into the worldwide viewing audience for men's racing is a logical place to start. The quality of the racing is high, often more exciting than a lot of men's races, so if you expose the fan pool to the women's events, the racing will sell itself.

Flanders peloton on the Muur. Photo by Elizabeth Freer

But it's not just optics; there are some major practical advantages as well. Pro races bring road closures, a significant use of manpower, material and money (for barriers, vehicles, police patrols, insurance policies, etc.). So why not have a women's race before the men take over the road, and take advantage of all that's been set up already -- the roads, the staging areas (start, finish, podium, etc.), the media. Two for the price of one, or one and a quarter maybe. Heck there are even heli and moto cameras on hand, sending pictures to network trucks for beaming out to you and me. Obviously this plays into the media too, which is the key to the survival of cycling, men or women. Sponsors only pony up because they want exposure to help their brand. Holding a women's race in obscurity is far less attractive than being an hour or so up the road from the men's Tour of Flanders, while helicopters circle around Belgium looking for something to show.

The downside is that the women wind up serving as the opening act to the main event, which could be interpreted as second-class citizenship. Now, let's be frank, women's cycling *is* second-class to the men right now, in races like the Tour of Flanders. Not because of the athletes or the races, but simply because they don't have anywhere near the legacy of their dude counterparts, now entering (or well into) its second century. The money gap, the TV gap, the fanhood gap -- it's all there, and while usually it's pointless to think in terms of these comparisons, holding the races together forces you to.

But the women hold up their end, looking like they belong on the big stage, and IMHO on balance, the benefits of having at least some events teamed up with the men outweigh the negatives. So far, the Belgians are the best at taking advantage of this natural efficiency. The Tour of Qatar, Tour of Flanders, Gent-Wevelgem, Omloop Het Nieuwsblad, La Fleche Wallonne, Dwars door Vlaanderen and the GP Ouest

France-Plouay are the biggest names sharing their facilities (including organization) with a women's event, along with the Tour de France dipping its toe in the water, as mentioned above. Calls go out for more and more of these. In most cases TV coverage happens to some extent or another. A half-hour highlights show is the industry standard, but some live video isn't unheard-of, and the GP Ouest France-Plouay features full live coverage, adding to the excitement of one of my favorite events, a rolling classic around the cycling-mad province of Brittany.

3.   National Team Events

The biggest single-day showcases on the calendar are the Olympic women's road race and time trial, every four years, and the annual UCI World Cycling Championships. These races benefit from their prestige, but they also step out of the shadow of the men's scene, devoting whole race days or large portions thereof to the women's events. No need to make reference to the men's race coming up from behind, or to the men's scene at all. Just the women in the spotlight, all by themselves.

The races themselves are big-time events. Both hosts -- the UCI for its championships and the Olympics -- have set the ladies up for full live TV coverage, on par with the men's events. Nowadays the Olympic Movement seems to draw more attention to humanity's flaws than to its possibilities, but it can still be counted on to showcase numerous sports, particularly women's events, which otherwise go overlooked. And the UCI World Cycling Championships are an annual high-point for both competition and attention. For road cycling, the

Olympics and Worlds courses are monument-level challenges, and the tendency in both cases is to rig the course to draw out the climbers and sprinters equally. Lots of access for fans, lots of action to watch, and they give a fancy jersey or a medal to the winner. What's not to like?

The wrinkle is that both are national team formats, where riders are assembled by country and divorced from their trade team alliances in favor of national unity. It's a mixed bag. Women's cycling can't muster this kind of stage very often, and it would be nice for some of the big trade team races to get this same level of prestige (Trofeo Alfredo Binda maybe?), as a way to strengthen the sponsorship the athletes so desperately need.[124] Also, year-long trade teams foster deep relationships, leading to strong team tactics, while national teams assemble just for a week or two at season's end and may or may not meld into a coherent unit. But it's good to have these events setting the bar high.

4.   Best of the Rest

And then there's everything else. Like today's race, the GP de Dottignies. It's a circuit race, with a *grand circuit*[125] looping around Mouscron and East Flanders, taking in some 77km, before homing back to Dottignies for four shorter loops over the local 14km circuit, ending on a long, slightly uphill drag over the Rue du Meunier just south of the town center. It's a

---

[124] National teams sometimes enjoy a decent level of sponsorship, but they can be a pretty poor substitute at other times. USA Cycling isn't known for being terribly lavish or effective, for reasons I haven't bothered to explore, but American trade teams like BMC or Trek are very much among the elite programs. The point is, trade-team cycling is the sport's foundation and national team events are outliers in many ways. So for the latter to get prime TV coverage and the former to go begging is a very weird way to present the sport.

[125] My command of French is impressive, *non*?

day for sprinters, but the course is long and rolling, exposed to the wind, and the sprint itself is no cakewalk.

We arrived in Dottignies sometime during the *grand circuit*, parked the car about three blocks away from the first sign of a street closure, and strolled up to the finish area. A few hundred people were milling around, lining the Rue du Meunier around the one block of open space between the main street and the Rijzendezonstraat, where a beer truck and sausage vendor had set up shop for the day.

It wasn't hard to find the people in charge, who then permitted me a spot to shoot pictures and gave me a startlist, which itself was a clue to life at the GP Dottignies. The first draft was studded with many of the biggest names in women's cycling, but coming a day after the exhausting and monumental Ronde van Vlaanderen, the rosters were replete with strikeouts and names added. The spring classics season is packed with important races and if you're a petite climber ill-suited to the flats around Mouscron, you might hedge your bets in Dottignies. Several riders fitting that bill (such as the previous day's winner Grace Verbeke) started the race but dropped out when they'd accomplished their goal, presumably a stretch of the legs as a way to recover from the yesterday and get ready for tomorrow.

But if that sounds disrespectful to the GP Dottignies, a) that's cycling, and b) making way for the sprinters and the powerful teams is no disgrace. Particularly when those teams consist (in 2010) of the Cervelo Test Team juggernaut, Nederland Bloeit, and others, and the sprinters' peloton consists of Giorgia

Bronzini (just before her run of consecutive world titles), Italian Champion Monica Baccaille, and Dutch sprinter Kirsten Wild.

Belgian champion Ludovic Henrion at GP Dottignies. Photo by Chris Fontecchio

Respect for women's cycling is an ongoing topic of discussion, on forums like the Podium Cafe and practically every other outlet with a taste for the sport. There isn't anything resembling consensus on the main topics -- how to structure the races, how to make sure riders get paid, how to maximize sponsorship potential, how to get the sport better exposure, and so on. The exception, the one thing there is consensus on, is that the sport deserves a better fate. This is more or less fact, considering there are frequent stories of riders unable to count on making enough money to continue as pro cyclists. Whether you think they should embody the Olympian ideal or whether they should cash in big time like the boys, I guess that gets us back to arguing again. But without question, the sport deserves at least enough support to keep itself afloat.

Apart from the inevitable physiological differences between women and men, which translate in cycling to shorter races and less ferocious climbs for the ladies, there are few visible differences in women's racing. Riders turn themselves inside out, physically and emotionally, in search of victory, riding at speeds that seem frightening to us mortals. Technical proficiency is pitted against terrifying risk. Strategy varies hardly at all from the men's version; if anything the women seem to hold back a bit less, thanks to the shorter times and distances involved. Charismatic stars drive the narratives -- like Dutch megachampion Marianne Vos, the friendly, mild-mannered cannibal; or Emma Pooley, a pint-sized attacking British climber who retired from the sport on top to complete her PhD (in geotechnical engineering); or Evie Stevens, the wide-smiling American former investment banker whose positivity has driven her to the sport's summit in seemingly no time,[126] or Pauline Ferrand-Prevot, an emerging French star

---

[126] Stevens kicked off her 2016 campaign by setting the Hour Record, a traditional cycling milestone consisting of seeing how far you can ride in an hour. Hour record attempts have to be in velodromes, to normalize things, as opposed to getting on an open road and riding a tailwind to the record books. And the record underwent radical changes as aerodynamic bike shapes departed from the traditional setup. Nowadays, however, we are back to a unified record that allows typical time trial bikes, with a standard shaped frame, aero bars and disc wheels. Stevens rode 47.98km in an hour, shattering the record of Bridie O'Donnell set barely a month earlier.

who is currently her nation's champion in road racing, time trialling, mountain biking and cyclocross.

So what's holding it back? I'll dodge the specifics, out of deference to your sanity and mine, apart from acknowledging the gender gap that prevails throughout humankind. Perhaps the biggest *legitimate* difference between men's and women's cycling, though, is history. In fact, women and bicycles do not lack history; the American cycling craze of the late 19th century coincided with the early days of the modern women's movement, and the ladies took to their bicycles as a sign of, or result of, their increased freedom and stature. But the heady days of Six-Days at Madison Square Garden dead-ended in the Depression, and women's liberation evolved without the bicycle's help.

Subsequently, professional women's racing at the big-time level didn't take off much before the 1980s. The Tour de France Feminin debuted in 1984, as did the Olympic women's road race. The Giro Rosa only goes back to 1988. The women's Tour of Flanders traces itself all the way back to 2004. The UCI World Championships for women's road racing ran its inaugural event in 1958. The Trofeo Alfredo Binda started in 1974. The GP de Plouay began in 1999. Obviously these events didn't invent the sport itself; they reflected a sufficient level of development among the races that had undoubtedly gone on for some time before someone said in the 1950s that we should think about having a women's world championships. Regardless, though, this history simply isn't of a kind with the men's events, the largest of which are all in the midst of celebrating their 100th anniversary. If the men's scene is on a completely different scale than the women's, there are some reasons for that, ranging from disappointing to shameful, but all else being (truly) equal, it's possible that women's cycling would be a lot closer to the men's scene if it too had a century's worth of stories to tell. By this token, the good days are coming, and a century from now this dichotomy will be a dim memory. It's just a question of when.[127]

Dottignies sprint for the line. Photo by Chris Fontecchio

Like most sprinters' races, the GP Dottignies can sound dull and unworthy of much description in hindsight, with breaks going out and coming back before the inevitable last kilometer leadouts and sprints. But like most sprinters' races, that would sell the action quite a bit short. In reality, being a one-day race (in Belgium no less), and with some tricks to the course, the possibility of a breakaway victory was real. And to the extent a sprint was likely, well, the disadvantaged teams weren't taking

---

[127] Worth mentioning: in 2016, the Oudenaarde Grote Markt (main square) drew a crowd as large or larger than it did for the race start in 2010... for the previous day's team presentation. The fact that women's cycling is now having team presentations the day before the actual race is itself telling.

it lying down. Nederland Bloeit had Annemiek Van Vleuten, now one of the sport's brightest stars, up the road for much of the local circuits. Cervelo marked her with Sharon Laws, and when that duo came back, Cervelo flexed another muscle by putting Liselot Decroix on a break, allowing their sprinter Wild and her helpers to relax a bit in the final 20 minutes. All these moves and countermoves played into Cervelo's hands perfectly, and Wild, a big, powerful sprinter, finished the job by a couple bike lengths over the two Italians.

Kirsten Wild celebrates Dottignies win. Photo by Mark Blacknell

This was a textbook bike race, full of chess games and hard riding, limited only slightly by the presence of a monument the day before. A big team flexed its muscles and won. Two more distant foreigners kept it close, but didn't have enough cards to play. All of this we watched from the front row.

Women's cycling has all the ingredients for success baked into the batter. Fans of the men don't have to like it, but if they think about what they love about watching men's cycling and approach the women's game with an open mind, they should have no trouble getting interested.

Grand Prix de Dottignies Results:
1. Kirsten Wild, Cervelo Test Team
2. Giorgia Bronzini, Safi – Pasta Zara, s.t.
3. Monia Baccaille, Team Valdarno Umbria, s.t.
4. Emma Johnasson, Red Sun, s.t.
5. Martine Bras, Gauss Rdz Ormu – Colnago, s.t.

Photo by Chris Fontecchio

12: The Fietsroutes, Belgium's Network of Cycling Routes

By Tuesday after *de Ronde* life began to slow down to a more survivable pace. The after-Easter bank holiday was done (and we could buy actual food again). Two days of races and the cyclosportive were in the books. For the first time since I arrived in Belgium, I woke up with nothing in particular to do.

Same went for Pete, so of course we immediately started planning our redemption ride, i.e. the ride to make up for all the climbs we meant to complete Saturday if there hadn't been so many other people in the way. It was a gorgeous day, mild and clear, and Tiffany from London was poking around for some riding company.

Mind you, nobody was proposing another marathon day in the saddle, a reprise of Saturday; 40-50 miles would be enough, with the goal of getting up some of the climbs we couldn't ride in style the first time -- namely, the Paterberg, Koppenberg and Muur. That left endless options on the table, except we all agreed we had to get back to Geraardsbergen, to the east, and we all wanted revenge on the Paterberg, to the west. Just those two items from the menu would entail a good three hours of riding, so we left the other details as blanks to be filled in along the way.

By way of the Oude Kwaremont we were at the Paterberg within a half hour. We approached from the north, as the race does, along the quiet, two-lane Stooktestraat, a pretty tree-lined road from which you can spy the famous Paterberg fenceline ascending to the right as you come into range. The stones themselves aren't especially visible, and the hill would just look like a steeply sloping field if not for the fence, which climbs in sharply staggered sections that show just how far from level the surface is.

Still approaching, the road twists one last time before reaching this intersection of Belgian solitude and cobbled hell. A signpost points you upward, and the climb shifts into gear within a few pedalstrokes. The stones on this day were touched by nothing more than the sun's rays, the Cycling Gods' way of saying "if not today, when?" Being in OK shape, not terribly heavy, and a grinder by nature, I was more or less prepared when the slope hit 20% and stayed there for a few turns. Even when the road relaxed a bit, it was still double digits, on the cobbles, all the way to the top. But I was ready.

My guess is that guys like me get over the Paterberg all the time, for one main reason: you can see the top. At 325 meters in length, and a straight line with a next to no shade cover, you can peek up ahead and tell yourself that the searing pain in your legs won't be around much longer. There is no respite before the top, just a solid block of anaerobic grinding. I made it, turned left onto the tarmac where there's a dirt patch opening by the roadside before the trees close in again, and spent the next five minutes catching my breath.

Photo by Chris Fontecchio

Aerobically, this is a max effort climb, harder on the lungs than the legs, though just barely. To this day I believe it's the hardest 300-meter effort of any of the regularly featured Ronde hellingen, even if it's less tricky than some of the other headliners. You can will yourself to the top, as I did, but without rhythm, without any mellower ramps where you can slowly take your effort up and/or down to mitigate the effect of the brutal midsection. One minute your strolling through the valley, then for 60 seconds or so you're killing it, then you're done. With no buffers, the effect is akin to blunt force trauma.

Pete had led the way, and made it more or less the same way I did. Tiffany came last, and I stopped for a few photos while she approached. The top of the Paterberg is one of the few places along the route with a notable vista, in this case of fields and Oudenaarde and the dour-looking Ruien Power Plant in Kluisbergen.

Rather than taking in the other nearby climbs, like the Koppenberg or Taaienberg, we decided to head straight for Brakel and regroup for the Muur. At least, until Opbrakel, where we peeled off to see if we could use quieter fietsroutes to get there, rather than the main road, which gets pretty busy and unpleasant coming through the main part of town. Ah, the Fietsroutes…
*****

The Fietsroutes are famous throughout the cycling world for providing a (mostly) pleasant way across all of Flanders. They vary from segregated pathways, of the rails-to-trails pedigree, to the shoulder of a four-lane highway. The two most typical versions are the canal routes,[128] which vary between bike-only and theoretically open to (almost nonexistent) cars, and the country lanes most beloved across the pedaling universe.

---

[128] See Chapter 2 for my day along the canals.

The Fietsnetwerk boasts over 24,000 km of designated bikeable ways (in addition to however many thousands of roads which, lacking in designation, are still highly bikeable by American standards). There is a website -- www.fietsnet.be -- where you can plan your route, clicking on any two points, prompting a list of routes to take and compilation of the distance. It's pretty slick. All of Flemish Belgium is included as well as Zuid-Holland in the Netherlands. Click on any city between Koksijde and Leiden, Maastricht and Aalst, and you'll be treated to more than enough peaceful options for pedaling your way in to, out of, and around your chosen destination. I know from reading that there are other places, like Denmark, where the options are no less awesome, but to a cyclist, if this isn't heaven, it's close enough.

And yet I can't get too far into this discussion without taking a moment to vent.[129] As great as the network is, its maps are a disaster. The Fietsroutes system is complex enough that you need a map, and not a single map, because to capture all the Fietsroutes of Flanders on a single piece of paper would require an immense piece of paper or some horribly small print.

So instead the network is embedded into a series of maps -- seven covering West Flanders, another seven covering East Flanders -- costing 6 Euros a pop. The scale is rather large, 1:50,000, making them easy to read and raising the possibility that on an ambitious day you'll need 3-4 maps if you're after complete coverage. I know I dipped (inexplicably) off the Leiestreek map from the Gent map despite not changing

---

[129] This might be a good time to jump forward a page or so.

routes, since I traversed an area where three maps met, only two of which I bought. The situation cries out for a phone app, but to date I don't see one out there. Maybe the point of it all is to sell maps.

And those maps will drive you crazy. We spent hours getting completely lost, for one simple reason: the maps put the route numbers at the intersection. Are you looking at a four-way intersection with the number 14 stamped on it? Fantastic! Now tell me, is that the number for the X-axis route or the Y-axis? Give up yet? Me too.

In practice what this means is that when you're riding you will come to an intersection, which will be very well marked as to which route goes in which direction. Maybe you're on Westhoek Fietsroute 26. You come to an intersection, Moortelweg and Briekstraat, and you see signs showing 26 heading straight while signs for 64 go left and 32 go right. You want to go to Boezinge, so you open your map.

The map shows the intersection where you are. It doesn't give any street names, and in the middle of the intersection is a green circle with "26". Does 26 end at this intersection? If so, maybe that's not where you are. Does 26 pass straight through it? If so, so does at least one other route, but it or they aren't marked at this location on the map, only 26 is. There are routes extending on the map toward each of the Four Directions. From the signs you can easily follow 26, but should you? The map says it's three km from there to another intersection with a 64 in it, very close to Boezinge. Does that mean you take 64 to get there, or that you take 26 and when you get to that intersection you'll see 64?

I can't tell you how maddening this is -- all you have to do is put the number *between* the intersections, and then I know it connects this juncture to that one -- but I can tell you that it caused us constant problems. I suppose you get to memorize routes if you live there. I also suppose, in retrospect, that we could have brought a compass, found our position on the map, determined from the map that (for example) Boezinge is to the west, and taken whichever route went west from where we stood. I further suppose that at times visual cues are available to help. Sometimes there are additional signs. Or, Boezinge is west; it's 10am so the sun is in the southeast. Or there's a highway on the map to the north, and I saw some trucks going straight.

Or! The good people of the Fietsroute Network, who have invested so much money and effort into making a truly world class system of numbered cycle-ways, complete with very slick and reasonably waterproof maps, could have labeled the routes on the map in a way which actually told you not only where you were but what route you needed to take next. Like, you know, every single auto highway map in the universe, including the Belgian ones. And no, I am not very calm right now.

[/rant]

Update! There does appear to be an iPhone app, finally, that should solve this problem, simply by placing you on the map before said intersection, so you can tell where you came from, and in turn, where you're going. It's listed under the name "Fietsknoop" and covers the entire Netherlands and the

Flemish region of Belgium. I plan to test this out in 2017 and, hopefully, put this painful experience behind me.

*****

Anyway, we took some familiar, larger routes from Greater Oudenaarde to Opbrakel, just above the descent into Brakel proper which would have linked us directly to Geraardsbergen, but by highway. So we cut north on a Fietsroute for what looked like a minor and pleasant detour which would serve up the Valkenberg as an appetizer to the our main course on the Muur, but instead sank back into a morass of Fietsroute confusion, and wound up about 10km northeast of where we intended to go, in Sint-Maria-Lierde, before doubling back to the N-route that we knew would take us to Geraardsbergen. I have no doubt in my mind that we could have done the entire day on positively lovely, quiet fietsroutes, featuring man of the climbs of de Ronde, if the map... let's move on.

As we finally managed to point ourselves to Geraardsbergen, however, instinct took over. The race route rolls into town from the west, and on the N-route connecting Brakel to Parike to Geraardsbergen you can see the village sprawling up the side of the next wrinkle of hills. No other towns of this size are around, so it's unmistakeable where you are headed. And before long the Kapelmuur is visible, the chapel itself peeking out from the forest atop the town. On a normal day, Geraardsbergen is a busy town down below and the Kapelmuur a natural escape up above, with trails disappearing into the forest from the barely-navigable cobbled roads that constitute the sport of cycling's holiest terrain.

When we reached the arching bridge across the train tracks that drops you directly into downtown Geraardsbergen, we knew it was time to conquer the Muur. All of it.

Once we got through the initial blast of urbanity down by the train tracks and the busy shopping area nearby, the traffic thinned out and the road turned upward. There was no mistaking the race route, from memory and road signs and probably some other clues that I don't remember. Were all the little lion flags swept up by then? Was the giant video screen dismantled? Can't recall. But as we hit the Old Muur, it was everyone for themselves and see you at the church.

I wasn't killing it on the lower slopes, knowing that the real trouble was waiting up above, but from the Cyclosportive I had the sense that, of all the *hellingen* where I had been forced to dismount, the Muur was the least treacherous. I *had* it on Saturday before that giant monstrosity of a guy spread his tentacles and gear across the road, and I knew I had it today. If it were raining, the *kinderkopje* of the upper slopes could have slid me off into failure with one blotch of mud on my tire. But on a beautiful day? I had this.

I turned right at the top of the Old Muur onto the narrowing approach to the Kapelmuur. The gradient stiffened but the stones weren't too demanding, until I entered the forest, the ramp just below our race-day viewing spot, the first of three brief plagues visited upon riders by the race. Now the stones were big and bumpy, but the friction was there, and as I turned left from the first ramp to the second -- our ramp, Cancellara's ramp -- the road began to test me.

Like Saturday, though, I honestly felt tingles down my spine riding over these majestic, infernal stones, knowing I had to get to the top, turn past the bar, and kick a few more times to make the summit. Pain and lactic acid mixed with euphoria and light madness, an ideal brew for any cyclist honing in on his or her goal. I simply kept turning over the pedals, because nobody and nothing was going to stop me from doing so, and whatever the cost was I was ready to pay. I'm sure I was smiling as I swung left and passed by the pub. I know I was smiling 20 seconds later when I dismounted and leaned my bike on the wall of the Chapel overlooking the Muur.

And that's all well and good... except I think this experience, like so much of cycling, sheds some light on the pros. Ask any rider and they'll tell you the Muur is special. And in the majority of cases they'll really mean it, as in, if you probe them further they'll start talking excitedly about the experience. As I mentioned earlier, it's hard but not fall-off-your-bike hard. It lasts a long, long time. But if you love the essence of the Tour of Flanders, which is so prominently on display in Geraardsbergen, then adrenaline alone will carry you 50 percent of the way up.

Which is a long way of saying, context matters, to them and to us. Flanders comes with a lot of the basic elements -- quiet, narrow, muddy, bumpy old roads -- but the layers of history and intense adoration transform places like the Muur into something unforgettable. And just because riding up it is part of your day job doesn't change things. Even if you've done 100 reps over the last two months on the Muur, being there on race day is something else. For me, being there on any day is like stepping into the batter's box at Fenway Park. We get it.

*****

A day later Pete insisted on giving the Koppenberg one more try, and I figured, why not? Truthfully, I was nervous about it. Two attempts gave me little confidence about the third time being the charm. On the plus side, I'd had a backpack on for the first attempt -- not the kit of a serious *hellingen* rider -- and the second was wiped out by other people getting stuck in front of me. Even more importantly was my sense of shame for not trying again. Turns out I was more afraid of not trying than of what would happen if I did. But the reality is that I didn't think I had the legs. I didn't think I could push through that much pain.

But I made it this time -- the mud had dried out considerably, leaving the gradient as the only serious obstacle to getting up. It was close; my legs were locking up toward the summit, but I made it. The reality is that when it's dry, it's far easier. I got through the bottom section, with the gradient ticking up to 9%... 12%... 14%... and it wasn't killing me. I hit the deadly 22% trench, and that hurt. But the difference was that I could keep turning the pedals and my back wheel would push onward. No slippage meant that as long as I didn't lock up I was in control of my destiny. The gradient was no longer a treacherous nightmare, but just a big, beautiful block of suffering. That I could handle, for a little bit anyway.

I ground my way up the gut of the climb, one revolution at a time, til the slope eased off a bit. At that point my legs were screaming, but knowing you've survived the hard part has the effect of sealing the deal. No cyclist is going to get that far and give in to the pain. Physically speaking, there is no relief as the road goes from madness to 11% with not much end in sight. Not even a whiff of recovery, even for someone in way better shape than me. But the psychological lift of knowing you won't slip out in the mud and there's nobody else to knock you over, well... you're not stopping. End of story, and if your legs don't like it they can sod off.

Finally I crested the hill, as the 11% backs off to a barely perceptible false flat, a point where you can safely call it a done deal. I pulled over to wait for Pete. A couple guys in a truck were watching, while sipping coffee on a break from some task. Maybe working on the farm that lives next to the Kopp. When I made the summit, they gave me a little cheer. Like there was something in my body language, a combination of accomplishment and oxygen debt, that brought out their show of support. Or maybe everyone in Flanders has the same regard for a cyclist cresting the Kopp. You just cheer, like cheering your kid's first soccer goal. You just do it. Me, I heard "welcome to the club of guys who got up the Koppenberg" in that cheer. It's silly and unimportant if you really think about it, but that was exactly what I'd hoped for.

13: Schoten and the Grote Scheldeprijs

Our last full day in Belgium may have started with that one last assault of the Koppenberg, but it ended like any good day in Flanders... standing by the side of the road watching a bike race. Today was the palate-cleansing Scheldeprijs, the Schelde Prize, named after the river whose banks graze the first few kilometers of the course. For years it's been a bit of an afterthought to the infinitely more demanding cobbled marches of Flanders and northern France. There are some cobbles, but look up "Oelegembaan" and "Broekstraat" on YouTube and prepare to laugh. Yes, there are "cobbles." No, they are nothing to worry about. Compared to the Holleweg these stretches of road look like a putting green.

But the race does fit several useful purposes. First, it celebrates Antwerp, the country's second-largest city, and one of the cultural and historical hubs of western Europe. The Schelde (or l'Escaut in French) means shallow river, a modest descriptor for a 350-km waterway that has been fought over periodically since the days of Rome. The river, connecting Dutch Zeeland, Antwerp, Gent, the Vlaamse Ardennen, and Valenciennes in France, always served as a way move freight, passengers and the various other elements. This all combined to make Antwerp the richest city in Europe some 400 years ago... which in turn, of course, got them in a heap of trouble. The Spanish Inquisition came calling, looking for gold or lost souls or both, and left enough of an impression that, according to the internet gnomes, people still refer to each other as "sinjoren," the Dutch revision of "señor". In both 20th century world wars, the Schelde provided a means for shipping goods in Flanders and northern France, largely in the hands of the Entente/Allies... except for around Antwerp, of which the German army took frequent control. The effort by Canadian forces to reopen the river in the Battle of the Schelde was one of the war's late highlights. Or harbingers, depending on your perspective.

Anyway, the river and the surrounding region have more than enough to celebrate, starting with the fact that nobody is under siege at the moment. And as far as cycling is concerned, the sport's roots are well anchored in Antwerp Province, with stars like Rik Van Steenbergen and Tom Boonen to boast about. De Ronde studiously avoids the area, to the point where the local media, via the Gazet van Atwerpen, has agitated for a Ronde van Antwerpen. Dunno about that; if the promo video featuring Geert Omloop is any indication, the climbs and cobbles are a pale imitation of the proper Ronde. And besides, the area already has a race that tells its story quite clearly. That's the race we were headed for that Wednesday.

Born in 1907, the Scheldeprijs might not get the headlines, but it is in fact the oldest current race in Flanders, surpassed in Belgium by only Liege-Bastogne-Liege and Paris-Brussels. When Karel van Wijnendaele was casting about for an emblematic race to trumpet the virtues of the Flemish people, it's not a total shock that he overlooked the race right under his nose. The Scheldeprijs, being located around Antwerp, wasn't entirely a "Flemish" event; Antwerp is historically part of the Duchy of Brabant, not the County of Flanders, so its connection to "Flanders" depends on which definition you're using. The modern Dutch-speaking half of Belgium? Antwerp's there. The ancient definitions, not so much. It stands to reason, then, that Van Wijnendaele didn't bite at this flat race in Antwerp Province to help fulfill his ambition to bring cycling to the Flemish people.

But there are other reasons Van Wijnendaele would likely have looked askance at the Scheldeprijs, and a prime one has to be difficulty. A century ago, all the respectable races were interminable death marches, like the 1903 Tour de France and its 470-km stages. Van Wijnendaele's inaugural Tour of Flanders was a 324-km slog across all of Flanders; by contrast, in 1913 the Scheldeprijs was just getting up to 170km, after being limited to just 85km the previous season. The winners of the Scheldeprijs, prior to the first Ronde van Vlaanderen, were names like Maurice Leturgie, Adrien Kranskens, Raymond Van Parijs (Ray from Paris), Florent Luyckx and Joseph Van Wetter -- all riders with no great palmares or win totals next to their names. Of the group, only Leturgie stands out... as the only Frenchman ever, to this day, to win the Scheldeprijs.[130]

The race itself bounced around the summer calendar for decades, landing mostly and most recently on a slot within a few days of August 1 but with plenty of editions in June, July, later August, September, even an occasional May date. Not until 1987 did the race find a home among the spring classics. And even then, the race was held in late April -- an afterthought -- most years. The running in 2012 on April 4 marked the earliest start date in the race's 105-year history.

---

[130] This should change any moment now, actually, as Arnaud Démare and Nacer Bouhanni tackle the race in 2016 and beyond.

When the organizers in 1987 finally decided to hold the race as an aperitif to the cobbles season, it began to find a new identity, at least among the fans. The list of riders didn't change much -- bunch sprinter Jean-Paul van Poppel, winner in August, 1986, came second in '87 and won again in '88. But for a race that traditionally followed the Tour de France like a limpet following a whale shark, sidling up next to the Cobbled Classics at least played into a narrative theme. Springtime in Flanders, gotta love it! Even if it's a lightly-cobbled course in the suburbs of Antwerp.

In the early 2000s the Scheldeprijs functioned more as a victory lap by the conquering heroes of Paris-Roubaix and de Ronde, coming back to Belgium (or passing through) en route to a short, in-season break. Then, the headlines were about Tom Boonen, the hero returning from battle and feeling like he should show something on his home roads.[131] Boonen notched a couple Scheldeprijs victories -- a foreshadowing triumph in 2004 following wins at E3 Prijs and Gent-Wevelgem, and a crowning victory in 2006, wearing the rainbow jersey, and with a second Ronde in his pocket. Having checked that box, Boonen passed on the race in 2007, lost in 2008 to Mark Cavendish, and has since only come back to keep the legs fresh for Paris-Roubaix.[132]

By 2010, when the UCI and race organizers signed off on the plan to move Gent-Wevelgem to a Sunday and the climber-

---

[131] Boonen is from Mol, about 50km east of Antwerp.

[132] Boonen's two wins trail only Cavendish, Marcel Kittel and Piet Oellibrandt, a track-and-crit star in Belgium back in the 1960s, with three wins each. Another local hero, the Emperor of the Herentals himself, Rik Van Looy, is level with Boonen at two wins. Kittel, however, has taken the last three in a row, has modest ambitions in the remaining classics, and is 27 as of this writing. So I think we know where this record is going.

friendly Brabantse Pijl to the week before Amstel Gold, suddenly there was a spot between the two most important dates on the spring calendar, a massive opportunity to step into one of the sport's brightest spotlights. Now the Scheldeprijs is mentioned as the (low-calorie) meat between the Monument sandwich, or maybe one of the condiments. Just being in the same sentence as de Ronde and Paris-Roubaix is instant cred in Classics Season.

Still, there is arguably a downside to its new-found positioning, one that the organizers of Gent-Wevelgem knew all too well. Riders with their eyes on Paris-Roubaix will refrain from digging too deep four days prior to the departure in Compiègne. And riders coming off racing de Ronde to win may still be too shredded to mount a serious challenge at the Scheldeprijs. The startlist tends to outshine the order of finish, and watching the riders depart intact from downtown Antwerp might be more rewarding than taking in the last dash in Schoten.[133]

If the course came with another heaping helping of cobbles and hills, it might have difficulty convincing anyone to target the Scheldeprijs. But the lure for the riders to this slot are twofold: the cobbled heroes need a reduced level of effort to expend on Wednesday of Flanders-Roubaix week; and the pure sprinters who won't be saving themselves for an unlikely chance at Paris-Roubaix need something to get excited about. Gent-Wevelgem didn't play the role of "gentle mid-week semi-classic" very willingly, with the Kemmelberg and occasionally vicious weather to dissuade the stars from applying themselves, and leapt at the chance to change dates

[133] Actually, some of the most prominent rider quotes about the race highlight the lovely start in the Great Market of Antwerp — a cultural landmark, sure, and a nice moment, but not exactly a compliment to the 99.9% of the race yet to come.

and go big. The Scheldeprijs has no apparent ambitions to be anything more than it has been; a 200km sprinters' event with a few modest cobble stretches thrown in for kicks.

*****

All of these decisions about how to order the Belgian race calendar could not seem more distant to your average bar patron in Wenatchee, Washington. For starters, the TV is probably not tuned to cycling but to football, if there's any to watch, that being the sport of choice in this western-style town along the Columbia River. [Maybe hockey; there's a junior team in town, the Wild.] Downtown Wenatchee gives off a hint of Old West, from its days as a mid-point stop on the Great Northern Railroad between Seattle and Spokane, but with plenty more New West than you often find east of the Cascade Mountains. This isn't your traditional cattle-and-timber village grown up. This is the heart of Apple Country.

Billing itself as the "Apple Capital of the World," Wenatchee's relationship to the world's most popular fruit is no joke. The capital part, maybe -- roughly half of the world's entire apple production comes from China. But the US is #2 in apple production, and 60% of that in recent years comes from Washington State. Sure, you can grow a decent apple almost anywhere. Sitting at home in Seattle, I watch wayward apples roll down the street in October. But if you want a perfect piece of fruit, Wenatchee is a good place to look. Its 300 days of sunshine per year combine nicely with the inexhaustible water supply the Columbia River represents (and other biological niceties... temperature? soil constitution?), to make fruit not just grow but thrive. Apples get the headlines, but peaches, grapes, cherries and pears are just some of the crops paying the bills. Vineyards are an established presence throughout the Columbia Valley, and golf courses are popping up to keep the tourists' attention and dollars.

But drive out of downtown Wenatchee in summer and what you'll notice are that the colorful orchards can't quite mask the brown, sun-scorched hills from showing the valley's true nature. Where the Cascade Mountains give way to the Columbia Plateau is where the verdant Northwest becomes desert, shadowed from the incessant rains of the coast by a north-south wall of peaks reaching 8,000 feet (not including the volcanoes, which top out at over 14,000). Wenatchee's nine inches of average annual rainfall are what we call a month in Seattle, in the fall anyway.

Twenty miles west of Wenatchee, you reach Leavenworth, a small, Bavarian-themed tourist town snug up against the granite wall of the Cascades. Just short of Leavenworth, you can turn south and ascend Blewett Pass, a 15-mile ascent rising 3,000 feet... though what few other roads leave Wenatchee, hitting their dead end in the national forest, are probably quieter than Blewett Pass. These are the roads where Tyler Farrar became... a cobbled classics devotee.

You'd think a professional cyclist born in a country that looks more like a detour off the Vuelta a Espana would be a wispy, 130-pound climbing ace. But Farrar, at six feet tall, is a power rider, strong enough to compete with the world's best sprinters even without a built-in advantage like Mark Cavendish's lower physical profile. Granted, Cavendish has many gifts, physical and psychological, that briefly made him the world's undisputed sprinting champion for the second decade of the new millenium.[134] But Farrar has a handful of wins over Cavendish, dozens of close calls, and in his peak years from 2009-12 he compiled a fine sprinter's resume, with victories in all three grand tours.

Farrar has made a good living off of his closing speed, but it's not the cycling discipline that's nearest and dearest to his heart. Cyclists typically dream of winning with nobody else in the picture, gloriously crushing the competition well before the final 50 meters, and sprint wins... well, it's always best to win. In talking with Farrar, he makes it very clear that the races he dreams of winning are the cobbled classics, by any means necessary, that the thrill of racing on the world's hardest flat roads and trickiest short hills are what make the sport so beautiful.

"I've always had a fascination with the classics," Farrar told me years ago. "[As a kid] the first race that really caught my attention was the Tour of Flanders. I kinda got into riding bikes and got into this mad hunt for any magazines about bike racing, and for whatever reason the first one I found was a classics edition. I was just studying any magazine I could get my hands on."

Dreams started evolving into reality for Farrar when he was 17. That was when USA Cycling brought Farrar to Belgium to race, doing junior and/or *espoir* versions of the classics, where he started to develop a feel for the pulse of these aggressive races. To supplement that experience, Farrar did what everyone in Belgium does: rode the Kermesses.

---

[134] Marcel Kittel has since taken away the title, and after a year lost to injury Kittel himself seems about to yield to one of a handful of young challengers.

Tyler Farrar in Schoten. Photo by Chris Fontecchio

"I started Junior kermesses when I was a junior -- where we lived when I was on the US national team, now that I've lived there a long time I know there is good training around there, but at the time I didn't know where to go to train and all that, like the training's no good here. And there are so many amateur kermesses here, there's five a week. Some days there's three happening on the same day around the country. So I would basically use the kermesses as training while I was over there. So at the same time we have our actual race program, and any time I had more than about three days between races I would just go and do kermesses until the next big race. And even as a pro, there's much less pro kermesse racing than amateur but there's still a decent circuit. I've done pretty much every pro kermesse in Belgium at least once, some of them many times. Actually I love doing them, I think they're a lot of fun."

"The team this year clamped down on me and told me I couldn't do as many of them. In 2008 I probably did 12 or 13 pro kermesses. In 2009 I think I did just five or six. The team this year (2010) said, 'you're doing a massive schedule already with us in just UCI races, we don't really want you doing all these other races in between,' so I only did one or two this year. I really enjoy them though. it's real racing, it's really hard -- it's some of the hardest races you'll do all year, because there's not that controlled team tactics going on."

Farrar has long since graduated from the Kermesses, and worked himself into the big-time Classics, showing enough potential after a few seasons for his Garmin/Slipstream squad to ride for him.[135] Starting in 2010, Farrar was the team's designated sprinter at Gent-Wevelgem and a protected rider for the Tour of Flanders. All of his years in Belgium and France had primed him to take his shot at the classics.

"Well, I've been racing over there since I was 17 years old, I did a lot of the juniors versions of the classics, and the *espoirs* versions,[136] and those are races where there's a lot more

[135] A/k/a Garmin-Cervelo, Garmin-Transitions, Garmin-Sharp and now Cannondale-Garmin. And in 2015 Farrar signed with the MTN Qhubeka squad, now Dimension Data.

[136] "Espoirs" literally means "hopefuls" in French, cycling's native language, but generally refers to under-23 events. It isn't terribly obvious from a continent away but in fact cycling has a fairly well-established development structure to it, so riders don't just parachute in from their local race circuit to a professional environment. The U23-level Ronde van Vlaanderen Beloften traces its roots to 1936, for example.

attacking involved. You have to learn the courses, when to make your move, when the crucial moves happen. So you know, all the guys who are really serious about the classics, they know, OK, when we hit this point in the race, you know its gonna go. I started out considering myself a classics rider who had a quick sprint, but I didn't see myself as someone who was going to be one of the top sprinters in the world. And as I got older and developed, that was one of the first areas where I excelled, in field sprinting."

The main target has always been the Tour of Flanders, but in Farrar's mind it's a longshot. "I handle distance fairly well, the distance itself is never really the issue. The issue is if they blow up my engine on a climb, there's not much you can do. So in Flanders, the fact that it's 250k isn't the issue; the issue is whether I can get over all those hills.

"You know, Flanders has never been won in a field sprint. Yeah, you can get third through tenth sprinting from that group of 30-40 riders that come through the finish. But there's always one or two guys fighting for the win, and I want to develop to the point where I can be one of those guys. But it's going to be a matter of time before I can tell if that's realistic or not."

That time arrived in 2012. Farrar trained his focus entirely on the classics, cutting out the sprint training that normally takes up a fair amount of his offseason program. He called it an "experiment," which sounds about right, because riders in their mid-to-late 20s, who have carved out a successful place in the peloton, don't often change their focus toward a different set of races. But Farrar didn't have too much to lose; he'd won nearly every major sprinters' target at least once, including a stage of the Tour de France in 2011, but with Mark Cavendish at the top of his game, sporting the World Champion's rainbow jersey, Farrar was finding it harder to win big sprints consistently or otherwise plough new ground. The Team would also need Farrar in the classics, and if he could raise his game to, say, Thor Hushovd levels (strong to the end with a good sprint), he could compliment 2011 Paris-Roubaix winner Johan Van Summeren and rising cobbles star Sep Vanmarcke rather nicely.

But the results didn't come, and in the end he experienced the worst of both worlds, not advancing in the classics and lacking the sprinters' speed when it might have come in handy. The most realistic big target, Gent-Wevelgem, got away from Farrar when he missed the move launched by Fabian Cancellara on the final ascent of the Kemmelberg. Next up, in Flanders, Garmin's directors thought the new course offered little hope for Farrar to stay close in the final climbs, and asked him to join an early breakaway to take pressure off his teammates. And finally in the Scheldeprijs, where once again he did everything right, Marcel Kittel snuck past him in the sprint to win by half a wheel.

"It was good to answer the question for myself, if I only trained for more aerobic training and power climbs of Flanders and cobblestones of Roubaix, what would happen? And now I know. The reality is I'm a sprinter, and no matter how much I train, I don't think I can train myself at this point in my career to be able to attack with the attacking riders of the classics. No matter how much I would love to be able to do that I have to be realistic about what my strengths and weaknesses are."

Farrar sounded critical and unhappy about the big picture, but a funny thing happened when I ask him about how it felt to be in the sacrificial breakaway. Was it thankless duty, or was there something different about leading the Tour of Flanders for several hours, including moments such as the first ascent of the Oude Kwaremont or the Paddestraat, where Farrar was on the very front of the breakaway, not a random guy wasting his energy but a former fifth-place finisher, and a student/veteran of the Cobbled Classics powering across the stones to the shouts of half a million excited onlookers. The smile on his face came through the phone.

"Oh, I think that will go down as one of the more special experiences of my cycling career. You know, it's funny, you have these moments in your career, and they're rarely your big victories or your big results. They're the days like Flanders was, a special day. The cool thing for me was I'm pretty well known in Belgium, so when I was in the break in front of the peloton, people know me so it really felt like all of Belgium was screaming my name. That's something I'll never forget. That was really special."

Most Americans can barely appreciate the significance of the fabled Ronde van Vlaanderen, but of those who do, only George Hincapie and Tyler Farrar can talk of it as something they experienced from the rarified place at the head of the peloton. Hincapie has left the sport without a win (and with his best results expunged from the books). Farrar has a fifth place,[137] so far, and a day at the head of the race. The list of

---

[137] Oh, did I mention this? On top of all else, the 2010 Ronde van Vlaanderen marked one of the high points for American classics cycling when Farrar won the field sprint for fifth place, after Cancellara, Boonen, Gilbert and Leukemans rolled into Ninove. Farrar's hopes in

Belgian cyclists who would gladly trade places with him on this basis alone is long.

*****

Back to 2010... With 7km to go, the peloton swings left onto a wide road along the banks of the Schlede. Quick Step were drilling it for Wouter Weylandt, their backup sprinter that day behind Tom Boonen. Weylandt and Farrar were best friends off the bike, back in Gent, but on this day it's all business.[138] Quick Step needed a win, facing a classics-long drought that had Belgian fans feeling down. But they had plenty of company at the front of the race, including Sky, HTC and Vacansoleil crowding them for position.

At the 4km mark, the race turned left again, saying goodbye to the Schelde and heading for Schoten. Like a flat stage of a grand tour, the prevailing strategy could be detected from outer space, and everyone with skin in the game was present and accounted for. The exception at the moment was Farrar's Garmin squad, but no matter: Farrar himself was there, and Quick Step's predictable approach meant that the American had a leadout -- his friend Wouter. Boonen himself launched at 500 meters to go, aiming to propel Weylandt into the

---

the race, back then, relied on the race coming back together after the hills, leaving him in position to sprint it out for a top place, something he could do even after a hard day. The new course doesn't really leave him in position to do that, with the finishing climbs coming in bunches close to the end. Though in 2012, the first edition on the new course, the day they sent Farrar up the road, the race did sort of come together at the end as teams struggled to figure out how to work with the altered route. The winning trio, led by Boonen, were a mere 38 seconds ahead of the chasing pack.

[138] These were truly happier times in 2010, as Wouter Weylandt tragically died in a crash on a descent in stage 3 of the 2011 Giro d'Italia. When the race resumed the next day, it was run as a moving funeral procession with results neutralized. Weylandt's teammates from Leopard-Trek led home the procession in one of the most emotional scenes of any sporting event, and invited a visibly anguished Farrar, from a rival team, to cross the line arm-in-arm with them in honor of Farrar's close friendship with Weylandt. Farrar and the Leopard-Trek riders departed the race after the stage.

stratosphere. But Weylandt had crashed in training earlier in the week, and his bruised body wasn't ready to respond. When Weylandt came around Boonen's left, Farrar went to the right, and Farrar summoned his burst of speed to drop his friend. Finally Farrar had his classic.

Farrar wins Scheldeprijs sprint. Photo by Chris Fontecchio

Later Farrar thanked his team for doing all the detailed, hardly-noticed chores necessary to keep a race together for a sprint, when a hundred or so non-sprinters have other ideas. The Scheldeprijs ends in a sprint often enough that it's easy to overlook what it takes to reach this point, but it's worth remembering that, compared to a stage of the Tour, none of the non-sprinters were saving themselves for the next day. So even when his leadout disappeared and he was forced to poach the Quick Step train, it was still a job well done for the whole unit.

Fans serenade the American winner. Photo by Chris Fontecchio

Beaming with delight, Farrar was ushered to the podium and brought out in due course. He's fluent in Flemish, as Belgian fans were aware, so maybe that's what was on the mind of the several hundred fans crowding around the stage in downtown Schoten for the podium celebration, cheering loudly for the American. Or maybe beer has worked its magic again. Regardless, while we awaited his coronation, a bunch of fans began singing a boisterous Flemish number in tribute to Wenatchee's Fastest Human.[139]

---

[139] Or so it seemed, honestly "Tyler Farrar" were the only words I could pick out. But there seemed to be nothing but admiration in the podium atmosphere that day.

Greatness, measured in Classic victories, may elude Farrar when it's all said and done, and he's running short on time pad his resume... though the Classics are something of an older rider's game. But even if Farrar's cobbled results have peaked, he has still gone where no American has gone before. He's officially the second American winner of a classic,[140] and his Ronde van Vlaanderen exploits are very much something to write home about.[141] But competitive juices aside, Farrar's love of the classics comes down to the history and spectacle of the races, their deep significance to the people standing by the road. They matter broadly to the Flemish fans, and to Farrar. So whether it's thru his results or his expressions of appreciation or his ability to make those expressions in Flemish or his living in Gent, or some combination of the above, Farrar has inserted himself deeply into the Cobbled Classics, into the hearts of fans, and into the Cobbled Classics Roll of Honor.

---

[140] George Hincapie's 2001 victory in Gent-Wevelgem is still on the books. Hincapie had several other results from 2004-06 stricken from his record after admitting to doping in that time.

[141] If Farrar has peaked, he'll finish with a pretty fair list of close calls in the cobbled classics. In addition to his fifth at de Ronde, he's been second and third in Dwars door Vlaanderen (2014 and 2011, respectively), third in Gent-Wevelgem (2011), and 8th in E3 Prijs (2014).

Garmin bus with displaced American arm. Photo by Chris Fontecchio

14: Previewing Paris-Roubaix, In Person and On Paper

On the occasion of this book leaving Belgium and heading south in the direction of the Queen of the Classics, the Hell of the North, the venerable Paris-Roubaix, let me start by declaring unequivocally that this is a French race. Wait, what? Last I checked, France is home to the entire course; and as far as I know it has never veered into Belgium, despite skirting the border. French is the language spoken all along the route. The race's origins are steeped in French provincial history. It's a settled question.

And yet there can be no denying that the little neighbor to the north has adopted this race in some significant way. France is far larger than Belgium, just based on population. France has historically (if not so much of late) been the center of the sport of cycling, from the Tour to the big sponsors and teams to the famous riders. And yet...

Number of Paris-Roubaix wins, by country:

1. Belgium, 54
2. France 28
3. Italy, 13
4. Netherlands, 5

I mean, not to be too simplistic, but how can those numbers not mean what they appear to mean? Belgians have some advantages in the proliferation of cobbles back home, but they race on cobbles in the Netherlands too, and look where that's gotten the Dutch. It's not merely the product of experience. The connection between Flanders and Paris-Roubaix is something much deeper.

In cycling terms, the connection is easy to spot. To the French cycling scene Paris-Roubaix is an outlier. The big French races (setting aside *the* big French race), from GP Plouay to Paris-Tours to Paris-Nice, don't feature many cobbled stretches. French riders seeking victory in the Hell of the North need to hone their craft in Belgium as much as anywhere. A French powerhouse who thinks he has a chance at the Cobbled trophy can race on actual cobblestones how many days a year in Belgium? 30? 50? He can enjoy the slow buildup to the major events by starting in the Omloop, ramping up at Dwars door Vlaanderen and E3 Prijs, and stretching himself out at the Tour of Flanders. He can hone his subtler skills by running the kermis circuit. This is nothing new. Not that you can never race on cobbles in France outside the second Sunday in April — I am sure in the cycling-mad Nord-Pas de Calais region you can find a few bouncy kermesses here and there. But on the elite level, Belgium is the only place to be. As a practical matter, the soul of the Paris-Roubaix — the experience of riding on the cobbles — is inseparable from Flanders.

And so are the people by the side of the road. The thickest Belgian presence in Paris-Roubaix happens at the Carrefour de l'Arbe, a punishing little strip of stones some 2km in length, bordered chiefly by 4km of screaming, quite probably inebriated Flemish fans. At this point the race is honing in on Roubaix, and passing through a region known occasionally as French Flanders. This is where France and Belgium not only meet, but blend cultures in ways too subtle for American civics textbooks to have ever taught me.

Officially the Department du Nord which hosts the business end of Paris-Roubaix is half of the Nord-Pas-de-Calais Region, bordering Belgian Flanders from the North Sea to the Ardennes (the taller, more dramatic Wallonian ones, southeast of the Flemish Ardennes). Historically, though, the north-westernmost half of the Nord Department was part of the County of Flanders, the ninth-century fiefdom responsible for modern Flanders' distinct identity. "Royal Flanders" fell periodically under French or Dutch control before the modern Belgian state came into being, and a series of settlements in the late 17th century between France and Spain (then running the Netherlands) led to the Flemish districts of Dunkirk and Lille being pared off from the old County and made part of France. To this day you can visit French villages with names like Steenwoorde or Hondschoote or Hazebroucke. You stand a decent chance of hearing the unique West Flemish dialect spoken, at least among some of the old timers closer to the coastal areas.

Back in Lille, I never saw any Dutch signs, but the city of Douai, 25km west of the Arenberg Forest, was host to the (French) Parliament of Flanders in the 17th and 18th centuries. The Nord Department crest is an elaborate black lion on a yellow shield -- sound familiar? All of this blurs the border between Flanders and France, which my brother and I crossed somewhere along the way the day after the Scheldeprijs. To this day I have absolutely no clue where that border actually was. I just know we found ourselves in Roubaix after a while, so we surely crossed it somewhere.

All of these cultural ties and practical similarities may draw Flemish cycling fans to the race, and that's important for putting Paris-Roubaix in its proper context among the rest of the spring classics. But having established this connection, let me emphasize the fact that in no way is the race not still uniquely French. No amount of Flemish victories and spectators can overcome the race's historical and geographical identity. The race came into existence because two Roubaix entrepreneurs, Theodore Vienne and Maurice Perez, had lobbied for the construction of a velodrome there and needed a way to draw greater attention to it from potential supporters in Paris. In 1895 they hit on the idea of a race from Paris to Roubaix -- a marginally appealing draw for April until they pitched it as the ideal training exercise for the 560km Bordeaux-Paris race scheduled for the following month. They called Le Velo, the sports newspaper responsible for promoting the sport, and got to work selling their idea.

Obviously you know how it came out, but my favorite detail from the race's origins comes from when Le Velo decided to inspect a potential route for the race. They sent a M. Victor Breyer to observe the route, which he did over two days, the second entirely by bike. Breyer spent a hard, cold, wet, bumpy day in the saddle, and arrived in Roubaix covered in mud. He urged the organizers to call off their *projet diabolique*," a dead-on description of what was to come. Thankfully, his advice went unheeded. We can only speculate that had all the potential organizers ridden the course, the race may never have come into existence.

By 1896 the race was underway, but just barely. Of the one hundred riders registered to compete, only 51 showed up at the start. The race's reputation as one to think twice about was already growing before the first-ever starting gun was fired. Another alleged controversy regarding the 1896 opener involved a potential clash with Easter Sunday. The story goes that the original plan was for an Easter running; the Catholic Church, supposedly then protested the interference with the riders' opportunity to worship on the holiest day of the year. Vienne and Perez, in turn, promised to organize a mass at 4am, to quell the criticism, then canceled it on the grounds that it was patently ridiculous to have mass at that hour. In fact, the 1896 edition ended up happening April 19, two weeks after Easter, so this controversy is likely fabricated, but by the following year the race *did* run on Easter Sunday, and became known as the *Pascale* for its tendency to take place on the holiday. In 2012, Easter took place April 8th, as did Paris-Roubaix— of the last 25 editions thru 2016, six took place on Easter Sunday.

Like many races that survive from that era, Paris-Roubaix struggled to define itself and was forced to continually evolve, with history both interrupting and reforming the race. In this case, that history comes down primarily to one event -- World War I -- and its imprint on the race is truly indelible.

The rolling countryside between the capital and French Flanders gave the early Paris-Roubaix a gentler flavor, and the stretch of the course through Doullens -- well west of the modern route -- lent the race its most distinguishing feature, a moderate climb where many a winning break was made. The rough roads common to this unremarkable region of France certainly took its toll on the peloton in those early years, but prior to the war nobody spoke about Paris-Roubaix the way they do today.

The Great War changed everything. You can get a pretty good sense of this when you drive the A1 route which parallels the modern Paris-Roubaix. All along the road are exit signs indicating cemeteries and historical points of interest regarding the terrible battles of the Western Front. The old Paris-Roubaix route through Doullens traces perilously close to the 1915-1916 battle line, while the Race to the Sea battle line (1914) runs slightly further east, in a straight line from Compiègne to Lille, the terminals of modern Paris-Roubaix. The Hindenberg line (1917) swings still further east, as does the race. Which means virtually this entire parcours, both its early and its modern versions, takes place along several of the hottest battle fronts of history's most devastating war.

What this meant to France is hard to overstate. The country lost 1.7 million people, military and civilian, in the conflict, while another 4+ million were wounded. The land was churned into a muddy hellscape of trenches and bombed-out structures.[142] In Roubaix, the wooden track where the finish had regularly been staged was gone. Simply getting from Paris to

---

[142] If this is hard to picture, look up the term "creeping barrage" and imagine what that would do to a landscape. Also, it bears mentioning that the presence of buried munitions is so vast that farmers refer to the hundreds of tons of bombs and shells recovered each year in Belgium and France as the "Iron Harvest." Tragically, this harvest includes highly explosive shells and poisonous substances like mustard gas, and hundreds of people have died since the Great War from encounters with its deadly legacy. We Americans take for granted the ability to wander off trails when the mood strikes us, but Belgium and France are among the many places in the world where this sometimes is not advisable.

Roubaix in 1919 was an uncertain prospect, let alone racing there. The organizers sent a crew to investigate... and the "hell of the north" was born. Spoke *L'Auto*:

"We enter into the centre of the battlefield. There's not a tree, everything is flattened! Not a square metre that has not been hurled upside down. There's one shell hole after another. The only things that stand out in this churned earth are the crosses with their ribbons in blue, white and red. It is hell!"

The nickname "Hell of the North" eventually morphed into a description of the race itself, which maybe isn't such a bad thing: after all, people of the Nord Department might prefer we all stop calling their neighborhood "hell" at some point. But the poignant origin of the phrase is part of the race's character that should never be forgotten. Paris-Roubaix is one of many races started in part to connect distant people, and if the original impulse was commercially motivated, the post-war reconnection gave the event a new, weightier meaning. Lille had been cut off from Paris by the devastation that lay between. I don't have any record of how people felt in 1919 when the race came back, but it was surely a sign that life would return to normal again.[143] Someday.

If "Hell" is found in the cobblestones nowadays rather than in muddy, corpse-filled trenches, that too is not without its

---

[143] There is a thoroughly moving chapter in Dino Buzzati's all-time cycling master work *Giro d'Italia*, from the 1949 race, where Buzzati describes the scene in Trieste when the Giro came to town. Trieste had been detached from Italy during World War II, occupied by Germany, fought for by Italian and Yugoslav partisans, and bombed by the Allies. So when peace and freedom came in the war's aftermath (Trieste was declared a free, independent state), the rebuilding began. And in 1949, finally, the Giro d'Italia came to town, at which point, according to Buzzati, the disconnected Italian population felt like they'd been thrown a lifeline at long last. One can only infer that, at the end of WWI, the people of French Flanders were thoroughly isolated from Paris by the devastation that lay between. And what better way to connect Roubaix to Paris than a bike race called "Paris-Roubaix"?

convoluted history. Paris-Roubaix was never designed to be a "cobblestone race" but rather just a race, in a region where it so happened that the roads weren't generally paved. In fact, the cobblestones themselves largely didn't exist in the area until after WWI, when people set about repairing the old dirt and gravel roads that had been shattered by the fighting. Following WWII, however, cars became more prevalent throughout Europe, and the cobbled stretches of road began to disappear under smooth tarmac in the name of progress. As with races in any other civilizing part of Europe, Paris-Roubaix was assumed to be eager and proud to adapt to the ways of modern transportation.

Somewhere along the way, however, riders and fans alike noticed that the cobbles were disappearing, and began to ask if this was good for the race after all. However influential the Doullens climb was in the earliest days of the race, it wasn't much of a hill, even less so when paved. On smooth surfaces, Paris-Roubaix would have trouble finding ways to challenge riders over the rolling-to-flat geography. And nobody likes a boring six-hour race.

At last people began to acknowledge that the race's challenge lay in traversing the cobbles, and the race began to look for ways to stay ahead of the paving machines. In the postwar era, if progress meant smooth, fast pavement, then having cobblestone roads built for Napoleon's armies was seen as a sign of backwardness. The onset of televised races made the matter worse. It was one thing for the newspaper to say that Paris-Roubaix passed over some rough roads; it was something else for the world to see your village sporting 17th century transportation infrastructure. Forget about new investment coming your way. In response, local governments couldn't pave over the streets fast enough, proclaiming proudly in the late 30s that "all roads of Paris-Roubaix will be modernized."[144]

But eventually the race supporters and organizers noticed the race was losing its appeal. "If things don't change, we'll soon be calling it Paris-Valenciennes," muttered race organizer Albert Bouvet, apparently not a compliment. Flat, paved roads meant dull racing ending in a sprint, and nobody outside a few sprinters wanted that.[145] But by 1965, only 22km of the race remained on cobblestones, compared to 60km in earlier times. The race's all-time speed record of 45.129 kilometers per hour was set in 1964.[146]

Word got out. Former winner Jean Stablinksi, one of the great names of Paris-Roubaix, notified the race in 1967 that there was a hidden stretch of (ahem) cobblestones in the Forest of Arenberg that might warrant a detour. But little progress was being made to undo progress in the name of cycling, until a Mr. Jean-Claude Vallaeys kicked off a conversation with local mayors and news media, an effort that launched the notion that the pave were worth saving. They took some small steps -- a photo exhibit in the Nord-Pas de Calais museum; a citizens' ride; a petition with 10,000 signatures calling for preserving

---

[144] It's probably worth noting that World War II slowed down these ambitions by at least six years, if not more. But for yet another devastating interruption to the progress of northern France, the now-famous roads might well have been paved over before anyone thought to speak up. Not that this is an acceptable trade-off, but it is one more way of seeing how our modern, beloved race hung by a thread for many of it middle years.

[145] Well, there is Paris-Brussels, a somewhat prestigious and historical race between the two capital cities that does simply run the flat, smooth surfaces of northern France. It remains popular with some fans, particularly in Belgium (of course), where folks can come out to watch a sprint finish. But despite connecting two of Europe's most venerable cities, Paris-Brussels rates barely a blip on the radar of worldwide cycling fans. It's safe to say this is a reminder of the fate that awaited Paris-Roubaix.

[146] By 2002, in the heyday of EPO, the average speed was back down to 39 kph.

the pave -- seemingly minor matters but which, taken together, coalesced into a genuine issue. Newspapers and politicians began to join in the cause, and Bouvet and Vallaeys formed Les Amis de Paris-Roubaix (Friends of Paris-Roubaix), a citizens' organization dedicated to preserving enough cobbled stretches to support a good race.

Les Amis undertook the difficult tasks of finding more pavé to use, and helping restore the secteurs already in use. Searching far and wide, the Friends found one secteur after another and gradually rebuilt the available route -- in consultation with the actual race organization -- back to the pro cycling world's hardest, craziest single day in the saddle. Not that it was easy, but things eventually turned the corner. Here is Alain Bernard, President of Les Amis:

"A few years ago, there was barely a village or an area that wanted anything to do with us. If Paris–Roubaix came their way, they felt they were shamed because we were exposing their bad roads. They went out and surfaced them, did all they could to obstruct us. Now they can't get enough of us. I have mayors ringing me to say they've found another stretch of cobbles and would we like to use them."

Basically, the beauty and challenge represented by the pavé firmly took hold in the popular mind, enough for the local mayors to stop feeling ashamed of their rough roads. That plus the advancement of the media, which elevated the race to an international sensation by the mid-80s, meant that having Paris-Roubaix pass through your town was too big an opportunity to let pass. My own initial connection to cycling, seeing that epic, muddy 1985 race and the Tour de France stage passing over the same roads three months later, made it clear that there was something special in the raw brutality of racing on such poor cobblestones. There was challenge in the effort, honor in finishing, terror in the process -- all to levels unique even to the Tour de France. It made fantastic television, in America and elsewhere, and from there, as they say, the rest is history.

Bernard himself contributed a jewel of a secteur, the Carrefour de l'Arbe double-stretch late in the race. As of 2011, Bernard reported that while there are few options beside the ones currently in use from the Carrefour to the Velodrome, in the prior 100km he knows of enough alternative stretches of pavé to keep the race bouncing around for the foreseeable future. Tarmac graders no longer threaten the character of Paris-Roubaix, and the basic contours of the race are set in (ahem) stone.

But Les Amis' work is hardly done. Every year multiple *secteurs* are in danger of being removed from the race due to degrading conditions -- dramatic enough that even this race won't have them. The typical problems are caused by flooding, by heavy farm equipment churning up the stones during spring mud season, and of course by thieving tourists -- a sign that people really *do* value the cobbles, for better or worse. Les Amis raise funds and gather work crews to rebuild broken *secteurs* by hand. They remove bits of road, lay sand (or maybe cement on hills, which are more vulnerable to water damage), then piece the road back together, one 25-pound stone at a time. They fix potholes and sinkholes, the hidden and more dangerous nuisances to the race. They even help remove moss from the Arenberg stones, which can get slick with plant growth in springtime. Volunteer crews do the work. The organization doggedly raises funds to keep up with the race's needs. The people have spoken clearly that they want the savage nature of the race preserved, so on that level the battle has been won. But implementing victory still requires eternal vigilance.

Oh, and the 2016 edition of Paris-Roubaix? A total of 52.8 kilometers of *pave*.

*****

On Thursday, after packing up and departing Oudenaarde, Pete and I set off for France. We drove to Ronse, through the heart of the *Vlaamse Ardennen* one last time. Drove past the turnoff for Dottignies. And noting the location of Roubaix just over the border, we pointed the car straight for the Velodrome, come what may. The maps showed streets crossing the international boundary, and before we knew it (literally), we were in France.

This was an unsettling experience -- crossing an international boundary without so much as a sign to take a picture of. I have lived most of my life within a leisurely drive of Canada, and I can enumerate the limited number of crossings in western Washington (or, previously, northern Vermont) where it was possible to gain access to our neighboring country, provided i show the guards my passport and nothing comes up to dissuade them from welcoming me. Canada, which in many ways is far less distinguishable from the US than Belgium is from France, might as well be on another continent, reachable only via expensive international flights, as far as the political connectivity is concerned. And then there's Mexico, our other neighbor, which some Americans would like to sever from us with a giant saw blade, allowing what's left of the continent to drift far enough away to protect us, once and for all, from our friends, neighbors, business partners and a substantial portion of our low-income workforce. Even more distinct than entrances to Canada, crossings to Mexico have a distinctly war-zone feel to them. So Europe's lack of identifiable borders defied everything I had been taught by both the way we Americans do business and by decades of history underlining the vast distinctions between European nations. One minute we were in Belgium, a minute later France, and within about another ten minutes we determined that we were, in fact, in France. We celebrated with a stop at a fast-food joint.

After lunch we tracked down the velodrome, which was wide-open to casual visitors as a few workers made preparations for Sunday's race arrival. I don't know if we would have been held up if we'd arrived on a bike and started circling the oval, but we were on foot, sporting cameras and reverential expressions, and the work crew couldn't have cared less.

There has always been something quaint about the colors of the velodrome to me. Paris-Roubaix is synonymous with crappy weather, World War hellscapes, dust and mud, and industrial neighborhoods. By French standards, it's a brooding landscape used by the race at a time of year when dark clouds drain away virtually all the color. Sometimes even the racers, outfitted like Christmas trees most of the time, get a coating of mud and blend into the drabness. The Velodrome is the exception.

The infield is a manicured lawn, as green as the sunlight will allow it to be. Circling that is your basic cinder layer, moderately reddish-brown. Then the signature: a stripe of baby blue paint covering the flat concrete outlining the surface of the track. The track itself is the color of a band-aid, caucasian pink, punctuated by a few ads for the regional government and some local businesses. It's an odd mix of color, striking but not in a truly cheerful way; more in a third-rate-Caribbean resort swimming pool way. It's not beautiful, but it's ... I dunno, it works. It's like the drab version of a colorful scene, so it makes total sense. And there is no scene like it anywhere else.

Roubaix Velodrome. Photo by Chris Fontecchio

Apart from hosting one of the biggest days in the cycling calendar, the Roubaix Velodrome is home to amateur races and clubs, as well as the Roubaix-Lille-Metropole pro team run by Cyrille Guimard, legendary *directeur sportif* of the Renault teams of Lemond, Hinault and Fignon. Guimard had his day in the limelight, and the stories of him and Hinault are fascinating little dramas, but nowadays he apparently lives a quieter existence getting young neo-pro riders ready for the big show. But all of this activity amounts to almost nothing, even a few days before the big race, as far as we could tell. Pete and I walked around the silent *parc*, poked our heads in the offices, and went on our way.[147]

Our main destination for the day was Paris, where we would be staying with friends, but not til we pulled over long enough to sample the pavé. For that, of course, we made a beeline for the town of Wallers. A small coal-mining town, Wallers could easily have faded into the coal-dusted anonymity of the Nord-Pas-de-Calais region, but for 2300 meters of pure magic... the most unique and enigmantic road segment in all of cycling. The Arenberg Forest.

Officially the "Drève des Boules d'Hérin," known lovingly as the "Trenchee" (trench) or "Trouée" (gap) d'Arenberg, this "road" is an arrow-straight path of stones bisecting a thick swatch of forest on the north side of Wallers, just past the old Anzin Mining Company, with its long barracks straddled by two strange steel "well" towers with giant rotors in the top sections for lifting coal into loading position. Approaching through town, the peloton and the steady stream of curious amateur riders course slightly downhill past old brick homes and businesses, all the time with the well towers visible, reminding

---

[147] How quiet it remains going forward is another matter. A new indoor velodrome was recently completed next door, called the Stab Vélodrome, named not after the act of knifing someone but after the aforementioned Jean Stablinski. Covered velodromes are the standard for professional track racing, not outdoor facilities, and the Nord-Pas-de-Calais Départment has a beautiful new one to raise a new generation of track-trained hard men and women. Personally I am not a fan of watching track — why go around in circles when you could ride your bike to ... anywhere? Lhasa? Timbuktu? Flanders? But there is a trend of very strong riders entering the sport following success in track.

everyone what's coming long before the forest pathway itself comes into view. The forest is some 10,000 acres, sprawling far to the east of Wallers, named for the Duke of Arenberg, whose lineage is based in Belgium but named after a town (Aremberg) in Germany. Anyway, back in town there is little evidence of the threat the mines once posed to the woods, apart from the large open pit behind the mining company.

But threaten they did. Mines devour wood with gusto, and in this case the mine shafts run directly under the forest. Today the only visible evidence of this is subsidence, mostly marked by pretty little ponds where the ground has sunk into the water table. The fearsome "*Trouée*" road itself pitches downhill at three percent from the moment it begins for a good 500 meters or so, well after the peloton passes under the other iconic bit of steel on the course, a defunct rail bridge crossing in a short, straight line over the road, connecting the treetops. The downward pitch is not attributed to subsidence, which doesn't tend to happen on such a large scale (it would be in the hundreds of acres), but it does serve as a nice reminder.

As for the road itself, the real star, there do not appear to be any surviving stories on its origin, but it was dramatically rescued from obscurity by one of the most recognizable people in the race's history, former world champion Jean Stablinski. Born in Thun-Saint-Amand just a few KM north of the forest and a veteran of Paris-Roubaix, Stablinski (née Stablewski until the media got in the habit of misspelling it) was the son of Polish immigrants and lost his dad to a mining accident when he was 14. Out of necessity, young Jean went to work in the mines until he got a pro cycling contract at 21. He went on to record 111 victories in a hall-of-fame quality career, including a world title, four French titles, a Vuelta a España, and stages of the Tour de France. "Stab" was a climber, which meant he wasn't exactly suited to his hometown race, but he did well enough, coming as high as 7th in 1964.

But his most memorable mark on Paris-Roubaix came toward the end of his career. In 1967, with the race in a struggle to survive against the paving machines, Stablinski alerted the organizers to a very challenging stretch of cobbles in his neighborhood, a rough stretch of stones through the forest that weren't on anybody's list of roads to smooth over. In fact, it wasn't even open to cars (and remains closed to them, even on race day when they are diverted around the forest). By 1968 the Arenberg Trench was included in Paris-Roubaix, and when Stablinski conquered the familiar stones with the peloton that day, he became the first and only person ever to have worked underneath the cobblestones and raced over the top of them as well. This wonderful nugget is celebrated with a monument at the entrance to the forest. What you give to the race is sometimes much bigger than what you take from it.

All of this mystique would all add up to nothing, however, if it weren't for the Arenberg cobbles themselves. They are considered, more or less unanimously, the worst cobbles anywhere in the sport of cycling. I can think of three reasons:

* Disorganization: The stones in the Trench look like they weren't so much laid down, like typical cobbles, as that they were dropped from a helicopter.[148] Even the worst secteurs

---

[148] Credit to American stage-racer Chris Horner for this image. His exact quote is, "The best I could do would be to describe it like this — they plowed a dirt road, flew over it with a helicopter, and then just dropped a bunch of rocks out of the helicopter!" This was not intended as a compliment.

elsewhere in the race have a line to follow, often the crown of the road, where you can limit the risk. There is no line through Arenberg, or not one that lasts very long.

* Quality: in the civilized world we think of paving stones as smooth and regular. In the Forest, they are nothing of the sort. Each piece of rock is different, varying from flat and navigable to something resembling a primitive carving tool. Sharp edges are deadly to tires, and the Trench has enough of those to take out half the peloton.

* Traction: Being an old forest, the stones are set in dirt, and being a humid environment that dirt tends to grow plants. Hither and yon tufts of grass, moss and other greenery pop up between rocks. When it rains, these plants and the dirt holding them and the stones in place all amount to a terribly treacherous environment. Before the 2012 edition the race organizers issued some vague threat to remove the Trench from the race if something wasn't done about a moss buildup on the stones. Something was, and the race went on.

Arenberg Trench cobbles. Photo by Chris Fontecchio

And then there's the initial descent, which adds a terrifying rate of speed to the above. Grischa Janorschke entered the forest on April 8, 2012 as part of the daily breakaway at the head of Paris-Roubaix. A powerful then-24-year-old rider from Bavaria built in the cobbles-master mold, Janorschke was riding his first-ever Hell of the North, repping his NetApp squad with distinction at the race's very front as they steered into the Forest from the south end. Hitting the stones at 50km-per-hour aided by the three-percent downslope, Janorschke was hanging on gamely for a few seconds until his front tire suddenly burst, another victim of an unforgiving stone edge. Janorschke helplessly stuck out a leg before flipping to the ground, taking out break-mates Guillaume Van Kiersbulck and Yaroslav Popovich in the process. Janorschke suffered some elbow fractures and other minor bruises. He was lucky.

The Forest has claimed some gruesome scalps over the years, and the high speed at the entrance is often to blame. In 1998, Johan Museeuw shattered his knee here, almost losing his leg to infection afterward. In 2001 Frenchman Philippe Gaumont suffered a broken leg too gruesome to recount here, again a victim of the speed at the mouth of the Trench. As Filippo Pozzato recounts, "It's the true definition of hell. It's very dangerous, especially in the first kilometre when we enter it at more than 60KPH. It's unbelievable. The bike goes in all directions."

Eventually the road levels off and turns slightly uphill all the way to the exit at the north end. The action tends to calm down after the first kilometer. Janorschke, for his part, says that the speed over the flat and uphill sections, in the 30-40kph range, is not terribly difficult to control, at least not by comparison to the downhill speed. By this point, however, the Trench has claimed its share of victims. Like the Koppenberg, this is one place where you can count on the bizarre spectacle of professional cyclists walking their bike. Less dramatic slips on the stones are happening here and there, as the cohesiveness of the pack is shattered into pieces. Popped tires and trashed wheels are a certainty, and other malfunctions are commonplace, to the point where no edition of the race goes by without a few poor souls lacking a teammate or support vehicle, and just hoofing it out of the forest where they can get help.

*****

With some or all of this in mind, Pete and I parked at the north end -- the exit, on race day -- which is steps from the highway and has a nice little dirt parking lot for the cyclotourists looking to try their luck. Our bikes needed some assembly -- Pete's was packed in his travel case and mine was wedged in a few places in our miniature Mercedes rental -- and then there was the process of getting dressed. It was one of those moments where you don't talk a whole lot, out of awe and fear of what you're getting yourself into. I wouldn't say that I was sitting there afraid of crashing; it was more just fear of the unknown. I'd ridden a good number of cobbles by this point. Some of it hurt. How much worse was this gonna be?

Eventually we got going, and it was definitely worse. In Flanders you're on a road that happens to be really bumpy (and steep and maybe wet and slippery and long...) but at least you're on a road. If you go a foot or so to the left or right, it doesn't really matter. This was more like an obstacle course.

One of the big differences from the Flanders stones is the crown. In Flanders, the older roads can have a round, sloping shape to them (horizontally speaking), like the pre-repair Koppenberg. In Paris-Roubaix, the crowns vary from non-existent, to sharp and severe, to intermittent — creating a whole separate category of ways your ride can go wrong. When there is a crown, and you can stay on it, you're maybe in better shape. But with the sharper ones, it's possible to slip down the side of the crown and veer off the road.[149] At high speed I guess you just take your chances, but at lower speed (ahem!) I felt compelled to turn a bit so as not to create a nice little, slippable side-angle. Which meant I was no longer going in a straight line. After a couple stops and starts I got my nerve up a little more about staying on the crown... but the crown comes and goes with no warning, leaving you to pick another line, or stay in the center, even though it's now a double fall line, and hope that the crown resumes soon.

Again, at high speed you can't pick your way through; you just blast forward and hope for the best. The guys capable of this have mostly taken the time to actually figure out where the ideal lines are, so maybe when you see Boonen and Cancellara on the front of the peloton every year, they are in complete control. But I can't relate to any of this. The middle section is a bit better as it flattens out and gives back a modicum of control, and climbing up the last bit is best of all, control-wise. But in general it's a doomed exercise the first time through. I must have taken ten minutes to complete the 2.4km stretch.

---

[149] In the 1985 Paris-Roubaix, Francesco Moser — then a three-time winner of the race — can be seen getting dropped from the breakaway with Eric Vanderaerden, then veering off to the side, coming to a halt in a puddle and keeling over. That's what happens when you're riding the crown and lose your line.

Yours truly, trying out the Trench. Photo by Peter Fontecchio

As I write this, a veteran of two passings of the Trench, I have to say in complete honesty I can't wait to try it again. It *has* to be easier at speed. And with a couple years of cyclocross in my legs now, the sense of being in complete control of my front wheel is no longer as important as it used to be. I've rattled that bike over dirt, stones, sand pits, branches, and so forth, without serious incident (somersaults in the sand are the opposite of serious). Granted that's on a 'Cross bike with an extra 10mm of rubber touching the road, but the psychological barrier formed by decades of riding exclusively smooth roads has been broken. I ride my skinny tire road bike in dirt and gravel when it suits me. I cut through grass if need be. I bump over bricks and even a few American cobbles with no concern for what might happen, including a few meters of pathway that looks eerily similar to the *Tranchée*, right down to the moss.

And nearly every time, some synapse in my brain harkens back to the Arenberg Forest.

From the south end of Arenberg, Pete and I decided to keep going to take in one more secteur of cobbles. We were due in Paris for dinner, or at least planning to arrive at a decent hour, and there was only one stretch of stones within an easy ride: the Wallers-Haveluy secteur. At 2500 meters it's about equal in length to the longest stretch in Flanders, so this was definitely going to be a challenge. Doing an out-and-back ride meant two times across both this and Arenberg, making for just under 10km of unpleasantness on our lovely day out. The ride between Haveluy and Arenberg is a pretty good cross-section of the race, passing over medium-sized traffic roads, past boulangeries and factories and homes in town and picking up speed in the open space between villages. The only real trick was spotting the yellow arrows, marking the race course, while riding in reverse direction.

Nevertheless, as we passed through Haveluy and into farmers' fields again, the yellow arrow stuck on a utility pole showed the race apparently emerging onto the street from a pasture. This was the exit of the *Secteur Bernard Hinault* (Wallers-Haveluy), a classic tractor path of cobbles. Rated at four stars, the *secteur* is board-flat with a dog-leg or two in the middle -- as it's raced, it starts heading west but turns north for the second, harder half. In dry weather it ranges from passable to miserable, with mouthfuls of dust for your troubles. The crown is grassy and in places it becomes pronounced, punishing anyone who drifts toward the margin with a slippery off-camber line. The stones are plenty rough enough, and on a good day this is a hard-riding couple kilometers of stones, though you can avoid stretches of it by riding in the hard-packed dirt on the margin. One struggles to imagine what it's like on a bad day, though. There haven't been too many of those since the *secteur* was added in 2001, but the combination of mud, wet grass, rough stones and tricky crown alignments would make for quite the cobbled soup.

Secteur Bernard Hinault, a/k/a Wallers-Haveluy. Photo by Chris Fontecchio

In the race this is a hot little stretch. Everyone knows that the peloton will split in the forest, which is only about 7-8km from the end of the *Secteur Hinault*, so if you want to be in position in the forest, it's here or earlier where you need to win the battle for space. It's full-gas on the stones here, and in between the two secteurs, so if you're far back coming into the Hinault *secteur*, only a superhuman effort is going to help you move up at that speed. Worse, there are plenty of thrills and spills in the Hinault *secteur* itself, so the guys in the back can't count on coming off this *secteur* still in contention. It's hard to say reliably where the race will officially hit high gear, but it's definitely on by the end of Arenberg, and could well be on leading into Haveluy.

In 2010 this *secteur* saw Garmin-Cervelo effectively exit the race, when their key riders all got held up in a minor crash. Tyler Farrar's bars got messed up and he found himself a few km later attempting to navigate the Trench without control of his front wheel. He emerged in one piece (and eventually finished the race), so in that sense things went swimmingly, compared to what would happen if a mortal being tried such a stunt. In any event, despite being overshadowed by the big bad Forest, this stretch of stones and the way it's raced makes for a healthy dose of treachery.

In 2005 the people of Haveluy, or some delegation thereof, dedicated the *secteur* to the Badger himself, in person, which must have been a nervous moment for the local poobahs. Hinault is a Michael Jordan-like figure in France... or maybe more like Larry Bird, whose greatness is fading a bit into the past, but otherwise unmistakeable. Hinault won the Tour de France five times, with panache, along with Monuments, world championships, and just about everything else a great champion should have on his curriculum vitae. Having the Badger in town would mean a great deal to a small northern town.

How that day must have gone is another matter. Hinault is known for being very gracious in person, but blunt-spoken, occasionally volatile, and famous for hating Paris-Roubaix. In his racing years *le Blaireau* referred to it as a "shitty race," which led to rumors that he disdained the race because he couldn't win it. Like many great athletes Hinault rode with a chip on his shoulder -- nothing drove him like being told he couldn't do something. He won the race in 1981 to silence the heretics and to relieve himself of the obligation to ever ride it again. If I know this, you can bet the citizens of Haveluy knew this too when they decided to honor him with the dedication. My guess, in the absence of any surviving accounts, is that the honor contained an explicit note of wry humor, and the proud champion -- now employed as an ambassador for ASO, owners of Paris-Roubaix -- accepted the humor along with the kind gesture, without repeating his opinion of the race.

Anyway, Pete and I made it over the secteur OK, with Pete clearly getting his legs under him and putting a good two minutes into me, though at least half of that can be attributed to my photo stops. We cruised through Haveluy for a few minutes, found a community center where we refilled our bottles, and pivoted back toward the car. Retracing our steps meant rerunning these two brutal *secteurs* in the direction of the race, and while Pete dusted me again, I would proudly say that I passed over the cobbles this second time with at least ten percent more confidence than the first running. We put the bikes away after about 25km total, and I can honestly say I was tired.

15: Paris-Roubaix, All Day

The highways circling Paris and heading north are quiet at 7am on a Sunday, despite providing access to two of the country's biggest sporting events taking place that day -- the Paris Marathon downtown and Paris-Roubaix up north. Compiègne, where Paris-Roubaix now starts, is about an hour from downtown, far enough that you won't really find any evidence of this iconic event, half-named after the City of Lights, in the city itself... save for the pages of L'Équipe, the national sports daily newspaper. There is a trickle of traffic consisting of people like us, sucking up the prospect of a long day for the chance to chase the Hell of the North over the sport's most terrifying roads. But the race scene is all encamped in Compiègne, and has been for days.

Compiègne is a perfect alternative to Paris as the jumping off point. For starters, Paris is too far from Roubaix to accommodate a modern classic, where 250km or so is considered reasonable and 300k is not. The early races started from Porte Maillot, on the northwest edge of Paris proper, and were 280km long, relatively short by comparison to the other major classics of the day. Starting in Paris wasn't any crazier than coming in from Bordeaux. Sanity became an element of the sport sometime between the pneumatic tire and the disc wheel.

More than logistics, Compiègne feels right as the gateway to the race's heart. This is a northern race, one whose landscape was distinctively scarred by the ravages of the Great War. Well, Compiègne is fittingly located at the southern end of the gently rolling open spaces of the north (as opposed to the busy, less distinct suburban areas). The town was also a command center at the western end of the battle line at various points in World War I and the site of the eventual armistice with Germany.[150]

With another long day in the saddle on tap, the race departed before 9:30, which meant we had to leave Paris at about 7am. A sizeable crowd was gathering, and available parking was half a mile from the startline or so. In case we had any trouble remembering Compiègne's history, winding through Compiègne's streets -- with names like Avenue de l'Armistice, Avenue de President Georges Clemenceau and Rue de President Roosevelt -- will provide you with relentless reminders. The start happens just behind the Town Hall, built in 1505 and towering over the center square. The space was pretty tight around the start area and packed with fans. A roped off area provided some comfort for the VIPs, but none of it felt like a big deal. The Tour of Flanders feels like a big show, from the organization of the start area all the way through to the finish. Paris-Roubaix is much more... provincial. Unadorned.

After the usual drill -- guys coming up on stage in singles and groups, riders sitting around chatting, the gun going off, the caravan rolling out -- the flag dropped on the spectators too. Like the peloton, we didn't exactly hit the gas right away. We had a long day in store for us, and if we were to make it to

---

[150] That would be the armistice which ended the fighting phase of WWI and eventually led to the Treaty of Versailles, which became a symbol of Nazi grievance in the lead-in to WWII. So naturally, when Germany prevailed in the Battle of France in early 1940, Hitler selected Compiègne to host the signing of another armistice, emphasizing the element of revenge.

Roubaix in decent shape, the first stop would have to be for food. A bakery on the route back to the car was filling up with fans, but before long we had bags full of breakfast and lunch, plus some caffes-au-lait.

At the car, as we sorted ourselves out Paul chatted with the guys next to us in the lot, who had a plan to see the race next at Saint-Python. We figured on catching an early secteur, far enough from the Trench to make that the second stop, and Quievy-Saint-Python sounded good enough to us. They told us to follow them, and we did, for a while, though eventually we lost them and found Saint-Python ourselves. Not that it's hard to find. This area of France is quiet, especially on a Sunday morning, so the commotion and traffic of the race is unmistakeable. We drove to the road closure at the juncture where the race course crosses a railroad track, coming downhill slightly over modest cobbles. Dumping the car strategically near the exit, we settled in with a few dozen other fans, including the obligatory Belgians, and waited for the commotion.

A sizable breakaway came by first, more than a dozen guys, looking pretty determined. Several minutes later the peloton rolled through, intact and very business-like, in a decidedly restrained way. The latter kicked up a fair amount of dust, suggesting that it was going to be one of *those* Paris-Roubaix editions. The mud gets all the attention, but the dust leaves its mark too.

There wasn't much to take away from the experience of seeing one of the world's hardest sporting events at an early phase when the combatants are still saving themselves that we couldn't have figured out on our own. But this wasn't anthropology, it was sport. Cool to see it in and of itself. Still, they number the *secteurs* for a reason: so people can engage in their own competition to see as many race passages as possible. Not that we were competing; being rank amateurs in this category and completely bereft of local knowledge, we planned to stick to the fundamentals -- four stops, with Arenberg and the finish yet to come.

Early Paris-Roubaix breakaway group, in Quiévy. Photo by Chris Fontecchio

As soon as the peloton passed, the mad scramble for the next location was underway. The effort was led in part by a couple team cars, HTC and another one, driven by soigneurs who had

handed out some water bottles at our Saint-Python crossing and were off to their next appointment. Behind them formed a high-speed caravan, including us, of people off to their next race passing too, and figuring that these guys might know something we didn't, on the theory that they couldn't afford to be wrong. They weren't, and more so they put on a brief clinic in how to get to the next spot without wasting two seconds. Both lanes of the road were fair game. Country roads were good enough, if they presented a chance at a shortcut. Speed limits were more or less irrelevant. The only limiting factor was the potential for churchgoers in the road, but you can see the steeples from a distance, and when you have a big enough caravan, even that's not a threat. By the time we made it back to the A route, we were ahead of schedule again.
*****

The Paris-Roubaix parcours has settled into something of a routine, whereby the race includes 27 or 28 *secteurs* of cobblestones, numbered in a countdown (i.e. reverse order), deliberately grinding down the peloton en route to Roubaix. As of 2007 the race organizers instituted a system that formalized what everyone was already thinking, actually rating each *secteur* with 1-5 stars to indicate its difficulty. Every year brings slight changes to the exact order, and some secteurs[151] get an occasional year off, but the following analysis (based on the 2011 course) is more or less what you can expect each year.[152]

---

[151] Is it getting annoying that I keep putting this word in italics? By now you know it's French for sector. The whole "-eur" thing is a dead giveaway, since that sound is about as English as bright sunshine or Renee Zellweger. So anyway, I'm dropping the italics... but I just can't bring myself to call a stretch of cobblestones in Paris-Roubaix a "sector." That's not their name. You understand, right?

[152] If you think it sounds lame that I'm going off the 2011 map, here are some stats for 2016: 27 secteurs of cobbles; every single one of them is included in this list; 52.8km total.

Each secteur has its own story, but not all of them are terribly fascinating, so perhaps it's best to view the race in phases.

Phase 1: Compiègne -- Troisvilles

Each year there are approximately 98 km of smooth tarmac before the race assumes its full identity. This phase is notable for the favorites biding their time in the comfort and safety of their surrounding teammates, and the inevitable break up the road, because sponsors need their due in big races, and because teams like to use breaks to tactical advantage, and because... well, some people just need to ride away from the pack. For some two and a half hours the race glides through the gentle landscape of the Aisne Department, whose otherwise quiet history was interrupted by the most severe ravages of the Great War. It's a landscape dotted with monuments and cemeteries, a place bearing witness to the birth of trench warfare and the death of a generation. The helicopters and TV cameras largely take a pass on this segment of the race, joining the action just in time for the first stretch of stones.[153]

Phase 2: Troisvilles -- St-Python

The cobbles get underway, with four quick secteurs in succession, totalling 9.2km of pave out of 15.5km of "road."

---

[153] We are getting closer to the arrival of full-race coverage. The Tour of Flanders leaves out the first two hours or so, and really, these seven hour days have nothing going on at first. But the Tour de France has had some full-stage video presentations and we live in an era where you can watch your dog sleep on the couch from your office workstation. So a Compiègne-to-Roubaix video option can't be far off.

The sheer length of the pavé secteurs means that the riders start burning a few matches, though of course the Bigs do their best to minimize the work.

27. Troisvilles - Inchy (km 98, 2200 meters), Rating: ***

Downhill on the cobbles... this is a good way to get out your early terrors. Said to be in good shape.

26. Viesly - Quiévy (km 104.5, 1800 meters), Rating: ***

Straight and generally lacking in surprises.

25. Quiévy - Saint-Python (km 107, 3700 meters), Rating: ****

They're not big bruisers. On the other hand, 3.7km is forever, and there's a long, slow uphill drag. Also, I bet these stones get pretty slick on a wet day. The road consists of smooth, square pavers set in dirt that comes all the way to the surface, to minimize the bouncing around.

24. Saint-Python (km 115.5, 1500 meters), Rating: **

Unless the internet is lying to me, there is no actual St. Python. Too bad; I was never all that inspired by the stories of the saints. Maybe if one of them had been named after a deadly snake or a troupe of British comedy geniuses, I would have paid more attention. Anyway, these 1500 meters are still just preamble.

Phase 3: Saint-Python -- Maing/Monchaux-sur-Écaillon

This has to be the worst part of the race. After the last half hour, you've said your hellos to the cobbles, but you are still some 40km from the true start of hostilities. So you wait. And pedal. And bounce around some more: nearly 12 of the next 40k are on cobbles. At least there's a feed zone early on.

One note: just because the race hasn't gotten interesting doesn't mean nothing is happening. Winning or meaningfully contesting Paris-Roubaix requires above all else a lack of bad luck (nothing distinguishes this from "good luck" quite as nicely as Paris-Roubaix). In these first ten secteurs of pavé are just as many flat tires as any other portion of the race, and the number of crashes is tempered only slightly by the reduced urgency. Lots of guys crash and/or flat in this phase of the race, and even if they get back to the front -- a likely occurrence -- they've already burned more matches than they planned.

Oh, and one other note: this is the portion of the race where cobbles secteurs are most likely to come and go from one year to the next. To stay abreast of the rotating course design, I've thrown in a few alternates to our standard secteur countdown.

23. Vertain (km 119.5, 2300 meters), Rating: ***

No doubt the distance is the issue. Also, at this point the cobbled secteurs are starting to feel a bit relentless, you'd think. This one makes it 9.3km of stones from km 104 to 121.

Alternate 23: Solesmes - Haussy (km 119, 800 meters), Rating: **

Used in 2014, the cobbles seem relatively flat and smooth, packed in dirt. No great tricks in store.

22. Capelle-sur-Ecaillon - Le Buat (km 126.5, 1700 meters) ***

Interesting section, it starts with a 4% descent and then a long 7% uphill, the steepest of the cobbled secteurs.[154] It was only unearthed from a farmer's field in time for the 2005 race. The dust will be flying here.

Alternate 22: Saulzoir (km 126, 1200 meters), Rating: **

Another of the 2014 additions, the only grainy video I can find shows them to be pretty typical of the early cobbles, flat and unremarkable.

Possible 21. Aulnoy-lez-Valenciennes - Famars (km 130, 2600 meters) *****

The first of two consecutive sectors which were briefly returned to the race after an absence of... here the info gets a little murky. I'm also a little short on details as to why they rate five stars. But this is probably the first big moment of the race. Still 120km from the velodrome, this secteur kicks off a brutal stretch of four secteurs in quick succession, 8km of stones in 12km of riding. The race has avoided it most years, so file this

---

[154] The 2016 edition includes a secteur called Hameau de Buat and has been advertised as being an uphill set of cobbles. The Hameau de Buat stones have not appeared previously, but might be associated in some way with the secteur 22 menu listed above, like a parallel track or something.

one away as a remote possibility. A five-star secteur at the halfway mark is a bit sadistic, I suppose.

More likely 21: Verchain-Maugré - Quérénaing (km 130, 1600 meters), Rating: ***

The sensible option. So sensible, in fact, that this sector appeared in the 2015 Tour de France. From that you can infer that these stones are on the polite side, and they are. Three stars has more to do with the distance.

Bonus Secteur. Famars - Quérénaing (km 135, 1200 meters), Rating: **

The other returning/mystery secteur. It might be run in reverse, as it seems to have been in 2014, in which case you can skip the next secteur, or flip the order.

Alternate Bonus. Quérénaing - Maing (km 135-ish - 2500 meters), Rating: ***

I'm no longer sure where to place this sector. Present in 2013 at km 133 and in 2016 as well, it was absent in 2014, but a similar sector ran in reverse, before the Famars sector, and started at Verchain-Maugré, also rating three stars but only running 1600 meters. Up and down a bit. In good condition.

20. Maing - Monchaux-sur-Ecaillon (km 136, 1600 m), Rating: ***

Apparently there are some big holes early on, but after that it's more of the same.

Phase 4a: Monchaux -- Arenberg

Finally, it's business time… and time to get back on track with the secteur order and statistics.

This is where the race descends into madness — not mythical course madness but actual flippin' crazy behavior. Everybody knows that the rapidly-approaching Arenberg Trench and Haveluy secteurs are strategically dangerous and selective. Even if you don't crash, chances are someone near you will, unless you are riding very close to the front. So working backward -- you need to be in the front in Arenberg or your day could well be over. This means you need to survive Haveluy in great shape, which means you need to *start* Haveluy near the front, which means you'd better move up in time... but everyone else has the same idea, so the sooner you move up, the better, except everyone else has *that* idea too. Bottom line: once you get off the Monchaux stones, you need be ready for the real action.

19. Haveluy (km 153, 2500 meters), Rating: ****

The "Secteur Bernard Hinault," named after the famous Bretagne who hated this race. Maybe the Haveluiennes named it after him following a night of drunken revelry, and it was one of those joking ideas that everyone loved, even if they can't quite remember why. Anyway, Pete and I rode it, it's one of the classic dug-out-of-a-field secteur, with a high crown in the middle and cobbles on the perimeter in varying stages of merging with the adjoining fields. Actually, even the crown is grassy. Anyway, this is where Garmin came a-cropper in 2010, and between that and our recon I can tell you that the stones are OK but there's plenty of treachery lurking.

18. Arenberg Trench (km 161, 2400 meters), Rating: *****

Any questions? Truly one of the greatest scenes in cycling.

Also, the race is most certainly on at this stage. The stones are pretty difficult to deal with; the crown comes and goes; and there are plenty of holes to add a layer of treachery. Whatever riders say about Arenberg (not considered the worst), it does hurt. Of that 2400 meters probably 1500 is slightly uphill on bad, disorganized stones which keep you on high alert.

Phase 4b -- Post-Arenberg

Another stretch of the race where cobbled sectors come and go. Briefly there was a three-star Millonfosse secteur, 1400 meters and close to the end of the trench, but that has been replaced starting in 2013 by the Pont Gibus stones and the Wandignies-Hamage marathon. These variations can really affect the tempo of the race — if bunched tightly enough, they can add up to a very heavy phase of the race. But if spread out, they tend to encourage more regrouping, where riders keep their powder mostly dry for another 20km or so. Certainly right after Arenberg the lead groups tend to slow down and regroup on the highway for a bit. We are still some 90km from the finish.

17. Wallers - Hélesmes (Pont Gibus) (km 167, 1600 meters), Rating: ***

This sector begins a trio that were adopted for the 2014 Tour de France, one of that race's more exciting recent chapters.[155]

---

[155] Paris-Roubaix secteurs in the Tour de France have a nice little history to them. There have been too many cobblestone stages over the years to recount here, but suffice to

Which is all well and good, but the requirements of the Tour are quite different from those of Paris-Roubaix. Cobbles need to be relatively non-threatening, or at least not likely to arbitrarily remove the favorites for the three-week spectacle before the first mountain stage.

This sector was refurbished by ASO for the 2013 race, at the cost of EUR1 million. The result is a very nice set of stones... which is not exactly a compliment. The "Pont Gibus" nickname is a tribute to Gilbert Duclos-Lasalle, a/k/a Gibus, who would have powered across these rocks with no great difficulty. Before refurbishing, I gather from old photos that this road was truly nasty, with a high, rounded crown and plenty of mud to help riders fall off it. But if progress no longer means paving over cobblestones, it does now seem to mean making them a bit less sadistic.

16. Hornaing - Wandignies-Hamage (km 174.5, 3700 meters), Rating: ****

Another of the Tour de France-approved sectors, and a fairly tidy set of square stones. No gradient to them, just a couple gentle turns. But the road is narrow and on a wet day the

---

say they are a recurring feature, particularly now that the Cobbled Classics have received such worldwide attention. I certainly recall a riveting stage from the 1985 Tour on the cobbles, though that was a stage battle with no consequences for the overall. After that they didn't show up much, but were brought back with some fanfare in 2010 (just a great year in cycling), where they produced some separation among the favorites and a small-group stage sprint won by Thor Hushovd.

They returned in 2014, where Vincenzo Nibali didn't merely gain separation from his rivals — he won the Tour. Gliding across the rain-slicked stones, Nibali accelerated multiple times, along with teammate Jakob Fuglsang and stage winner Lars Boom, even dropping Fabian Cancellara along the way. Chris Froome, the defending winner, abandoned after crashing (unrelated to the cobbles). Every threat to Nibali lost at least two minutes on the day, including Alberto Contador nearly three minutes down as well as a group of favorites at 2.28. The race was never close again. Another cobbled stage featured in 2015 but featured nice weather and produced no fireworks.

shoulder would be treacherous. Beyond that... 3.7km is a long time for your wrists and arms to be in crisis.

15. Warlaing - Brillon (km 182, 2400 meters), Rating: ★★★

Re-pointed in 2009 (again, for Tour de France usage), this is yet another beastly long stretch of stones. On its own, it might not impress, but the proximity of this sector to the next one is what brings the hurt to the riders.

14. Tilloy - Sars-et-Rosieres (km 185, 2400 meters), Rating: ★★★★

Good god, another 2.4km? By this point in the race the riders might not care about anything less than the four-star, seriously bumpy stuff, which this isn't, but for some reason this sector got up-rated to four stars anyway. Again, the character of the rocks themselves is only part of the challenge; the sheer number of them, and how they are sequenced, can be equally hard to deal with.

Phase 5: Orchies

The last feed zone of the day comes right after the Tilloy secteur, and in Hell there is no chance anyone monkeys around here. Food is a complete necessity for what's coming.

As to what that is, the short answer is the decisive action of the race. Winning breaks have happened earlier than here, but only when they involve a non-favorite or a dark horse who is given some leeway by teams who don't want their top riders emptying the tank with 80k to go. But by Orchies you can no longer assume that any move is a feint. Tom Boonen won from here in 2012, and Fabian Cancellara did the same in 2010.

13. Beuvry-la-Forêt - Orchies (km 192, 1400 meters), Rating: ***

The "Secteur Marc Madiot," it consists of 700 meters of unearthed cobbledy madness and 700 meters of new stones, laid down for the race prior to the 2007 edition. While lacking in any truly awful features, the older stuff is dirty and rough, and on a wet day this could be a quagmire.

12. Orchies (km 197, 1700 meters), Rating: ***

Not banging, but muddy (or dusty) and irregular. Kind of a messy stretch, with a noticeable, occasionally pronounced, crown in the middle. Where the crown gets sharp, riders must balance themselves along the narrow line, but there are acceptable alternative routes on the margins.

11. Auchy-lez-Orchies - Bersée (km 203, 2600 meters), Rating: ****

Recent repairs got this secteur a modest rating in the past, but it's been up-rated to four stars' worth of pounding and mess. Strategic importance is very high, since it precedes the Mons-en-Pévèle secteur by just a few km. And it has a bit of everything: smooth sections, parts with a crown, margins made of dirt or of sharp, rough stones, and so forth. Another thing to be alert for: changing from one type of challenge to another. The fourth star is as much about the variable conditions as the length.

Phase 6: Bersee -- Vertain

Prime attacking territory. The pack has thinned out enough by now that getting to the front is no longer a priority in the smooth-tarmac gaps between terrifying pave secteurs; those moments are for taking your foot off the gas and gathering your wits. Of course, taking a breather and letting your guard down are two different things, a lesson many riders have learned the hard way. If there's already a danger man up the road, those gaps are also a good place to make up ground for a chasing group that is willing to work together. Assuming such a thing still exists.

More conventionally, though, the Mons-en-Pévèle secteur is the big feature, one where riders are either attacking or trying to survive. In 2006, these stones became notorious for picking up George Hincapie and his bike, snapping his steerer tube in half, and spitting him out into a ditch holding his newly-separated shoulder. Crashes happen enough so that fans may struggle to remember one from another, but the haunting sight of a very-fit HIncapie suddenly sitting up holding his dismembered handlebars was one I'll never forget. As if this race wasn't scary enough, imagine rumbling over some of the worst stones and suddenly losing all control over your front wheel. Swerving off the road was by no means the worst possible outcome there.

10. Mons-en-Pévèle (km 208, 3000 meters), Rating: ★★★★★

On the podium of famous secteurs, along with Arenberg and Carrefour de l'Arbe, this sector has featured almost every year since 1978. Owing to its length (ugh), its position in the race, and the varying conditions, it's a five-star beauty. At times the road can be full of dirt or mud, and the latter portions are rough, crowned, and treacherous as a viper. In recent times it's seen critical moves go away, or as mentioned above, seen riders disappear.

9. Mérignies - Avelin (km 214, 700 meters), Rating: **

A mere trifle, perhaps? The distance is short and the stones aren't bad in any way. But the road is narrow and there's a slight crown.

8. Pont-Thibaut (km 217.5, 1400 meters), Rating: ***

Dirty, big crown, lots of grass for slippage. This looks more like cyclocross terrain than a road. The race has escaped rain for several years running as of 2016, but when its luck runs out, this will be another possible Waterloo for riders.

7. Templeuve l'Epinette (km 223.5, 200 meters), Rating: * / Le Moulin de Vertain (km 224, 500 meters), Rating: **

First of a couple sectors listed in tandem, because though distinct from one another, they are so close together that they function as more or less a single entity. The Templeuve stones are more classic Paris-Roubaix cobbles, unearthed for the 2002 race and now a fixture in the race. Not bruisers but narrow and slick. Also, the crown is a tad pronounced, making it easy to slide sideways if you're not in position. The good news is that at this point in the race there won't be any peloton to speak of.

Phase 7: Vertain -- Gruson

Now time is running out, and any rider who doesn't fancy their chances in a velodrome sprint has to pick a spot to attack. The good news is, if you're still in contention heading into this stretch, it's because you're good at riding on cobbles, in which case the next 12km present a target-rich environment. The

5.2km of cobbles found in the next three secteurs are simply classic Paris-Roubaix stones, big and nasty, with the roads in conditions that vary from theoretically manageable to making grown men cry.

6. Cysoing - Bourghelles (km 230, 1300 meters), Rating: **** / Bourghelles - Wannehain (km 232.5, 1100 meters), Rating: ***

The Secteur Duclos-LaSalle, because apparently France has run out of riders to name Paris-Roubaix cobbles after. In fairness, this one predates Pont Gibus. Still, if anyone deserves a double honor, it's France's double-winner Madiot. Anyway, the Bourghelles sectors have a nasty stretch with some holes on the side, but mostly they are comparatively regular and manageable. The crown is pretty mellow, at least.

5. Camphin en Pévèle (km 237, 1800 meters), Rating: ****

Poetically named the "Pavé de la Justice," though I think that has more to do with being connected to a street in Camphin-en-Pévèle called Rue de la Justice. Anyway it sounds super cool, and it's also the remnants of a Roman road, long and straight, which is even cooler. The cobbles are old, rough, crowned and sporting some grass in the particularly bad last 300 meters. It's also a full 1.8km long, though much of it is a bit smoother than what comes next.

4. Carrefour de l'Arbre (km 240, 2100 meters), Rating: *****

This really has to be the worst of it, right? This most famous of sectors is named the "crossroad of the trees," which I don't fully understand, but it consists of five turns at or near 90 degrees, and an exhausting array of challenges.[156] The cobbles are irregular, the crown is a mess, there's mud or dust a-plenty, and the strategic importance is through the roof. When it's wet, puddles can conceal race-ending potholes. Maybe even a collarbone if you hit it just right. The race is regularly won and lost in this stretch.

3. Gruson (km 242, 1100 meters), Rating: **

After what's just gone down, this is child's play, right? In truth, the road is narrow, straight, not horribly bumpy, but prone to treachery on the margins in the form of puddles disguising holes. By any normal measure, such as that of the 2014 Tour which rolled over these stones, this is a difficult, dangerous couple of minutes. In Paris-Roubaix, their more likely significance is that riders are really, really gassed coming off the Carrefour de l'Arbe, and if someone has the strength to attack, it's not a bad place to win the race.

Phase 8: The finish

If a group of any size survives past Gruson, the chances of them entering the velodrome together for a sprint suddenly go way up. The Hem cobbles come after a break from the bouncing, and barely count as cobbles after what the riders have been through. The final 300 meters of pave in Roubaix are city stones, which is code for not really cobblestones at all, as far as the race is concerned. In short, if you haven't ditched

---

[156] Among the special challenges would be the race's highest concentration of drunk Belgian fans. Throughout cycling, from Alpe d'Huez to the Tour of California, the proximity of a large concentration of spectators is a constant disruptive threat. But I can't think of any place in the sport where fans are more likely to cause riders problems than here. It's a tiny road on a flat field with people closing in on both sides in huge numbers, and nothing to stop them from darting across the road at the wrong time.

your companions by now, there is no reason you should be able to here.

One of my favorite editions of Paris-Roubaix was 2008, when at last you had a fairly complete set of champions riding alone. Cancellara was the 2006 winner and had only deferred his 2007 chances to his teammate O'Grady. Boonen has his 2005 win still in his pocket. Alessandro Ballan was the 2007 winner in Flanders, the only man strong enough to de-throne Boonen in his home race since his ascension in '05. [Teammates don't count.] The three rival champions rode alone, all other challengers rendered irrelevant, and the only question was whether anyone had the ability to drop Boonen before Roubaix. They couldn't -- this time -- and the result was predictable.

2. Hem (km 250 - 1400 m) **

Least of anyone's problems by now.[157] Flat, relatively smooth, bracketed by asphalt strips so you don't need to even think about riding the stones. There are still some 10km remaining in the race, so gamesmanship is still a possibility, but the cobbles add little to whatever plan one has in mind here. The race changes character shortly afterward as the peloton leaves behind the endless farmlands and reenters civilization in the outskirts of Lille.

1. Roubaix/Espace Crupelandt (km 258 to 300 m) *

Some of the coolest cobbles in the world. This harmless sector is named after the winner of the 1912 and 1914 editions,

---

[157] Subject to change. Apparently Hem is planning to lengthen its secteur to 3km sometime soon. Whether that features in the race is to be determined, but it could present a new determining factor.

Charles Crupelandt, one of those French Flemings I mentioned above. Crupelandt sounds like he could be the subject of a pretty amazing book: double-winner in Roubaix; winner of the *Croix de Guerre* for his WWI service; convicted post-war car battery thief; and scourge of cycling after he circumvented the French licensing commission and raced the 1923 edition (rather well, rumor has it) through a dissident federation, the *Société des Courses.* He lived out his later years running a bistro in Roubaix, and was honored 50 years after his death with this sector… fittingly, since both of his victories were won in bunch sprints in Roubaix.

Competitively speaking the cobbles are inconsequential, but spiritually they are as powerful a sight as any. The sector was created in 1996 (the day of its naming) in honor of the centenary edition of the race, by reforming the Avenue Alfred Motte to include a newly-cobbled median. Included in the array is one stone bearing the name of each Paris-Roubaix champion, with the year or years alongside.

The end of this sector is less than half a kilometer from the velodrome entrance. When you get to the *Espace Crupelandt*, it's either time for a parade to the finish, or for lining up your sprinting strategy.

*****

Our next stop was that most diabolical stretch of Hell, the Arenberg Trench. The same tranquil swatch of forest from the previous Thursday was now packed with humanity and crackling with excitement like Old Trafford on Derby Day. What would ordinarily be a two minute drive from the exit off the A23 to Route D40 was pretty much a logjam of occupied and parked cars. People were exiting coming from the south, from earlier points in the race, and traffic on the exit was a tad sticky, but we missed the exit anyway, then turned around at the next exit and came from the north, where the ramp traffic was more manageable. From there we slithered off the D40 at the next road, the Rue Les Glodennes, to dump the car. Across the street was a miniature shrine of some sort, set off in a field next to the edge of the trees with a small parking lot and worship space. The peace of this scene was disrupted by scads of cycling fans on foot or bike, plus the odd VIP-looking bus rolling by. We were a good half-hour or more ahead of the arrival of the race, so the ten minute walk meant nothing much, in hindsight. At the time it was the longest ten minutes of my life, especially given that we had no idea what would happen when we reached the Trench, or whether we would actually manage to squeeze into position along the route.

What happened was that we simply found a very good place to stand, watched the race, and rolled out to the next phase of the day with no trouble whatsoever. Since the *Trouée* is as long as it is, and parking is pretty scant, it never really fills up. Both ends get packed tight, the first choice of fans who can't or won't make an effort to get further into the Trench, and there were some mobile party structures encamped at the north end which ferried in a large chunk of humanity. The center of the Trench is substantially unfenced and not at all at viewing capacity, just a few spectators mingling and maybe a rope providing a theoretical separation between watchers and riders, until something goes wrong anyway. For us, once we walked into the Forest for a minute or two, the human chain along the fence began opening up, and we occupied a few spaces in a reasonably short time.

There really isn't any point along the Trench where you need to be more than anywhere else. I suppose the entrance is the most spectacular, watching guys react as they hit the brutal stones for the first time. At the opposite end, where we were standing, you have the benefit of seeing the race start to take shape. For all the adjectives used to describe the Trench, perhaps the most fitting from the racing perspective is "selective." Rarely does a big group emerge together from the north end. Often the race regroups after exiting the *Trouée*, if nobody is pushing the pace, so that selection may be temporary. But the combination of the Forest, the Secteur Bernard Hinault, and the smooth pavement in between constitute the traditional first big shakeup, and the pace and energy are frenetic until the end of the Forest, when the shaking and the madness stop and riders and teams often slow down to take stock before the hostilities boil over again.

Bottom line, standing at either end has its benefits, and watching in the middle of the Forest isn't so bad either. Things can go awry at any moment -- burst inner tubes, components gone missing, wheels slipping, chains dropping, and of course riders hitting the deck -- be it you or someone inconveniently placed in your path. In 2011 some people watching the race from a quiet point in the middle found themselves standing with Tom Boonen, who had punctured a tire and was waiting for help. It's all pure Paris-Roubaix, from one end of the infernal Trench to the other.

Arenberg Trench on race day. Photo by Chris Fontecchio

Eventually the roar of the race arrived. Helicopter chopping came into earshot, if not view -- there is little daylight visible past the trees when you're in the Trench. But there is no mistaking the distant sight of movement. From the north end you're looking down a straight road with a pronounced dip in the middle, so the entire *Trouée* is in sight. Eventually a few official cars and motos pass by, and eventually they've got the breakaway in tow.[158]

---

[158] Most vehicular traffic is kept out of the Arenberg Trench during the race until the peloton is safely away — which is the other half of why this secteur is so threatening to the hopes of riders. Not only is it a likely place to suffer mechanical trouble or a flat tire, it's a place where your team car can't help you. Teams have people standing along the route with spare wheels, and neutral service or your team car will eventually show up, but cycling is like real life, and for 364 days a year vehicles are entirely prohibited from entering the Forest, full

The sound of a cyclist passing by on the pavé of Arenberg is a distinct rattling of bike parts, not too different from the sounds of the *kasseien* in Flanders. But the visual appearance of the riders was striking, as they weaved and wobbled, in obvious discomfort, like climbers struggling up the last few meters of some high-alpine super-ramp. There was no order, nobody was all that intent on drafting anyone else. The break on this day had been away for a few hours now, and although it included some cobbles warhorses like Jurgen Roelands, they had been pushing the pace for a long time, and it had taken its toll. The break had, to put it bluntly, shattered itself on the stones. Maarten Wynants, Adam Hansen, Jeremy Hunt and Chris Sutton, representing the post-Arenberg surviving remnants of the break, would stay away for another half hour before succumbing to the peloton outside Orchies.

A few minutes later it was the turn of the leaders. Nobody in attendance was left wondering where the favorites were. Riding at the tip of the spear, storming straight down the center crest of the stones, was Fabian Cancellara. Tom Boonen sat a couple spots back, behind Cancellara's teammate Matti Breschel. Thor Hushovd hovered close by, as did Juan Antonio Flecha. The best riders weren't merely afforded the prime position by reputation; they seized it, pouring the wattage on the pedals, exhibiting a stolid determination as they checked off another (particularly nasty) box.

From there it was another ten minutes, maybe, of riders going by, less numerous with each passing wave until all that

---

stop. When they say winning Paris-Roubaix requires you to avoid bad luck, this is what they mean.

remained were the quasi-hopeless stragglers and the team cars. For us there was still plenty to cheer: the sight of someone turning themselves inside out to survive these infernal stones is always inspiring. It's especially so if you can recognize them as the guy who set up Flecha by riding 50k or so on the front, for example, and frankly no less cool when you catch a pavé rookie being baptized by fire. The mere act of men racing bikes across this surface is the attraction. That some of them will have their names recorded in the ledgers of history... that's for later. This chapter is about suffering, in the baseline form that every rider today will experience.

Grinta on the march. Photo by Chris Fontecchio

When it was finally over and the last rider still competing (or wobbling home) had gone by, about half the crowd headed briskly for the exit -- the race chasers, people looking for a TV set, or folks who have someplace else to be. At the north end of the road the VIP mobile colossus wasn't going anywhere for a while. They may still be there, as far as I know.

Having far to walk means we were close to the highway on-ramp, and within a minute or two we were speeding up the A3 to Lille. None of us actually knew where the Roubaix Velodrome was, but we figured (correctly) that we wouldn't get very far before bumping into some evidence of the race route, whereupon we could just park and walk once it began to look at all crowded. The sports park is on the southeastern side of Roubaix, barely more than a couple kilometers outside the A-route ring around greater Lille, and barely inside the line border between the village and open farmland. As it should be -- this is a rural race with a mildly urban finish, and the Roubaix Velodrome's location minimizes the urbanity of greater Lille.

Once we dumped the car again we only walked a few blocks before we found ourselves on the Avenue Alfred Motte, the last city street on the race course before it turns into the Velodrome.[159] Monsieur Motte, from a noble Roubaix family, isn't well known around the internets, where he is listed as "chevalier," i.e. a dude on a horse. Anyway, if you can picture someone rolling into the finish and mugging for the moto cameras with red brick walls in the background, that's his namesake. At this point the finish line, including a lap around the track, is maybe 2km away or so, which means this isn't

---

[159] The finish line has mostly been on a track, specifically the Roubaix Vélodrome, since 1943, except for 1966-68, when the parcours was first overhauled into the modern configuration. Prior to 1915 the race ended on the grounds of what is now the Parc des Sports, including the Vélodrome. From 1915-1942, however, the race frequently finished on the broad boulevards of Roubaix, or even neighboring towns Wattrelos or Marcq.

exactly where the hottest action can be found, and as a consequence the people out and about are all moving in one direction. A few minutes later, we reached the day's last stretch of stones.

By this point the avenue, which runs in a straight line from the end of the rural paths to the velodrome, has been renamed the Avenue Roger Salengro, after a French Interior minister who was hounded to suicide at age 46 by his fascist political enemies.[160] Despite the cheerlessness in that name, the road itself marks the promenade to one of cycling's great landmarks, the Roubaix Velodrome. The Avenue itself is two narrow lanes sandwiched around a cobbled track that's cordoned off from traffic by hedgerows and trees. Bicycle traffic -- the race, namely -- is directed off the car track and onto the stones, where the celebration often goes up a notch. The stones are not selective; they're modern and neatly arranged, even by Paris standards.

What makes them so cool is that each winner of Paris-Roubaix has a stone dedicated to him, with the winner's name etched into the very street. This must be especially sweet for multiple winners like Boonen and Cancellara to roll past their name on the way to another victory. For the rest of us, names like Serse Coppi and Fischer and Pelissier and Merckx and Hinault and De Vlaeminck evoke the race's history in the very material that makes us care about these records. Nothing is fancy here. Roads are named after obscure, tragic politicians. Coal and cloth are the area's historical backbone. You win our race?

---

[160] People who bemoan the lack of decorum in modern politics haven't looked very far back into the past. Remember the Ides of March?

Here's a cobble. Monument to the winners? Let's carve up a cobble.

Within a block of the race's last turn before the Velodrome, human traffic backs up from the sweeping arc of the Rue Alexandre Fleming. Named for the Scot who discovered penicillin, this street leaves the city, eases the team cars into a lot behind Cyrille Guimard's office, and directs the racers to the Velodrome entrance. Once the velodrome is full, fans spill over onto the sidewalks of the Rue Alexandre Fleming. In the space of a block we went from light foot traffic to a wall of humanity. Pete, Paul and I swam through the crowd, looking for an opening where it might be possible to watch, and I departed for the press room located in the sports complex next door to the track.

My camera had died by now, but karma balanced things out a bit. There was a press pass waiting for me, and I parked my belongings and headed for the infield to watch the race come in. My first try was through the stands, the couple dozen rows of benches covered by a tin roof where the ladies and gentlemen traditionally take in the race without fear of getting soaked. But the guard only let in people with a certain type of pass, which mine was not. So I doubled back to Rue Alexandre Fleming where the gendarmes let me over the rope, assuming I knew what to do next.

So, with Fabian Cancellara some 10-15 minutes away, I found myself standing on the very road he would use to find his way home. My only choice was to walk down the road and onto the Roubaix Velodrome track, the sport's hallowed ground on the sport's hallowed day, from where I could tuck myself into the infield with the rest of the press. It was a dull, overcast day, the velodrome was packed to the limit with people, and if I didn't eventually move I would get run over by Cancellara. This is what I meant when I spoke of feeling like I was standing in the middle of a movie I've been watching my whole adult life. Where I walk to is where Greg LeMond and Sean Kelly tiptoed around a crash in 1985 -- the first race I ever saw -- as Eddy Planckaert and Jozef Lieckens slipped out on the wet track. They were racing for third on the day, behind Frenchmen Marc Madiot and Bruno Wojtinek. At this moment I was waiting for the winner.

Cancellara seals his Double. Photo by Elizabeth Freer

Eventually he made it, to the roaring delight of the crowd. A woman holding a child in a Saxo Bank Swiss champions' jersey identical to Cancellara's was standing a few feet from me: Cancellara's wife, and the child undoubtedly the little girl whose angel pendant Cancellara held up for the cameras as his good luck charm a week earlier. The Swiss Bear celebrated with a few fist pumps as he passed the line, signaled by the ringing of the one-lap-to-go bell. He was mostly business on that lap, gave one last celebration as he rolled over the line again for the win, went another 30 meters or so, and pulled over, exhausted and surrounded by some team folks -- management and soigneurs, then his family. It seemed like he needed time to gather his wits or strength or both. Having attacked from over 50km away, the final act in a devastating fortnight of cycling prowess, where he checked off a few of the biggest goals of his professional life, this was a man on empty.

Two minutes later the race for second came in, with Thor Hushovd outsprinting a sarcastically-clapping Juan Antonio Flecha, a sign of the latter's disapproval toward Hushovd's tactical approach on the day. An even more dispirited Boonen came in with the next group, another minute and 14 seconds later. Never much for a sprint when the win has evaporated, Boonen lost out on fourth place to Roger Hammond, one of the many riders whom the Belgian champion would bitterly accuse of riding for second that day, rather than working together to bring back the lone attacker, once Cancellara took off. Bjorn Leukemans was next, seconds back, followed by a black-clad Filippo Pozzato, whose Italian Champion's kit was darkened in mourning of the death of national team coach and former two-time Paris-Roubaix winner Franco Ballerini, who had died in a car accident in February. Pozzato was honored in

the post-race celebration with the Ballerini Prize, for the top
Italian finisher, before heading to the famous showers.[161]

Boonen home in fifth place. Photo by Elizabeth Freer

As we left the velodrome pointed in the direction of normal
life, Pete bid goodbye to the experience by chatting up a
Rabobank mechanic and getting a race-used bike bottle for his
troubles. The lesson is, of course, that around the professional

---

[161] Yes, there are famous showers, or at least famously unadorned concrete walls
shaped into shower stalls for the riders who survive to the line. The hard-man aesthetic
doesn't let up on this day until riders make it back to their team bus. Nor does the sense of
history, as the showers now bear small plaques with the names of former race winners on
them.

cycling scene good things happen to beautiful women and gear geeks, and what Pete lacks in feminine guile (e.g. all of it), he more than makes up for with the self-taught knowledge of a serious mechanic and gear nut. Gear, and the obsession around its numerous details, is one of those doors to the sport that I can't seem to walk through. I enjoy doing what I know how to do, but there is something[162] stopping me from going any further. I truly enjoy cleaning a drive train and assembling my bike for travel, but can't get my mind around making purposeful contact with a bottom bracket. I don't have the patience for catalogues, and have been taught to distrust most ads to the extent they are angled at getting people to buy bikes they don't need.

But to Pete's delight, gear is all that's happening by the time we head for the exits — mechanics cleaning and storing the day's fleet of bikes. The cobbled classics are over, and the riders who came for them are headed out too -- maybe to a victory party, maybe to a beach in Spain for a break before summer, or maybe just home. Some guys are staying around for Wednesday's Brabantse Pijl, a hilly, barely cobbled ride that combines the skill set of de Ronde with a good deal more climbing. A small number of combatants from Paris-Roubaix will continue racing through the Ardennes Classics, where they join forces or engage in battle with the elite climbers of the sport. Lars Boom would be pressed into duty a week later in the Amstel Gold Race by his Rabobank team, the unofficial hosts of the biggest Dutch classic, an all-hands-on-deck affair for the country's emblematic team.[163] The end of the cobbled classics is the end of a season-within-the-season, but your next

---

[162] Bandwidth?
[163] He took the DNF in that one.

mini-season could start as early as the next morning. That's cycling.

So the riders were washing up and heading for the exits, via team buses or private cars, but the end of the race is the start of the work day for the mechanics. They are not likely to be in a hurry unless a victory party is in the mix, and the friendlier ones might be happy to chat while they go about the scrubbing and tinkering tasks that lie ahead. They're nocturnal creatures by nature anyway, I'm told, and never more so than during a stage race where the deadline is tomorrow's race start. We lingered long enough to take in the scene at the gear trucks, a fitting place to close the chapter. Nothing is more final than seeing the specially-outfitted Paris-Roubaix bikes dismantled, cleaned, and stowed neatly like sardines hanging from the walls and roof of the gear truck. Tomorrow or the next day or maybe Wednesday in Brabantse Pijl -- a/k/a the Brabant Arrow, running from Leuven to the suburbs of Brussels along the linguistic border of Flemish and Wallonian Brabant Province -- as the riders head down to breakfast and the mechanics slowly unlock and open the doors to the gear trucks, the cycle of cycling renewal will begin again.

*****

The exodus from the classics was happening everywhere for the next 24 hours. Our friend Paul caught a train from Lille back home to Paris, proving that the city which gave the race its first name is still a decent home base for following the race. Pete and I headed to Brussels' Zaventem Airport, for a quick night's stay and a mid-morning departure back to the US. On Getaway Monday the airport is traditionally besieged by the sport of cycling. On this day, lines for security were at post-9/11 lengths, and Pete had to do some bargaining with the security staff to make his flight home via Zurich.

I had several hours to watch the scene around the American carriers, whose check-in area was a mountain of bike luggage: hard shell frame and wheel cases, duffle bags adorned with team or sponsor names, and so on. Standing close by was a gaggle of skinny guys in their late teens, clearly cyclists, and primped like pros with sculpted hair and performance eyewear, most sporting some kind of USA Cycling logo. This would be the US junior national team, which sponsors kids on the rise for parts of the season through a base in Izegem, West Flanders. Their bubbling enthusiasm and dash of bravado might have been attributable to their status as representatives of their nation, a heady thing for anyone, especially an 18-year-old. It might also have had to do with the performance of one Lawson Craddock of Houston, who finished third in the Paris-Roubaix Espoirs race a few days earlier.

Craddock joins Taylor Phinney, currently of BMC, as two prominent investments in cycling by the US national program, with an eye for the classics. Or, well, he did. By 2012 Craddock had graduated from the Juniors -- guys under 19 -- and left the USA Cycling program behind for the Bontrager-Livestrong team and the U23 racing world. Known in France as the *espoirs* ("hopefuls") category, this circuit is for riders aged 19-22, and both Paris-Roubaix and the Tour of Flanders hold U23 events, big targets for the guys in that age group. The Paris-Roubaix Espoirs version happens in late May while the Ronde van Vlaanderen *Beloften* runs sometime close to the senior event.

In 2010, Phinney became the first rider ever to win consecutive Paris-Roubaix Espoirs events, and at 6'5" in height, with tremendous raw power, the son of former 7-Eleven star Davis Phinney and Olympic silver medalist Connie Carpenter is on course for a classics career. He got his first ride in Paris-Roubaix with BMC in 2012, finishing a rather stunning 15th. This and his earlier promise don't make Phinney a lock to become the first American to win on the Pave, but they give reason for hope. The numbers don't lie, and Phinney's big frame can only emphasize the race for him even more. If he slots into the Magnus Backstedt category of riders who truly specialize in the Hell of the North, it wouldn't come as a major shock.

Craddock's podium spot in the junior Paris-Roubaix would be a logical springboard for success following in Phinney's footsteps. Also a son of a pro, Craddock's dad Tom was a pro downhiller in the 1990s, and dad has done much to nurture Lawson's and his older brother Parker's interest in the sport. Craddock grabbed a strong 11th at the Ronde van Vlaanderen Beloften in 2011 and targeted the race again the following spring, only to suffer bad luck and miss out on another big result. Like Phinney, these results can be filed alongside a suitcase worth of promising *beloften* hopes that were never realized, but if he does go on to bigger things, we will point to them as early shots across the bow of the sport. Time will tell.[164]

---

[164] But it probably won't tell us that Craddock is going to win big in the classics. As of 2016, Craddock had turned pro with Giant-Shimano/Alpecin, and two years later had signed on with the Cannondale team. But Giant saw potential in him as a climber, and by 2014 Craddock was on the podium at the Tour of California, followed by a role as the lead pacemaker for Tom Dumoulin at the 2015 Vuelta a España in the mountains. The classics aren't on his program in 2016, but big things might be around the corner regardless.

Anyway, back at the airport the scene goes on. Standing outside the Tintin bazaar I say hello to the VeloNews staffers who went over for the action. I'm rubbing elbows with a few cyclotourists who discovered the joys of riding up steep, awful surfaces in lousy weather, just like I did. I'm still in the cycling world, a bubble that doesn't pop til I change planes at Dulles Airport and drift back into the ordinary world of travelers, back home in America, back to Seattle and my family and my true life.

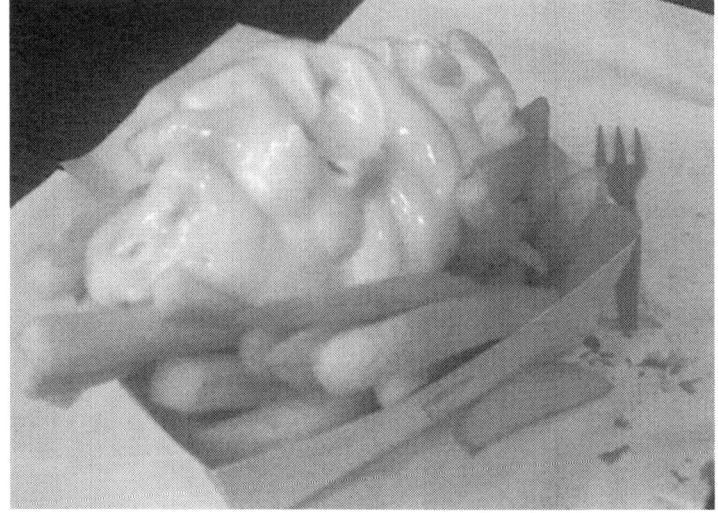

Photo by Chris Fontecchio

Epilogue

April 2, 2011, Seattle. Ronde van Vlaanderen Eve. With my wife on travel, the kitchen is all mine. It's time to prepare the frites. I've lived my entire life eating fries, without ever giving much thought to how to make them. In Vermont there was a place that pressed whole potatoes through a fry cutter and deep-fried them right in front of you, but only after a little searching did I discover that a time-honored technique is to fry them twice, once to soften them up and once more at higher heat to make them crisp. With the Ronde starting at midnight local time, and video to come around 3, I need to prepare everything I can. The first fry happens now. The second... around 4am.

Beer is chilling in the fridge. Leffe Blone and Chimay Blu, though the former will be the key. Sadly, nobody in Seattle took me up on my offer to host a 4am viewing party, and I would hate to open the Chimay without plans to finish it -- not an option with kid duty on tap. But a Leffe will happen, maybe around 4:30 or 5, pursuant to the Podium Cafe tradition, several years running. When the peloton hits the Koppenberg, we toast. We salute the great race and the great racers, we salute the madness of their task and to some degree ours. We salute the cameraderie we have found through connection, albeit a form that still defies human connection. And for those who are willing, we seal it with a nice malty Belgian beer.

Speaking of great racers, Fabian Cancellara is once more the favorite to win. According to his recent efforts in the E3 Prijs Vlaanderen, where he stomped away from the entire peloton for a 20km beat-down, and Milano-Sanremo, where he nearly outsprinted all the sprinters so immense was his strength, Cancellara seems all but unbeatable. There's a certain smiling resignation to the pre-race chatter. Talk of everyone parking in Cancellara's wheel is rampant. Boonen says bold things but his DS Lefevre is said to be giving pep talks. Barely an interview passes, with anyone, until mention has been made of the Swiss Bear. If he doesn't win, it will add to the legend of the race, one too hard and too fickle to predict when faced with even the clearest choices. And if he does... that's cycling.

Also done is the samourai sauce, but that's the easy part. It's just Vietnamese chili paste in mayo, at a 1:4 ratio or thereabouts. We tested this last November, on several unsuspecting potential future Vlaanderophiles who attended my birthday celebration in the city park not far from my house. That was the scene of my last cyclocross race of the season, a nicely rolling, wooded course that (for once) I knew pretty well before the race started. My event was the first of the day, which left a pretty long time afterward for the birthday part. We camped out in a nice viewing spot on the course, a small impromptu team of riders -- friends and their families. By 10:30 the first hibachis were in business. By 11:30, rounds of sausage and grill-heated frites were trickling out. Beer began flowing right after the race, albeit in moderation in light of the kids and the rules. The main accompaniment for the frites was a samourai sauce I had looked up online. Everyone eyed it with suspicion, but virtually all decided it was great.

Cyclocross.

Whether the Tour of Flanders ever becomes a household name in America remains to be seen. As cycling's popularity appears to grow, the spectacle of a race like de Ronde or Paris-Roubaix is sure to attract attention across the pond, but even now in 2016 a country accustomed to making space only for the Tour de France might collectively struggle to pay attention to races in April, overlapping with the postseasons of basketball and hockey as well as the start of baseball. Then there's doping, which could stunt the growth of interest pretty quickly among fans whose knowledge and interest isn't deep enough to withstand scandals. Never mind that the scandals peaked several years ago; it's still all the most casual watcher can be counted on to know about. So it's not a done deal.

One major factor in favor of Americans continuing to discover the classics is, oddly enough, the massive popularity surge of another Belgian import: cyclocross. The simplest description of Cyclocross is that it's the bicycle version of other cross-country sports: cross-country running, equestrian steeple chase, motocross, etc. Take a sport that is ordinarily confined to a clear, set space and unleash it on the natural world, and kapow! You've got a new sport. Personally, I love the term "steeple chase," a relic of a time when people galloped from town to town, with only the sight of the distant steeple to indicate which way to go. See the steeple? See the fields, stone walls, ponds, etc. between you and that steeple? Well... get to work.

Cyclocross grew out of road racing when, presumably in less formal settings, racers would short-cut their route by driving through farmers' fields. Bad idea? Don't knock it til you've tried it. If road racing is a chess match, or a battle of wills that plays out over hours or weeks, cyclocross is a nice, charmingly unsubtle interlude. It's full of bumps, twists, turns, never a dull moment, and the races have always run a bit on the short side, scarcely more than an hour even at the elite professional level. A modern race will simulate the ancient steeple chase concept with pre-existing features, if you can find them, like steep hills, mud, sand, stone walls, even the odd staircase. And when there aren't enough in place beforehand, you just build wooden barriers, typically 1-2 feet high.

Typical cyclocross races are short circuits, about ten minutes' worth of riding per loop. I rode my first amateur 'Cross season in 2011, the results of which I don't care to discuss in much detail, but anyway the courses were typically flat spaces that wandered off to small hills for variety. We raced around a pumpkin farm for one event; a couple schools, several more local or regional parks. We rode on lake beaches, slalomed through lots of Douglas firs, and zipped around the local velodrome, or at least the infield and the steep grassy embankments ringing the site. Courses get much crazier but you get the idea. How many circuits you do depends on your category, but the longest races are just over an hour.

Road racers love it for a couple other reasons besides that make it a nice complement to a season on the pavement. The rough terrain is great for mastering bike handling. Rocks, sticks and other debris toss your front wheel hither and yon, and sand and mud are worse. Every turn is a potential adventure: wet grass, soft dirt, gravel, mud, and so on. But without pavement to make you think twice about riding aggressively, you've got little to lose if you overcook a turn. Falling in a field or the woods costs relatively little in skin and broken bones.

Unless you hook a tree, chances are you're dusting yourself off after a typical crash and hopping back on your bike.

Another way in which cyclocross has caught the attention of roadies practically everywhere is the fitness effect. Churning through fields and forest requires a high-intensity effort that starts from the opening gun and ends when you cross the line. Most new crossers talk about how much their lungs hurt, even more than their legs. After racing a season of cross I sorta get that complaint, though afterwards it's my legs that are shaking like jelly all day, not my lungs.

Cyclocross in Seattle (and my son skillfully remounting his bike). Photo by Chris Fontecchio

The other thing people -- racers and friends, family, fans -- love about cyclocross is the atmosphere. The short circuit courses are viewer-friendly, the vibe is entirely casual, and the emphasis is on fun. Beer plays a major role in cyclocross, with races in Belgium occasionally routed right through the ever-present beer tent and fans worldwide upholding a long-standing tradition of handing beers to straggling riders still navigating the course. So too does silliness. Ask some of my kid neighbors who stood out on a course with my family last November cheering for the "Tighty Whiteys," a team of riders whose kit consisted of nothing more than tall colorful socks, white briefs with the Lion of Flanders on the back, and their number written on their ribcage in magic marker.

Donut handups. Photo by Chris Fontecchio

For all of these reasons cyclocross is exploding in popularity. Seattle, for example, started a second cyclocross series in 2009, because the first longstanding race series wasn't enough, and now a third one is honing in on the fun. If you're here you could conceivably drive to Bellingham, 90 minutes north, and ride their series. Or Spokane, four hours east, to ride theirs. It's three hours south to Portland where cross is taken to extremes, like everything in Portland. It's also three hours north to Vancouver, and if there isn't a burgeoning cross scene in the city that brought us extreme mountain biking courses from the North Shore, I'll eat my mud-strewn leg warmers.

Mud... beer... unusually hard riding... crazy terrain... thrills and spills... Belgium.... Wait a minute. Do you see what's happening here? All of the unique, lovable qualities of the Classics are essentially being consumed by the American public faster than smartphones, but under the easygoing brand of cyclocross. Several Seattle clubs have incorporated the Lion of Flanders into their kit -- in one case, chugging a frosty brew. Riders race in kits, costumes, underwear, or outfits that are even more difficult to explain to children, in November. For the less-dressed, their bare flesh and absurd costumes do not celebrate exhibitionism, but *suffering*, and the love of it. At least one of the Tighty Whitey guys showed signs of a crash, adding extra mud to the cold, the dampness, and the effort of 60 hard minutes to his list of afflictions. By all appearances he loved it as much as our kids.

Not every fan of cyclocross can be expected to transfer that admiration to the cobbled classics. I mean, if you're really just in it for a laugh, you might not find the gladiatorial scenes of Paris-Roubaix as gratifying as a guy racing through your local park with a papier-mache rendering of the Space Needle emanating from his crotch. But those fans who love a race that combines unthinkable challenges from the course and the conditions, and a race among hardened warriors brushing off those challenges, or even embracing them, to animate something more than just a bike race... those fans whose only contact with top-level European road racing is when they stray into a Tour de France feed in July would likely be pretty jazzed to find that there's a version of road racing that combines that elite performance with the madness of cyclocross.

World Cyclocross Championships, 2013, Louisville KY. Photo by Chris Fontecchio

But it's not just about the sport. The other obvious common thread is Belgian culture. Not all of it -- not the church or the squabbling across the language divide or whatever -- but the culture of Belgian cycling. A supposedly reserved people going mad in the freezing rain for a bike race, celebrating with beer and sausage and frietes and all the elements of a good, casual outdoor party. In the American mind Belgium doesn't stand out much, it's a small, civilized place in Europe which hasn't made a major impact on America through immigration or food or language, at least compared to a few of its neighbors. But cycling has long given Belgian fans and athletes a platform to distinguish themselves from the European sports scene, and the culture that has grown up around cycling is becoming a viable export.

Ultimately what makes me and many others admire the Belgian scene is quite simply love. Sports fanhood at its deepest depths has always had an infectious quality. It's what makes you want to watch college basketball involving two schools you didn't attend. The fans are so excited that surely it's worth your time to care a little about what is happening. And so it is with Belgium and its cycling — road, 'Cross, track, and so on. Except that the connection isn't merely some distant wavelength you may or may not detect. It's a feeling you can experience yourself, in person. And not just aesthetically but physically, on your own bike, gulping the same air as you hammer up the same hills that the greats of cycling once rolled across. You can wallow in cycling so much more thoroughly than any other sport I know of. In Flanders, it's all there: the roads, the people, the food and beer, the ancient history of suffering and glory, under brooding spring skies. Open up your senses — eyes, ears, voice, taste buds. Open up your body — lungs, legs, butt, shoulders. And experience the great sport of cycling the Flemish way, like no place else on Earth.

Belgian cyclocross legend Sven Nys wins in Louisville. Photo by Chris Fontecchio

Appendix: Welcome to BoonenWeek!

[Ed: This is a series of posts I wrote for the Podium Cafe in March, 2016 to celebrate the most important classics rider of the most recent generation, Tom Boonen. The posts also include a look back at Fabian Cancellara, on the eve of his retirement, and maybe Boonen's too, as the Great Rivalry entered its last lap. All posts copyright © 2016 Vox Media, Inc., reprinted with permission.]

Post #1: How Terrific Was Tom? The Ascension Years

This project is about taking stock of cycling at a time when we are forced to reckon with the changeover from Tom Boonen, cobbles hero, to... whatever happens next. To start in earnest, we need to assess what Boonen has accomplished in his career. I could recite the palmares but what we're really trying to get at is, what did it all mean? There can be no doubt that it all adds up to a storied career, and one with its share of good stories. Let's begin today with the happy early years, when nearly everything he touched eventually turned to gold.

Before the Dawn

Boonen is the son of Andre Boonen, who rode professionally from 1979-84 and racked up ten wins of minor import, while riding for teams with names as awesome as Mini-flat Vermeer

Thijs. Pop doesn't seem to have risen too far up the ranks, but from his palmares I gather he had a sprint on him. He once beat a guy named Verbrugge and another guy named Jules Van de Weyer -- Tom's life partner is Lore Van de Weyer. No idea if they're related. Even if not, though, it's clear that Andre was enough of a cyclist to have raised young Tom in that small world, though Boonen himself says he doesn't really remember Dad's active days, and cycling wasn't the focal point of the family. Still, he has a cousin, Jasper Melis, who has a page on Cycling Archives, and an Aunt, Annie Melis, who was a national champion in the 1960s. Unless he hated the sport or was bad at it, the door to cycling was always going to be open for young Tom, and he seems to have quite willingly and forcefully stepped through it.

As an amateur he wasn't necessarily ticketed for greatness, but the signs were there. The first time he entered a race, at age 14, he won, and he came in second in the national championships at age 15 to future teammate Gert Steegmans. Somewhere before his 19th birthday he began attending camps with the US Postal Service team, which in 1998 or so was starting to be a big deal, and not yet for all the wrong reasons. He broke out big time in 2000, winning seven times including the U23 Paris-Tours, and then crushed his age 20 season with a Belgian U23 championship, six other wins, second in races from the U23 Omloop to the U23 Liege-Bastogne-Liege, and top ten at the U23 Paris-Roubaix and World Championships. He turned pro with his now-familiar Postal outfit, despite offers from Patrick Lefevre's Domo team and the Mapei juggernaut. And by this time, he was ticketed for big things.

Auspicious Debut

Why Postal? It can be a little hard to remember, before they became known as the dopingest dopers that ever doped, that they were pretty seriously committed to a run at the Classics. Lance Armstrong himself was into winning in the Ardennes, though he only succeeded in a single Fleche Wallonne victory, but more to the point George Hincapie was coming off a victory at Gent-Wevelgem and had just missed podiums at Flanders and Roubaix. The support staff for the classics was thin -- Vlad Ekimov and Benoit Joaquim were the mainstays -- so there was a clear role to play. And Boonen himself, knowing Hincapie for a few years, was looking forward to learning by his side.

What changed Boonen's plans so soon after began on the morning of April 14. Arriving in Compienge for his first full appearance at Paris-Roubaix, Boonen had probably something like zero 260km races in his legs, so there was little reason to believe we were about to see one of the decade's legendary rides. But that's exactly what we got. Working for Hincapie, Boonen was on the front of the race for much of the final two hours, until the cards were played -- Museeuw attacked for the win, Hincapie attacked a drainage ditch, Boonen was let off the leash for good, and nothing was ever the same again. [We will have a longer treatment of this race later in the week.] The highlight of the day for Boonen was being anointed by Museeuw as his successor, which is bigger than anything the Archbishop of Canterbury ever presided over.

But words have consequences, and in this case they were really big words with really grave consequences for US Postal.

Can the next Lion of Flanders ride for a foreign team? An American team no less? [I guess it's more palatable than a Dutch one, but still.] We were spared when Boonen declared his intention to leave, despite a year left on his contract, citing a lack of chances to ride for himself that was slowing down his development. Now, Postal were already a first rate PR machine, so there is no reason to take official descriptions at face value.

Why exactly did Boonen leave? It's tempting to come up with a narrative around the team's then-unknown ethics, which I'm sure plenty of people would have been repelled by. But a cyclist in 2002 didn't have many clean-team choices, so there isn't much point wandering off into that wilderness of idle speculation. Another possibility -- strong one, actually -- is that personalities became less compatible. Contemporary reporting suggests Bruyneel found out about Boonen's desire to break his contract through the media. Not a good look.

More likely the pressure from home just became too much. Before becoming a star, Boonen cited the calm development he experienced at US Postal as part of the attraction, but once he was anointed a Lion In Waiting, the temptation to go big seems to have won out. Boonen discussed the process of buying his way out of his contract like a formality, a clear sign that Quick Step were going to shower him with money. Boonen seems by all accounts like a truly decent guy, disliked by few if anyone, but in future years you could detect signs that fame had gone to his head. Too good, too soon... it's an old story. But by fall of 2002, it couldn't be stopped.

Be Careful What You Wish For

Armed with money, some early fame, and the perfect team, Boonen set out to take on the world in 2003, only to find that the world -- especially that portion of it associated with cobbled classics -- had its own timetable for him. Here he is chasing his first whiff of cobbled glory, in Gent-Wevelgem, and it sums up how the season went in general.

No matter, he was working for Museeuw anyway, and managed top 25 in both Flanders and Roubaix, more realistic results than his breakout the previous April. Even if Boonen knew the cobbles like the back of his hand, as he once said (having raced the entire Paris-Roubaix minus the first 60km in the U23 event, for example), that doesn't mean he was ready to take over just yet. In cycling, even the most dynamic physical specimens take time to fully bake.

A year later, Boonen's sprinting power launched him into the stratosphere, while his cobbles endurance was still taking shape. It can be a little hard to remember but sprinting was his original calling card, not unlike a lot of large, ultra-powerful riders in their early years, and he didn't renounce even the big bunch gallops until I believe 2008, when he started to guard his safety a bit more, and as new sprint specialists began to crowd him out some. Anyway, in 2004 he racked up a full 19 victories, including a bunch sprint in E3 Prijs Vlaanderen (as it was then more commonly known), a reduced bunch sprint for his Gent-Wevelgem revenge against mostly classics guys, and finally the Scheldeprijs in a true field sprint. From there he began racking up sprint wins in stages of week-long races, before taking a pair of sprints in the Tour de France, including the prestigious final stage on the Champs-Elysees.

The fairest way to look at this phase of his career is that there weren't a ton of great sprinters around, though of course there were fast men. Oscar Freire, Stuart O'Grady, Guido Bontempi, Danilo Hondo -- these were his chief competitors back then. No disrespect. But you have to admit there was some luck involved in his turn as the world's best sprinter.

Belgian Nirvana

And anyway, as nice as that all was, Boonen clearly had a destiny with the cobbles. As Museeuw retired, the 2005 Quick Step team was his alone, and with three seasons under his belt Boonen finally figured it all out. He doubled up on his E3 palmares by outsprinting Andreas Klier, but when he got to the business end of the Ronde van Vlaanderen with five companions (including dangerous sprinters in Hincapie and Erik Zabel), he decided there would be no sprint. Boonen attacked with 9km to go and left his rivals for dead, taking his first Monument by 35 seconds. A week later it was time to take this fantasy into overdrive, as he outsprinted Hincapie and Juan Antonio Flecha to become the newest Flanders-Roubaix Double victor.

This was something Museeuw had never achieved, nor had Merckx. Among those who had, we're talking Peter Van Retegem, Roger De Vlaeminck, Rik Van Looy, Fred De Bruyne, and some guys from the pre-war era. That was it. To have achieved this milestone at age 24 made it all the more difficult to believe.

Could Boonen be stopped? Oscar Freire aimed to find out as the World Championships approached in Madrid. By then Boonen had 13 wins in his pocket, the only blemish being his withdrawal from the Tour de France -- while clad in the green Points Jersey lead -- due to crashes. If the organizers of the Worlds wanted a flat finish to give their hometown hero Freire a solid chance, they failed to properly anticipate just who was coming around the corner the following year (world championship courses tend to be laid out at least a year in advance, if not more).

Everything about the 2005 season was a dream, for Boonen of course, but for Belgian fans alike. As I said, this isn't just about the man. This is about the whole sport, and one large sliver of the sport -- Belgium -- was experiencing something almost beyond description. A young, handsome, smiling champion, slaying sprinters and hardmen alike, winning alone in Flanders, winning the excruciatingly elusive Double, winning the world championship to top it all off... I can't really say what that was like for them. I can only imagine that it was truly something memorable.

But this is why we have a whole week to digest the impact of Boonen on the sport of cycling. Nowadays he is always compared to Fabian Cancellara, not always favorably, but it's important to remember that there was a time when Boonen was the only rider in the conversation. And I don't mean just about his meteoric rise, I mean about anything. Boonen was the sport in 2005 -- apart I suppose from the endless Armstrong dirge finally grinding to a halt. By contrast, Boonen was an impossibly fresh face, in all ways. Boyish in his looks, because he was only 24 and prone to smiling a lot (who wouldn't?). And yet performing feats so remarkable, so soon. That meteoric rise really was a story like few others -- certainly unlike even Cancellara's arc. And sure, the excitement young champions generate can get a little overblown, but for whatever reason it's always fun. Besides, results like Boonen's really did suggest we were seeing the start of something special. Which we were.

Post #2: How Terrific Was Tom? Part II: Growing Up, Changing Course

2006: You Can't Have Everything

We left off our look back at the brilliant, game-changing, and still going career of Tom Boonen on the day he placed the world's biggest target on his back, that of the arc-en-ciel, the World Champion's rainbow jersey. Much is made of a "rainbow curse," and though much is also made of the Loch Ness Monster, there is a little something to wearing an insignia of your special status everywhere you go, in a sport where there are a million ways to lose -- including several beyond your control -- and only one way to win. Boonen put on that bull's-eye in 2006 and set out to dominate in spite of his status. It wasn't like all eyes weren't already on him anyway.

But in 2006 things got a little complicated. His old US Postal team, re-christened Discovery Channel, had succeeded in putting together its own Stop-Boonen movement, building around George Hincapie with Leif Hoste (2nd in Flanders in 2004), Stijn Devolder (former De Panne winner and E3 podium'er), Vlad Gusev and other useful assets. Hincapie himself had been knocking on the door at the Monuments for a few years, and came into the Ronde van Vlaanderen as an alternate favorite, should Boonen falter somehow. Lotto, T-Mobile, CSC and Rabobank also seemed loaded for bear. Boonen had his work cut out.

And he was up to the task. Boonen escaped on the Valkenberg, chasing after a flier by Hoste, whom he defeated in a sprint to win de Ronde in the rainbow kit, achieving another level of Flemish Nirvana. But the race rankled, and whispers went out that Boonen conspired with Hoste somehow to work together, an odd sight since Hoste's captain Hincapie was among the chasing hopefuls. On the other hand, the two Discovery riders took second and third, and there's no reason to believe another strategy would have resulted in dropping or outsprinting Boonen. That rumors still fly about "payoffs" and "conspiracies" indicates that Boonen had reached another level of success: the one where people get sick of losing to you and start nasty backbiting campaigns.

Little did Boonen know that his Ronde victory was the end of an era where he singlehandedly dominated the cobbled classics. He would dominate again in the future, to be sure, but the competition changed forever a week after his Ronde win when Fabian Cancellara broke away from the leading octet of riders, including Boonen, to win Paris-Roubaix and established himself as a credible threat to Boonen's cobbled dominance. Additionally, Boonen's finale consisted of him riding in the unfamiliar position of having no teammates -- up til then he could not only count on his power and finishing kick, but a cadre of threatening teammates like Paolo Bettini, Filippo Pozzato and Nick Nuyens ready to assist. In fact, Boonen lent them extra power by allowing them to win races, including a memorable move by Pozzato to take Milano-Sanremo just two weeks before Flanders. It seemed like he truly held all the cards, until Cancellara blew them all away -- his teammates, and finally Boonen himself -- to take a win that declared the cobbled monuments up for grabs again.

Yeah, that race, with the train crossing, pictured above, and George Hincapie's broken steerer tube. Karma went up the road on Boonen that day too. After the power of his victories it seemed like the Cobbled monuments were Boonen's to keep for a long while, but everything seemed different after this edition of the Hell of the North. Maybe the Cycling Gods just went a little crazy that day, but then again, maybe Boonen was human after all.

Boonen Was Human After All

One defeat did little to diminish the essential greatness of Boonen, and 21 total wins (counting jerseys) in 2006 amounted to a #1 world ranking and a Rainbow Defense to beat the band. But as Jens described in his post about Boonen's Weird Phases, this was around when Tommeke moved to Monaco (fleeing a Boonen-mad homeland, to be sure) and kinda maybe had a little too much fun. He is mostly remembered in 2007 for a Ronde when he couldn't follow Alessandro Ballan or Leif Hoste, a Roubaix when he stuck to Cancellara like glue while Stuart O'Grady disappeared up the road, and a Tour de France where he won the green jersey but missed out on a few sprints, while Cancellara was passing the moto cam in the prologue and sneaking away from him to win a sprint in the yellow jersey. A fairer representation might recall that Boonen won Kuurne-Brussels-Kuurne, Dwars door Vlaanderen and E3 Prijs, but guys like Boonen, or at least his fans, don't trade in semi-classics.

Things went from bad to worse for those fans, however, as Boonen began the process of renouncing the bunch sprints that had made him so stellar in the beginning, and replaced those headlines with stories of him testing positive for cocaine, landing him outside the Tour de France in 2008, and nearly again in 2009. Those two spring seasons were a bit unkind to Cancellara (save for his MSR win), with the Swiss rival being controlled by Quick Step in 2008 and not fully fit for 2009. That left a vacuum around Boonen, but it turns out that Stijn Devolder was the one who abhorred it the most, winning a first Ronde in 2008 that looked like a triumph of team tactics and a second one in 2009 that felt more like a humiliation of Boonen. Redemption came in the form of two more Paris-Roubaix wins, once in a sprint over Cancellara and Ballan, and a second when Thor Hushovd crashed out of a threatening finale involving teammate Heinrich Haussler, leaving Boonen to win alone. Great wins, and even the stories from de Ronde had more to do with everyone being too afraid of him to go after Devolder.

But if the aura of invincibility was diminishing by then, it disappeared for good in 2010. Directly in front of a group of fans from the Podium Cafe, I might add. This spot is halfway up the Kapelmuur, where one of the most legendary duels in the history of the Tour of Flanders was decided on that day, at that very moment. Racing on the old, classic Ronde course, the two race favorites Boonen and Cancellara -- who would go on to share the record of most Ronde victories (3) -- escaped on the Molenberg and thundered away toward some sort of dramatic conclusion, which came when Cancellara made the subtle acceleration you see here. By the top of this 50-meter hell-ramp, Boonen had cramped a bit, Cancellara had flown the coop, and their destinies were altered for good. Cancellara stayed away for the win, and to make things worse, this came a week after the Swiss Bear had outwitted Boonen in a tight corner to win E3 Harelbeke... and a week before he denied Boonen his customary Roubaix redemption, with an even more dominant and confirming victory for the CSC man. Fabian had the Double. Tommeke had become human again.

There is no question that this was the moment Boonen stopped being the God of the Cobbles he had started out as. Before this day, if you tossed out 2007 you could point to an almost-unbroken string of Classics seasons where either Boonen or one of his teammates (and therefore Boonen again) dominated Flanders and Roubaix. The 2005 Double. 2006 Flanders (but not Roubaix). 2008 and 2009 Devolder-Boonen team Doubles. His non-victories could be written off as something other than a sign of diminished strength on his part.

But this was something different. After this moment you could no longer call him the strongest rider. Cancellara's win was no fluke -- he had looked stronger than Boonen even when they were cooperating before the Kapelmuur -- and the next week's dominant Roubaix effort answered every question about who was better. Suddenly the 2008 and '09 results looked more like Boonen was merely hanging on until Cancellara figured it all out. Boonen was left as the unquestioned second-best rider in the world, clearly better than everyone else on the cobbles, except for one man. But in cycling there is the winner and there is everyone else, and for Boonen to join the latter group after the lofty status he had enjoyed was easily the story of the end of the decade.

Without the sprints to boost his statistics, Boonen's status as the #1 points-getter was also long gone by 2010, and he slipped into forgettable territories no matter what system you look at. Entering his thirties, he became something of a Champion Emeritus, and his place in Quick Step evolved into a top option in certain races, rather than an unquestioned leader everywhere he had a chance. His rematch with Cancellara in 2011 didn't amount to much, as the entire world focused their energy on marking the Swiss rider out of existence -- a more plausible strategy given Cancellara's lack of sprint -- with Nuyens coming around him for the Flanders win and Johan Van Summeren upsetting the favorites in Roubaix. There, Boonen was left holding the remains of his derailleur in the Forest of Arenberg, yet another blow to his former invincibility, as Boonen had a habit of exiting the Trenchee at the head of the peloton, where royalty rides. Boonen ended 2011 outside the top 100 riders in the world (105th -- Podium Cafe World Rankings), and we all sort of figured the party was over.

The Party Ain't Over

What happened next maybe deserves its own post, but it's well-known enough to everyone here that doing so might belabor the obvious. I'm referring, of course, to Boonen's record-smashing string of victories in 2012, which you can see in a few different lights. That run consists of victories in E3 Prijs, Gent-Wevelgem, the Tour of Flanders and Paris-Roubaix. What did that mean? Here's your historical context:

Back before the modern calendar, Gent-Wevelgem had been sandwiched between Flanders and Roubaix as the Holy Week, and nobody ever swept all three, until Boonen did so on three consecutive Sundays. So this was a precedent of sorts, albeit one slightly messed up by... oh, let's blame the UCI.

Once the new calendar sorted out E3 and Gent-Wevelgem, nobody had won both, in the span of three days, until Boonen managed it. The thinking a few years back was that riders could only go hard in one or the other if they wanted to stay fresh for the impending Monuments.

* Boonen became the first rider to win all four of what now shape up as the World Tour cobbled classics.
* Boonen became the first rider to win the Flanders-Roubaix Double on two occasions.
* Boonen tied Roger De Vlaeminck, a/k/a Mr. Paris-Roubaix, for the record of most career Paris-Roubaix wins (4).
* Boonen tied four other riders (later five with Cancellara) for the record of most career Tour of Flanders wins (3).
* Boonen tied four other riders for the record of most career Gent-Wevelgem triumphs (3).
* Boonen passed Rik Van Looy to set a new all-time record of most career E3 Prijs Harelbeke wins (5).

The first two wins came at Cancellara's expense, which was sweet enough, though the Swiss Bear's crash-out at Flanders took a bit of the lustre away from that victory, a sprint win over Pozzato. But if anyone had ideas about putting an asterisk on Boonen's 2012 accomplishments, he made mincemeat of such suggestions by launching a 53-km solo attack that even Cancellara could admire, to win in the velodrome and finish off his utterly historic run of excellence in the grandest fashion possible.

The following season it was Boonen's turn to crash out of de Ronde, and Cancellara's turn to pump up his palmares in his absence, with his own second Double over riders like Peter

Sagan and Sep Vanmarcke who were starting to represent a new breed of challengers to the two-man (increasingly) old guard. Boonen has spent the time since his 2012 season scoring minor stage sprint wins -- seems like old times? -- while failing to mount a challenge to either the still-dangerous Cancellara or the new breed of classics guys, though the only healthy spring campaign since, in 2014, Boonen was only a hair off the leaders' pace, including Paris-Roubaix where he finished in the back of the group that failed to reel in his teammate Niki Terpstra. Health remains a concern this year, after a horrific crash in Dubai last fall that left Boonen with a temporal fracture and permanent (?) hearing loss. The great champion is still with us, and while nothing this spring would come as a surprise, expectations are at their lowest point since he arrived in Compiegne on that fateful April day in 2002.

If I had to say what this period of time meant, I'd start by stealing from Jens' post about Boonen maybe drifting a bit, then catching himself and maturing back into the great champion he started out as. His personal life reverted back to his early days as he returned to living in Belgium with his partner Lore (they now have twin daughters), and with results that suggest he was back to his best, even if his best at age 30 and beyond couldn't live up to his incredible peak years from the first big run of success. And of course, he no longer had the top rung of the ladder to himself, with Cancellara fighting him tooth-and-nail. And he was no longer padding his resume with sprint wins.

But for Boonen to pull off that 2012 season suggests another form of greatness, one less magical and in some ways more awesome: he was a different rider, but knew exactly what his strengths and weaknesses were, knew exactly how to deal with his rivals, and got more from his lesser body than he ever did in his life. Some might put his 2005 season, including a world title, at the top, and I wouldn't fault them for doing so, but his 2012 run was as great as anything we've seen from a classics rider, ever.

For a single person to reach two very different, very incredible heights in his career, seven years apart, is maybe the real Boonen story in a nutshell. He has been, at varying times and in varying combinations, not just strong and fast, but smart, tough, consistent and resilient. He is a champion and a survivor. In this collection of qualities and achievements is every element of the challenge of these races themselves.

Post #3: What Constitutes a "New Boonen"?

The (eventual) retirement of a great champion like Tom Boonen is a seminal event for Belgian cycling fans as well as fans of the Classics everywhere, for reasons connected to the man himself and how much his fans have enjoyed watching him race, as well as to what it means to watch a race like the Tour of Flanders without him. After next month, or perhaps as late as a year from next month, it's a reality we will all have to face, whether we like it or not.

This post examines what exactly is the vacuum the departure of a great champion leaves behind, and what it will take to fill it. Want another Lion of Flanders? Me too! So let's generate a job description based on what we can glean from past Lions, and see whether anyone answers our call.

What, Where?

What makes a bona fide Lion of Flanders, or someone with a reasonable claim on the name? For starters, victory in the Tour of Flanders. Without that, the conversation is over. You might be a very good cyclist, revered in Belgium even for your qualities, but upon winning de Ronde van Vlaanderen you enter an exclusive club. Ah, but that club has an upper level. Someone must win de Ronde every year, whether there is a true champion racing that day or not. So no, not all Flanders victories are alike. To elevate yourself to a special place in the minds of Belgian fans, your resume had better run a little deeper than that.

A Paris-Roubaix win as well is a sure sign that you were no fluke, for that race rarely rewards flukes, and it is unreasonable to think a rider could feign his way into winning two races as special and selective as this. Those guys stuck down in the lobby of the club -- good for them, they did what they had to, and luck was on their side. But luck doesn't strike the same rider in such succession as this. So yes, the lifetime Double is a very good sign.

So too are multiple Ronde wins, it should go without saying. Any of the other revered Belgian races, that counts too, be it another cobbled semi-classic or the Belgian National Road Race Championships. A world championship, representing something of a trophy brought home from overseas, is a huge feather in a rider's cap. Some combination of the above definitely gets you upstairs, above the club's rabble.

And then there's the penthouse.

Who?

Do we have a definitive list of Lions of Flanders? That's a special designation given by the Belgian press, for feats that move them to... give the designation. Like most great titles, I guess you know it when you see it. Secondary to that, there are a small number of riders who are held up as the true "Flandriens," examples of the great qualities required to win these races, as well as riders who, by winning them, achieved a level of fame associated with the cobblestones. An element of myth is useful, or at least some sort of story that goes beyond mere success that captures the hearts and minds of Flemish fans. Johan Museeuw, flawed as he may have been, pointing to the leg he almost had amputated while crossing the line in the Roubaix velodrome -- that sort of thing. A quality that helps you rise above.

First on this list, chronologically, is Achiel Buysse, the first man to win three editions of de Ronde. Because nobody has yet to win a fourth, the three-winners club is a symbol of elite-ness that can't be denied. Because Buysse raced in the 1930s and 40s, the races available to him weren't what they are now, and his lone Kuurne-Brussels-Kuurne win along with his Ronde successes make for a thin resume. But like I said, those three wins can't be denied.

[You could argue that Cyrille Van Hauwaert is truly first on this list. The original Lion of Flanders is so original that his best days occurred before de Ronde van Vlaanderen existed. But his record is unmistakably classical: in a five year period he took Paris-Roubaix once and finished on the podium three other times. Plus a Milano-Sanremo win.]

Briek Schotte, the Iron Briek, is somewhat literally the poster child for the Cobbled Classics, his weathered face appearing on the cover of a comprehensive catalogue of his breed titled "Flandriens." Schotte bagged two world championships in 1948 and 1950, as well as two Flanders wins and six other podium places over his 19-year career. Longevity and regularity are two definite qualities worth noting. But yeah, the world titles help too.

Rik Van Steenbergen is next. Rik I won two Ronde titles right out of the gate, and by his third season had completed the Lifetime Double with a Paris-Roubaix win, his first of two. Add in three world championships and a variety of other wins, and you have a Flemish hero. Also notable was his success on the track -- the Six Day races are very much a part of the Belgian culture, so having a presence there too is maybe not something you put on top of your resume, but it's in there someplace.

Rik Van Looy -- Rik II -- was the first rider to win all five of cycling's one-day Monuments, in addition to two Rondes, three Roubaixs (including the 1962 Double), and back-to-back world championships in 1960-61. And track. The sheer breadth of his wins is what made him so notable.

Roger De Vlaeminck, the Gypsy, Mr. Paris-Roubaix... another unquestioned lifetime member of the classics penthouse. Four wins in the Hell of the North earned him an iconic nickname, not only for its style but for what it meant. Until Boonen, nobody had ever taken four titles in the Roubaix Velodrome (or wherever; the finish moved around some). Like Rik II, he swept the Monuments over the course of his career, though the one that eluded him longest was that pesky Tour of Flanders, which he finally secured in 1977. Absent that... who knows? But regardless, De Vlaeminck did everything, and added "iconic nickname" as a resume padder.

Eric Leman sneaks into this discussion because, like Buysse, he can point to three Ronde victories and drop the mic. His record thins out some from there -- K-B-K, Dwars, lots of stage sprints -- but when you take three Flanders wins, in the Age of Merckx, no less, you're in.

Walter Godefroot? Pushing it? He's got two Rondes and a Roubaix, plus a Belgian Championships win. And a string of doping offenses. Hmph.

Eddy Merckx barely needs discussion, but it's worth noting that he never did the Double in a single year, and doesn't hold a share of any of the "most wins" titles in either Flanders or Roubaix. But being unquestionably the best at every goddamn thing puts an end to any questions. Edwig Van Hooydonck merits a mention, with two Flanders wins (plus a U23 version as well) to go with four Brabantse Pijls, a K-B-K and a Dwars.

Johan Museeuw is still the last official Lion of Flanders, which is the reserved corner booth in the penthouse above the top floor of the club of elite cobbles champions. Whatever you think of him today, his record is undeniably top-shelf: he won a total of 27 one-day races (along with sprint stages, criteriums, cyclocross races, and so on), including three each of Flanders and Roubaix -- though never in the same year. His iconic comeback from nearly losing his leg, depicted above, is a scene practically everyone in Belgium remembers. No getting around his legend.

Oh, and if these guys had anything in common, besides palmares, it was a sense that they cast a shadow over the classics year after year. They delivered a lot, or came close to it, but even when they weren't on the podium, everyone knew where they were. They had a presence, and you don't get that merely by striking gold once or twice. You earn it one year at a time. That's maybe the ultimate criterion, but of course it's one we won't be able to assign to up-and-coming riders in advance.

OK, so to summarize, we have quite a list of characteristics to choose from in determining what makes a Classics great. For organizational purposes, I have borrowed a template from MS Word for compiling a quality checklist. See what you think... and if you like it, bring it with you wherever you may go to locate the Next Boonen.

CHECKLIST FOR MY IDEAL ~~CAR~~ CLASSICS RIDER

After filling out this checklist, print it and take it with you when you look for your next new ~~car~~ Classics hero.

Tour of Flanders Victory	
More Tour of Flanders Victories	
Paris-Roubaix Victory/-ies	
The In-Season Double?	
World Championship(s)	
Monuments Success	
Semi-classics successes	
Sprinting successes	
Belgian Championship(s)	
Tour de France success	
Other unrelated awesome wins	
Chiseled granite-like facial features?	
Awesome nickname?	
Career-defining rival?	
Anything in common with Merckx?	
Bunyanesque legends?	
Plausibly deniable ethics record?	
Lion of Flanders?	

Post #4: What Made Tommeke Great, Part Next: His Team!

We hardcore cycling nuts spend a lot of hot air educating the masses about the FACT that cycling is a team sport. [And then someone wins the Tour in a time trial.] The classics do a good job of driving this point home, particularly in years where for whatever reason the races get aggressive and team tactics become easier to spot from the race broadcast helicopter. If you have cards to play, and you use them well, you can win the classics.

In the era dominated largely by Tom Boonen, team tactics have been downright devastating... or they were, until Fabian Cancellara became impossible for any team to control. Let's take a quick run through the Boonen Years and look at the team that made him as great as he was.

2002: US Postal Service

Key Teammates: George Hincapie, Viatcheslav Ekimov, Benoit Joachim

Stats: 17 wins (t-20th), no classics wins.

Rival Teams: Er, a bit awkward since I'm not sure USPS were seen by anyone as their rival. But for reference, Mapei still existed, which is to say they dominated the victory totals, and Lotto-Adecco were the Belgian alternate. Telekom and Rabobank were in with a shout.

Power Plays: Yeah, no. Hincapie and his young protege were the entire presence for the team, with Big George getting taken to the cleaners at the end in Flanders (Tafi attacks... and attacks... and attacks again, finally going solo) and Young Tom cleaning up the team's mess in Roubaix. In Gent-Wevelgem the team did fine but simply couldn't reel in Cipollini in the sprint.

Verdict: Boonen was still a kid, so for him and Hincapie to get past large, veteran teams was too tall an order.

2003: Quick Step-Davitamon

Key Teammates: Johan Museeuw, Frank Vandenbroucke, Paolo Bettini, Nick Nuyens, Luca Paolini

Stats: 24 wins (9th), Het Volk, Milano-Sanremo

Rival Teams: Telekom, Lotto-Domo, Alessio, etc.

Power Plays: Nothing notable. QSD had riders near the front but not in numbers. Vandenbroucke, enjoying a brief revival of his early promise (or at least staving off his tragic end), got unleashed in de Ronde but beaten on the line. Boonen wasn't quick enough to finish off Gent-Wevelgem, or avoid the photographers' well. And Servais Knaven was their lone rider within a shout of the front of Paris-Roubaix.

Verdict: This was the calm between the storms. The eye of the Patrick Levefre hurricane. Others were free to move about. Peter Van Petegem did the Double and forever introduced

Brakel and his magical facial hair to the world. Just a weird moment in time.

2004: Quick Step-Davitamon

Key Teammates: Knaven, Bettini, Museeuw, Nuyens, Paolini

Stats: 46 wins (1st), Brabantse Pijl, E3 Prijs, Gent-Wevelgem, Scheldeprijs.

Rival Teams: T-Mobile, US Postal, Lotto-Domo. Lotto went into reloading mode as Van Petegem dropped off dramatically. Wesemann scored his big win in de Ronde and Zabel was still strong, but otherwise they were minor players.

Power Plays: I'm going to take something of a pass here. Obviously they swept the semi-classics, unless you count Hincapie's overall win in Driedaagse de Panne. Gent-Wevelgem video is lacking but from the results list Boonen had Museeuw, Knaven, Nuyens, Cretskens and Bodrogi all up there with him. Beyond that, I can't say much.

Verdict: The pieces were falling into place. Boonen the klassikoer was still a work in progress, but if it came to a sprint he was the favorite, and he usually had enough support to deliver him to the line.

2005: Quick Step

Key Teammates: Bettini, Nuyens, Knaven, Kevin Hulsmans, Paolini

Stats: 37 (4th), Omloop Het Volk, E3 Prijs, Ronde van Vlaanderen, Paris-Roubaix

Rival Teams: Discovery Channel, Davitamon Lotto, T-Mobile. The stakes started going up with the rivals, as Discovery picked up Leif Hoste and Stijn Devolder. Lotto were still pretty leaderless as PVP finished out, but the pieces were in place for later and they nabbed Davitamon as their big $$ sponsor from QS. Klier and Zabel led the Germans.

Power Plays: I'm not sure I'd say anything they did qualified as an outright power play. Boonen's monumental wins were won at the end on his own. I'm sure he had help getting and staying in position though.

Verdict: The best you could say is that nobody else had critical mass, and Boonen was so strong and so fast that he himself represented the center of power throughout the classics.

2006: Quick Step-Innergetic

Key Teammates: Bettini, Steven de Jongh, Nuyens, Filippo Pozzato, Wouter Weylandt

Stats: 45 wins (2nd), Kuurne-Brussels-Kuurne, Milano-Sanremo, E3 Prijs, Ronde van Vlaanderen

Rival Teams: Discovery, CSC, Davitamon-Lotto. CSC are the newcomers, formed in 2005, and adding Cancellara to Breschel, O'Grady and Kroon leads to immediate results. Lotto and Discovery are status quo.

Power Plays: De Ronde, where Bettini had begun talking up his chances of winning, and he stood guard for Boonen with Pozzato and Serge Baguet when Hoste made his fateful/fatal move. The presence of a lot of guys made it hard for Hincapie, among the favorites, to simply go bounding after Boonen. A week later, however, Boonen gets isolated and Discovery are the ones in charge. Well, of everyone except Cancellara.

Verdict: Not a great year for team tactics, but Boonen is good enough in the sprint to salt away a bunch of wins regardless.

2007: Quick Step-Innergetic

Key Teammates: Baguet, de Jongh, Bettini, Weylandt, Gert Steegmans, Peter Van Petegem

Stats: 38 wins (t-2nd), K-B-K, Dwars door Vlaanderen, E3 Prijs

Rival Teams: CSC, Predictor-Lotto, T-Mobile. CSC were as loaded as ever. Discovery announced it was finished at the end of the season. Lotto poached Hoste from them, paired with Johan Van Summeren.

Power Plays: From QSI, very little. Van Petegem did not really feature as he wrapped up his career. Weylandt was coming into his own as the team sprinter, which helped out Boonen quite a bit, but in the race it's telling that the guys in position at Paris-Roubaix were Matteo Tosatto and Kevin Van Impe, and nobody in the Flanders breakaway.

Verdict: CSC were the ones making the power plays that year. Boonen's boys were hardly weak; it's just cycling. Sometimes things come together nicely and other times they don't.

2008: Quick Step-Innergetic

Key Teammates: de Jongh, Stijn Devolder, Steegmans, Weylandt

Stats: 45 wins (3rd), K-B-K, Nokere Koerse, Flanders, Roubaix

Rival Teams: Columbia, CSC, Silence-Lotto. Columbia were an incredible assemblage of talent -- Hincapie, Boasson Hagen, Eisel, Hammond, Greipel, Cavendish and so on. They were a bit too young to really destroy the sport, but 77 wins is nothing to sneeze at.

Power Plays: The ultimate power play! Devolder had been in the all-important penultimate-hour break, putting CSC (primarily) on the defensive. Even two years before his confirmation, Cancellara was viewed as a major threat in Flanders, one Lefevre obviously took seriously. Cancellara and Boonen marked each other all day, while Devolder launched once -- and drew an all-star response from Hincapie, Ballan and Flecha -- then got caught and countered with a solo move from the Eikenmolen, some 20km away. The following week, CSC were quick to cover Devolder's probing attacks in northern France, and eventually launched Cancellara, only for Boonen to follow, ride stronger, and win the sprint.

Verdict: There has been a few volumes' worth of argument about the Devolder Ronde wins, but few would say he didn't deserve this one. Anyway, the spring campaign was the ultimate Quick Step master class, where you pick your poison one week, and die, then try the other one a week later, with the same end.

2009: Quick Step

Key Teammates: Devolder, de Jongh, Sylvain Chavanel, Allan Davis.

Stats: 24 wins (t-9th), K-B-K, Dwars, Ronde, Roubaix, Le Samyn

Rival Teams: Silence-Lotto, Rabo, Columbia-HTC, Saxo Bank, Garmin-Slipstream, Cervelo Test Team. Lotto nab Philippe Gilbert, staving off total collapse. Columbia crush everywhere but the cobbles, though Boasson Hagen took an epic Gent-Wevelgem and in general the team had HUGE talent. CTT got hot with Haussler and Hushovd. Garmin started sneaking into the conversation with Maaskant notching two fourths in the monuments. Really, this was probably the most competition QS had faced since the Boonen days began.

Power Plays: A two-man support job this time, as first Chava takes the break to the Muur, and then Devolder attacks the front of the pack over the top. And then, a week later, Boonen did the work for himself. [Possibly out of anger.]

Verdict: This was a definite milestone year in the team's development, with some of the old guard (e.g. Bettini) leaving and Lefevre stocking up with guys who could actually stand in for Boonen. Chavanel was a great signing, providing value right away. But it has to be said, they got immensely lucky both times. The Ronde group was weakened by Cancellara's withdrawal, and in Roubaix if Hushovd could stay on his damn bike, who knows how that one would have turned out?

2010: Quick Step

Key Teammates: No major changes

Stats: 17 wins (t-16th)

Rival Teams: Saxo Bank. And to a lesser extent, HTC, BMC, Rabo, Garmin, and Lotto. Saxo won Dwars (Breschel), E3 (Fabs), Ronde (Fabs) and Roubaix (Fabs), while HTC took Gent-Wevelgem (Eisel) and Garmin the Scheldeprijs (Farrar). BMC were just starting out. Gilbert was capable of anything, and a year away from his own milestone.

Power Plays: None. There simply was no way to check Cancellara at this point. Also, the Devolder-Boonen dynamic had officially turned into a problem. Stijn always apeapred to be a loyal teammate, but the temptation of three straight Rondes began to change that as he began to talk up his own chances for the first time. Which led Boonen to talk them down, and Lefevre to chastise Devolder in the papers, particularly when he had a poor run-up to the classics, and fell flat in them.

Verdict: In a way this year was a few years in the making. Two years before, Boonen was probably stronger than Cancellara, but the Swiss Bear was gaining strength and was held back by luck in '09. Breschel too was in top form, while QS just got older. Part of the problem is that it's hard to be on top for so long. But a much bigger problem -- still a big problem -- is that the rest of the world had discovered the cobbled classics by now. Foreigners won every single event until the post-Roubaix Brabantse Pijl, taken by Seb Rosseler... who had just left Quick Step.

2011: Quick Step

Key Teammates: Steegmans, Chavanel, Iljo Keisse, Niki Terpstra, Zdenek Stybar. Adieu Stijn.

Stats: 8 wins (t-50th), Nokere Koerse, Gent-Wevelgem

Rival Teams: Garmin-Cervelo, HTC, Sky, Leopard-Trek, Rabobank. The CSC/Saxo implosion was a major shakeup, with Breschel going to Rabo and Cancellara left a bit on his own (but Saxo getting the last laugh in Flanders anyway). Garmin and CTT merged, and the argyles nabbed stalwart Joahn Van Summeren from poor ol Lotto. And then the usual litany of strong teams without a major threat to win, unless you still counted Pozzato and Ballan as threats to win. Vacansoleil nabbed Devo to go with Leukemans and Marcato, which was... something.

Power Plays: I'm going to stretch this a bit and credit Quick Step for some powerful defense. By now Cancellara had passed Boonen by, and the onus was very clearly on Leopard to make the race, but Cancellara was simply surrounded by everyone with an interest in winning, and no escape route. Well, one, the long launch, which he tried in Flanders but drew an alert and very strong Chavanel for company. By the end of Paris-Roubaix, which Summie stole from the front group,

Cancellara got downright pissy about his situation, but it's his own damn fault for signing with the Schlecks.

Verdict: Year One of Life After Tom. Not Life After Tom literally, just Life After TOM! and the team did well to get on a podium. Also the move to hold Boonen back from E3 (then not WT) so he could go after points in G-W (WT) paid off with a win there. Doing the best with what they had.

2012: Omega Pharma-Quick Step

Key Teammates: Chavanel, Keisse, Grabsch, Stybar, Terpstra, Tony Martin

Stats: 51 wins (t-1st), all the classics. All of them.

Rival Teams: Pfft. Well, Lotto got smart and hired Andre Greipel once HTC shut down, staving off yet another disaster from losing their sponsor to Quick Step. Layopard morphed into Radioshack-Nissan, but that didn't bring Cancellara any relief. Garmin, Rabo, Sky... usual suspects. BMC became a solid classics team with Ballan, Hincapie, Gilbert and Van Avermaet. They were probably the second-strongest, but not fully baked as a unit.

Power Plays: 2012 will be remembered for sunny weather, Classics coming down to bunch sprints (all won by Boonen), and of course the greatest escape ever, Boonen's power play in Paris-Robuaix. Actually it was a two-man attack with Chavanel Terpstra (by now feeling maybe he was worthy of his own moment), and Boonen topped his lieutenant by going alone shortly after. This was winning from the front, an answer to Cancellara's whining about how everyone was out to get him the previous year. There's always a way out of the box, you just have to know when it happens. I don't know if this was a team thing or just brilliant instincts by Boonen.

Verdict: There will always be the asterisk next to it, with Cancellara having only been on hand for the first two drubbings, but Boonen put his mark on cycling history, and had largely himself to thank.

2013: OmegaPharma - Quick Step

Key Teammates: Chavanel, Stybar, Terpstra, Martin.

Stats: 55 wins (1st), Driedaagse de Panne

Rival Teams: Fabian Cancellara. Also a new guard of Cannondale (re: Sagan), Alexander Kristoff (Katusha) and the hordes from BMC. Lotto were hanging on with Greipel and Jurgen Roelands. Sep Vanmarcke's move to Rabo/Blanco was good for Blanco, if not Sep.

Power Plays: None to be had. Boonen crashed out early on and the field was cleared for Cancellara to do his thing.

Verdict: Boonen's loss and the team's lack of results without him signaled another changing of the guard was due. Not so much through transfers though. Stybar and Terpstra were both looking increasingly like major options for the next season. And reality suggested Boonen wouldn't be around much longer, not at his old level.

2014: Etixx-Quick Step

Key Teammates: Keisse, Stybar, Terpstra, Mark Cavendish, Guillaume Van Kiersbulck

Stats: 62 wins (1st), K-B-K, Paris-Roubaix

Rival Teams: Cancellara still, and still alone. Tinkoff-Saxo, Katusha, Giant-Shimano. Degenkolb's Gent-Wevelgem win was a hint at things to come.

Power Plays: Definitely Paris-Roubaix, as the team missed out entirely on the moves in Flanders. The race stayed together after the major cobbles, but Lefevre had Stybar -- now in his second display of excellence in Hell -- along with Boonen and Terpstra, so when Terpstra attacked with 6km to go, it was pretty standard tactics. But it also worked. Oh, and before then Stybar had sat in on an all-star attack featuring Sagan and Vanmarcke, which Terpstra and Boonen eventually reeled in.

Verdict: The team was fantastic, but Boonen could be heard grumbling about his teammate taking a win instead of him. Sure, it was aimed at their rivals, who sat on him, but you could sense him sensing a changing of the guard, or at least the sand running out in his career's hourglass.

2015: Etixx-Quick Step

Key Teammates: Stybar, Terpstra, Vandenberghe.

Stats: 54 wins (1st), K-B-K

Rival Teams: Katusha, Tinkoff, Giant, Sky, Lotto, BMC

Power Plays: None to be had without Boonen. Stybar got second in Roubaix, brilliantly enough, but EQS wasn't holding all the cards anymore.

Verdict: The torch is in need of passing. Stybar is the team's worthy successor by now, and Terpstra a wildcard co-leader as well. This was a year without Tommeke, and while it didn't go well, it was the team's new reality.

*****

The metaverdict here is that Boonen has almost always had an advantage over his rivals in his team support. Patrick Lefevre is unparalleled as a game-manager, along with his lieutenants (who probably deserve a ton of the credit). And roster-building? The best. Year after year they are #1 in wins, and that counts for a TON in Belgium. But there's also some luck involved. Taking on Stybar and in the process gaining Bakala money was a shrewd move that became a million times shrewder when Stybar blossomed into a brilliant rider all around. I doubt they were counting on that happening.

Still, with all the team support, Boonen has shown time and again that he was the strongest guy, capable of winning even without that special edge. His instincts have also gained him some great times (and cost him a few others). So you can't point to his team and discount Boonen's record. But you can't point to Boonen's record and discount the brilliance of his team either.

Post #5: Fabian and Tom Made History Together

Greatness came early for Tom Boonen, a monument winner in 2005 at the age of 24. Truly remarkable achievement. But do you know who nearly beat him by a year? Fabian Cancellara.

This is one of the more entertaining editions of Paris-Roubaix. with highlights including a devastating puncture by Johan Museeuw in his last cobbled classic, and of course the utterly prophetic spectacle of Leif Hoste on the attack, only to be felled by a Lion of Flanders flag getting wrapped in his wheel. Anyway, the end result was that four riders got free of Museeuw, Tom Boonen and George Hincapie, and sprinted it out in the velodrome. Cancellara was one, and finished last of the four, after pretty much leading out the sprint for an entire velodrome lap. That bit of inexperience prevented his story from getting off the ground before even Boonen's.

That's Fabs in Fassa Bortolo colors. Forgotten years to all but his die-hard fans.

A year later, with Museeuw's torch being passed in front of our eyes, Cancellara missed the winning move and got eighth, enough to serve future notice to those paying close attention. But by 2006, we all knew him. By then the stop-Boonen movement was in full force, and Cancellara was the guy who stopped him.

From that day forward, Cancellara and Boonen were spoken of as more or less equals, at least in the classics. They will always be different riders in important ways, but more than that, they will be linked together in cycling history for all time. They battled each other, not in a coincidental way but in a way that the Red Sox and Yankees do battle (or did in their peak years) -- deliberately, openly, and in ways which made both riders stronger, and all of us fans happier. You simply can't celebrate Boonen Week without talking about Cancellara.

Tale of the Tape!

Height and weight:

- Boonen -- 6'4" (1.92m), 181 lbs (82kg)
- Cancellara -- 6'1" (1.82m), 181 lbs (82kg)

Comment: Boonen possesses those most prized assets, long thighbones. Cancellara isn't de tank de tank de pletwals for nothing.[165]

Age:

- Boonen -- Born 15 October, 1980
- Cancellara -- Born 18 March, 1981 [Hey! Happy birthday big guy!]

Comment: No meaningful difference.

Team Progression:

- Boonen -- US Postal, Quick Step

---

[165] A famous call from Michel Wuyts, Sporza announcer, during Cancellara's attack in the 2010 E3 Prijs. Pletwals means steamroller.

- Cancellara -- Mapei, Fassa Bortolo, CSC, Leopard, Trek Factory Racing

Comment: Both have had pretty stable situations for a cyclist. Boonen especially so, starting with a full pro year abroad on a glamour team and then coming home. Cancellara had two early years on glamorous winners, then a stable situation at CSC, which broke off to become Leopard, the Guercilena project, which changed names and absorbed the remnants of the imploded Radio Shack post-Postal legacy squad.

First Pro Win:

- Boonen -- UNIQA classic, stage 2, July 7, 2002
- Cancellara -- Tour of Rhodes, prologue, Feb 21, 2001

Comment: Cancellara gets in the win column while Boonen is still racing U23 (though he was winning in 2001). Fittingly enough, Boonen's first pro win was a stage sprint, while Cancellara's was a time trial. For all their similarities, this is their primary difference.

Career Victories (per Pro Cycling Stats):

- Boonen -- 109 wins, including 36 classics, 14 Grand Tour stages, 1 World Championship (RR)
- Cancellara -- 72 wins, including 32 classics, 19 Grand Tour stages, 4 World Championships (all ITTs)

Comment: Hm, those GT numbers must include jerseys and/or TTTs, because Boonen, while a lot of things, is not a prolific grand tour stage winner. Cancellara's stats in the GTs consists largely of time trial successes, which is an entirely separate chapter in his book. As good as he got in the classics, he was/is the best stage race time triallist I ever saw.

Monuments:

- Boonen -- 3x Ronde van Vlaanderen, 4x Paris-Roubaix
- Cancellara -- 3x Ronde van Vlaanderen, 3x Paris-Roubaix, 1x Milano-Sanremo

Comment: It's weird, I always thought of Cancellara as the perfect engine for Paris-Roubaix, where you don't need to do anything dramatic but be strong as a goddam ox all day long. Pre-2012, de Ronde seemed more likely to encourage sprint winners. And yet, in their era, Boonen has sprinted to three victories in Roubaix, while Cancellara has sprinted four times in the velodrome, with one win and three defeats.

Other Classic Wins:

- Boonen -- 5x E3 Prijs, 3x Gent-Wevelgem, 2x Scheldeprijs, 3x K-B-K, 1x Paris-Brussels, 1x Dwars door Vlaanderen
- Cancellara -- 3x E3 Prijs, 3x Strade Bianche

Comment: Nationality counts for a lot in how their respective careers have panned out. Part of Boonen's greatness and importance to Belgian fans is the overwhelming number of wins he's scored in Belgium, or just over the border (Roubaix). Cancellara isn't Belgian. He's an honorary Belgian, but even that doesn't hone his focus on the classics the way national identity does for Boonen.

Head to Head:

- Total number of races: Boonen 1,093, Cancellara 1,062
- Total distance traveled: Cancellara 190,384km, Boonen 181,282km
- Finished first: Boonen 53%, Cancellara 47%
- Classic wins: Boonen 11, Cancellara 7

Comment: Boonen's sprinting is again a factor, with Gent-Wevelgem and E3 basically the difference.

Lost Spring Campaigns:

- Boonen -- 2013, 2015
- Cancellara -- 2009, 2012

Comment: Arguably 2011 was half-lost for Boonen, suffering a mechanical in Paris-Roubaix. Cancellara was around in 2009 but not himself and DNF'd in Flanders after breaking his chain on the Koppenberg. Each rider scored one Double in the other's absence.

How Did They Affect Each Other?

On to some narratives. It's nice to think that they drove each other to higher heights, and if you read their interviews they'll say sure, but it's hard to know exactly what they believe. I guess we can wait for their autobiographies. They seem to be friendly rivals, insofar as they seem to be friendly people in general and are often spotted making casual conversation at the start line, but that's about it. On the other hand, we can make some educated guesses based on how sports work in general and conclude that they were both probably very, very good for each other's career.

What Fab did for Tom: This is pure speculation, but there are a few big items I'd list. No question, having Cancellara around makes it impossible to devalue a lot of what Boonen accomplished. But for Cancellara people might say "he just beat up on guys like Hoste and Hincapie," but instead we have Boonen winning each of his major classics directly from Cancellara on at least one occasion, except de Ronde. Onto squishier concepts... Boonen drifted a bit as Jens described earlier in the week, vis-a-vis his Monaco years. Cancellara rose to the top in that time and seized the crown in 2010. By 2012 Boonen was the better rider again. Before 2010, Boonen had barely known real defeat -- just that weird Paris-Roubaix and the 2007 races which were during his not-good years. Maybe they didn't wake him up enough, particularly as Boonen came back to score two more Paris-Roubaix wins. 2010 changed everything. But Boonen's response in 2012 was huge, and surely was driven by the challenge of Cancellara. He was as good as ever, one last time. Oh, and the 60km attack in Paris-Roubaix? Cancellara-esque. If Tom ever thought about his legacy vs. the Swiss Bear, that was the day he did something about it. [Albeit not head-to-head, alas.]

What Tom did for Fab: Not as clear, for one reason -- doesn't Cancellara strike you as a guy who was 100% motivated from day 1? You can't really make someone more motivated than "completely motivated." On the other hand, Cancellara is conscious of his legacy, he mentions it a lot and it sounds a little pompous at times, except that he has 100%

earned the right to think about his legacy, because he has an amazing one. Well, Boonen is by far the biggest obstacle to his legacy, or was before 2013, and Cancellara has certainly been forced to reckon with that. The quality of Cancellara's 2010 rampage is through the roof, for one simple reason: Tom Boonen. Moreover, he has forced Cancellara to take risks not involving dragging Boonen to the line in a sprint (Cancellara is a pretty cagey sprinter in his own way). So tactically, Cancellara had to try stuff.

Who Was Best?

The question is begged. The answer is for you to decide, and argue about til the Judgment Day. A few points.

Pro-Fabs: The entire 2010 trilogy, all taken directly out of Boonen's hide. There is no counterargument to this that quashes this point. There are counterarguments, but they aren't as strong as this single three-week statement. Nothing is. Fabs at his best beat Tom at what was maybe his best. Also, there is the style of wins. Cancellara never really beat Boonen in a sprint, he had to be stronger, and we all know the strongest guy is the awesomest.

Pro-Tom: The numbers. Also, what's wrong with sprinting to win? Also, who owns the longest solo attack for a monument victory, between the two? Boonen does. Is it Boonen's fault that in his very best year, 2012, when he beat Cancellara twice (E3, G-W), that Cancellara crashed out and wasn't there to contest Flanders and Roubaix? Given how those went it's hard to picture Cancellara having evened the score. Sadly we will never know, but how is that Boonen's fault?

The Real Winners: Us. An era of Tom without Fab wouldn't have meant quite as much, and certainly wouldn't have been anywhere near as fun. Think of 2008-09 and spread that out over a decade. Just Boonen versus his teammates. Pass. Think of Fabs with no Tom. Who would have driven him to be so dramatic in his attacking? You can just picture him sauntering away from Flecha or Hushovd over and over again. Cool but nowhere near as fun.

Since 2006 we have gone into practically every season waiting for one or both of them to seize control. When one has done so over the other, it's been like witnessing history. And since the two combined were so effective, when they lost it felt like history too. The rising Boonen-Cancellara tide lifted all boats.

Tom Boonen and Fabian Cancellara. Photo by Elizabeth Freer

Acknowledgements

I would like to thank the people of SBNation for giving me a place to indulge and practice my love of the Classics, and cycling in general. In particular to Markos Moulitsas, who first invited me to join the SBNation family, and Tyler Bleszinski, SBNation co-Founder and President, who soon became the Podium Café's biggest in-house supporter.

I would also like to thank my co-Editors, Jens Hagström, Jen See, Douglas Ansel and Conor Kelly, for their inspiration and great work. Thanks to Bram Schittecatte for editorial assistance with this book. Thanks to all the Editors – Caro, Dan, Jimbo, Elaine, Skip, Ewoud, Mark, Ruthann, Susie, Jim, Antoine, Chris S., Marlys, Marvin, Will and of course Tony/Elvisgoat – for keeping things fun and friendly all these years. Thanks to my neighbor and friend Ron for being a fellow cycling nut and helping me gear up beyond all reason. Thanks to so many others at the Café for the same level of inspiration and support. Thanks to Sheriann for your wonderful graphical designs. Thanks to Elizabeth for your wonderful photos.

Special thanks also to my brother Pete and to Drew Davis, who got me going with the whole idea of a cycling blog. Thanks to old friend Steve Berthiaume for sitting me down in front of Paris-Roubaix in 1985, and for being my first cycling teammate. And thank you again to my beloved Stacey Schultz for being there throughout the writing of this book, including especially the time I was away in Europe, and for not thinking that my internet obsession over a European sport is as weird as it sounds.

Printed in Great Britain
by Amazon